Local Knowledge

Dennis Forster

UK Book Publishing.com

Editing, design, typesetting and publishing by UK Book Publishing

www.ukbookpublishing.com

ISBN: 978-1-916572-36-2

Local Knowledge

Dedication

In loving memory of my grandpa Thomas Harrison and my Harrison uncles: Rowley, Harry, Ted, Tommy, Jimmy and last, but not least, my dear mam, Isa Harrison; the youngest and only girl to have survived those times of high infant mortality. God bless them all.

Local Knowledge

In 1863, Americans were killing each other in a brutal, no-holds-barred, civil war.

In 1863 Newcastle-upon-Tyne was as important to the British economy as Silicon Valley is to America's today.

On a cold February morning in 1863 – it might snow but, then again, it might not – an express train from Liverpool pulled into Newcastle's brand new, but still unfinished, Central Station.

In a First Class carriage of this train – its seats upholstered like Chesterfields in a gentleman's London club – sat an American secret agent. His name was Jeb Prior Phelan. Today we'd call him a 'CIA Operative'. He was on what the families who'd lived on the border between England and Scotland in Tudor times would have called a 'hot trod'. A term they used when they were legally pursuing and breathing down the necks of rustlers.

Jeb was not hard on the heels of rustlers, he was hard on the heels of Confederate agents … agents who were on Tyneside to buy the Armstrong Gun. His paymaster was Abraham Lincoln. He was against slavery.

****

The driver of the Liverpool-Newcastle express that morning was called Charlie. Charlie loved being an engine driver. He'd heard that in the old days toffs had been keen to take the reins of a stagecoach.

Their reasoning? They were certain that only gentlemen knew how to handle horses.

As far as Charlie knew, no toff had ever driven a steam locomotive. Standing on the footplate of a steam locomotive doing forty miles an hour got you as dirty as a pitman or chimney sweep. Toffs didn't like soot spotting their cravats. They didn't mind mud thrown up by horses' hoofs but not, heaven forbid, industrial soot.

Charlie brought the train to a stop by pulling down hard on a red lever as long as his arm. No longer moving, the locomotive gave out the human equivalent of a relaxing sigh. Steam, under pressure, hissed from a pipe under its boiler. Feathers of white smoke, like a sea fret, drifted around it and hid its shiny wheels.

These exhalations always reminded Charlie of the way a dog, after a swim, shakes itself dry. And the locomotive had had a 'swim'. Its 'swim' had been pulling a train from Liverpool to Newcastle.

Wiping his hands on a rag, Charlie surveyed the crowd of folk on the platform the way a duke looks at his butler when the butler has served him burnt toast.

Charlie fancied himself a cut above porters and the like. What happened on the platform had nowt to do with him. He was a locomotive engineer. Yuh had to nar what yuh were deeing when yuh were driving a steam engine. Yuh had to nar your steam engine the way yuh had to nar the missus. When the missus wouldn't make yuh a mug of tea, yuh had to nar why. It was nee gud thumping the table. When your steam engine's wheels slipped yuh had to nar to pull the chain on the sand box. To give the wheels 'grip' yuh trickled sand on the line.

Bringing his head back into the cab, Charlie told Albert, his fireman: 'the vultures is hovering, Albert'.

'What duh yuh mean "vultures"?' said Albert.

'Porters, Albert … porters is "vultures". The passengers we carry are their carrion. Passengers is called "carrion", Albert, because they expect folk to carry their bags.'

'I've read about vultures in Mr Dickens' "All the Year Round". They have hooked beaks. They look like the Duke of Wellington. And they have bald heeds like me Uncle Harry. To try and make his hair grow me Uncle Harry rubs bone marrow on his heed.'

'Stop wittering … am not interested in your Uncle Harry. I wants a fried egg. Heat ya shovel on the fire. Have yuh got the lard? Before we gan back to the shed your driver wants his breakfast. If a divent have me breakfast I'll be a skeleton. If folk see a skeleton on the footplate they'll think they're seeing a ghost train.'

****

To be a railway porter in Newcastle, in 1863, without getting a black eye, that is, you had to be a member of the Porters' Guild. Its rules were made known to new members by word of mouth. Membership of the guild ensured you'd get your turn … nee pushing or shoving … to milk the First Class passengers.

This cold February morning it was the turn of a porter called 'Hooter' to have first bash at milking the 'toffs'.

Behind him … close behind him … in his shadow, knowing his place in the pecking order, pushing a barrow … sauntered 'Groveller'.

'Hooter' was called 'Hooter' because he had a big nose. 'Groveller' had earned his nickname because once, when a passenger had tipped him 'handsome', he'd been obsequious in his gratitude.

'Hooter' as well as being a self-styled 'senior porter' was also a philosopher. If he'd been captain of a man 'o war he'd have flogged with monologues and soliloquies.

Approaching the First Class carriages of the express from Liverpool, 'Hooter' told 'Groveller': 'In this game, Groveller, I'm "Big Barrow". You're the dog's bollocks.'

'If yuh say so, Hooter.'

'Aye … a dee and divent gan giv'n me the V behind me back. Yuh nar a have eyes in the back of me heed.'

On the back of his porter's cap 'Hooter' had two circles of white paper. In the centre of each there was a black dot.

'Passengers love a gimmick. If yuh can make a passenger smile you'll get a good tip. "Your bags are safe in my hands, sor. I have eyes in the back of me heed." If you've been to the "Telegraph" for a swift half … divent let them smell ya breath. A pissed porter gets piss aal tips. I had the honour of carrying Mr Dickens' bags when he came to the toon. Lovely man … didn't look well. A good tipper, Mr Dickens. When I telt him a had eyes in the back of me heed and showed him me cap, he said: "Cor blimey!" Then, yuh nar what he did? He took out his notebook. After writing in it, he told me a was a "Phenomenon". I'm not one to boast but am tell'n yuh, in Mr Dickens' next book look out for a porter with eyes in the back of his heed. Will I be lucky, Groveller? I should be. Yuh nar why? Because it's me granny's birthday. But we aal nar, as far as tipping gans, First Class passengers are as unpredictable as the weather. It might snow today but, then again, it might not. The rich might tip you handsome but, then again, they might give yuh nowt …not even a smile.'

The First Class carriages were painted a glossy canary yellow. 'Hooter' called them 'daffodils'. They were next to the engine. The wisps of white steam circling them made them look like egg yolks in a froth of albumen.

Opening the door of the First Class carriage closest to him and looking in, 'Hooter' said: 'Porter, sir? Bags, sir?'

'I am sorry to disappoint you, porter,' said Jeb. 'I am travelling light. I only have my valise and my banjo.'

Newcastle was a sea port. At the mouth of its river, the Tyne, at South Shields, there was a long established Somali community … tough little men who could reef a top sail in a typhoon. Men of colour in the town were by no means run of the mill, but they were not unusual.

What was different about this man of colour was that he was not a rough and ready seaman. Out of the corner of his eye 'Hooter' noticed 'Groveller' had struck lucky with a toff with so much luggage, 'Groveller' was using his barrow … the bastard!

This man of colour was a gentleman. If he didn't have money, he, 'Hooter', would eat tripe, which he hated.

'Yee, an American, sir?' said 'Hooter'.

'My accent has given me away?'

'That's reet, bonny lad, it has. I nar the twang 'cos when a was young and could dee handstands, I sailed … deckhand to Atlanta.'

'Not, I hope, on a slaver?'

'Nar! Nar! Cotton was the ship's cargo. God bless you, sir. Welcome to the toon.'

'And god bless you, porter,' said Jeb. 'Here …' tipping 'Hooter' a sixpence. 'That's for bidding me welcome to your town and for opening my carriage door. You are against slavery?'

'I hates slavery, sir, the way I hates tripe. If everyone hated tripe as much as I do, sir, every tripe shop in the toon would gan bust.'

'I am uncertain of your meaning, porter. I am hearing a foreign language. But you seem a good fellow. You have earned your gratuity,' giving 'Hooter' another sixpence. 'Which way out?'

JEB DOES SOME NECESSARY BUSINESS... HE FINDS THE NATIVES DIFFICULT TO UNDERSTAND

Jeb was travelling 'light' because he'd left Liverpool in a hurry. He'd had no time to pack. He'd travelled from Liverpool to Newcastle on a train which, at times, had reached a speed in excess of fifty miles an hour. He'd travelled the distance between the two towns in less time than it would have taken one of his black-slave-brothers to pick and pack a bail of cotton.

His luggage, as he'd told 'Hooter', consisted of a valise – what, today, we'd call an overnight bag – and a banjo. The banjo was in a bespoke case made from the skin of a Mississippi alligator. In a shoulder holster – made for him by his step-father's New York shoe maker – he carried a US Army Colt revolver.

For a provincial town the Central Station was larger than he'd expected. The northerners who'd built it – he believed they were called 'Geordies' – were clearly aspirational. They were not shrinking violets. The station heaved and hummed with New World energy.

That Newcastle was a sea port was brought home to him when a tall man, with clogs on his feet instead of boots, and smoking a clay pipe which, when he spoke, swivelled from one side of his mouth to the other, like Kay's flying shuttle, said: 'Excuse, vich vay to the river, peas?'

'You are a Dutchman?' said Jeb.

'Ja ... I am the Dutch.'

'I'm an American.'

'Zat is wery interesting … but, vich vay to ze river, peas?'

'You are a fisherman,' said, Jeb, pointing to the fishing net draped shawl-like over the man's shoulders.

'Ja … I fishermen … but, vich vay is ze river, peas?'

'Gangway! Gangway!' shouted a youngster pulling a barrow large enough to have been pulled by a shire horse. Its load of chickens, in cages, clucked the way clocks tick in quiet rooms. A rooster in a cage let everyone know he was chanticleer by, every now and again, letting rip with a good morning, the sun is above the horizon, 'Cock-a-doodle-doo'.

'Are yee two like those bairns lost in the forest?' said the urchin. 'A nar yuh divent think yuh are but you're in me way. If a divent get these cluckers on the Hexham train the boss'll give me a clip roond the earhole. Reet, the clog dancer forst. Ye want the river, reet?'

'Ja,' said the Dutchman, 'vich vay is ze river?'

'Yuh gan through that arch ower there,' pointing, 'it doesn't matter a monkey's whether yuh turn left or reet … take any street which gans doon and you'll come to the river. Now,' turning to Jeb, 'where duh yee want to gan, mista?'

It was clear to the Dutchman that the dark skinned, well dressed American hadn't a clue what he was being asked.

'Ze young man, sir, is asking ver you vont to go.'

'To a telegraph office,' said Jeb.

'In that case, bonny lad,' said the urchin, 'follow me and me chickens. If you lose me when am galloping shout, "Harry", and I'll stop till you catch up. Gee-up!'

After a few seconds of pulling the barrow at speed, all the time pretending he was a horse, the urchin shouted: 'Whoa there! Had up! Gan through that arch ower there, Mista, and turn left. If you've got eyes in your heed yuh can't miss the telegraph office. Gee-up!'

At which command the boy-horse, before Jeb had time to thank him, set off, at a canter, to catch the Hexham train.

******

In the Telegraph Office Jeb went to Poste Restante. Behind its counter a clerk was scrutinising his moustache in the reflection of a tin box.

'I'm bending the knee toneet,' he told Jeb. 'I want to look me best. What do yuh think?' letting Jeb see his moustache.

'A little more wax on the left side,' suggested Jeb.

'Do yuh really think so?'

'I do.'

'That's what I'll soon be saying in a church if Phyllis says she'll marry me. Before I ask her, am ganna spoil her. I'm ganna take her to the pie shop in New Bridge Street. If a mutton pie and a waxed moustache doesn't make her say yes … nowt will. Now, sir, how can I help you?'

'You are poste-restante?'

'That's what I am today, sir. Yesterday I was early deliveries but, today, I'm poste-restante.'

'Would it be too much trouble for you to check if there is anything in one of your pigeon holes for a, Mr J. P. Phelan?'

'Of course not, sir, that's what I'm paid to do.'

'In between asking your customers to admire your moustache?'

'Don't be like that, sir. All work and no play would make Geordie a dull fellow. And nobody likes a dull fellow, sir; do they? I know Phyllis doesn't. '

From the pigeon hole marked 'P', the love-besotted clerk handed Jeb a telegram.

'Thank you,' said Jeb.

'If only I had a mirror, instead of the bottom of a tin box,' said the clerk going back to admiring his moustache.

The telegram was from Henry Adams, the son of the US Minister to Great Britain. Henry wished Jeb to meet him off the London express arriving in Newcastle at eleven-thirty that evening.

Outside the station Jeb saw a brand new hotel. He knew it was brand new because its ashlar was still yellow. The town's smoky air had not yet had time to turn it black. And the town's air WAS smoky. The gods of heavy engineering had placed a halo of black smoke over the town.

The hotel's name, the 'County', puzzled him. Was it a French hotel? France was full of 'Counts'. England was full of Dukes. Then he remembered how, for administration purposes, England was chopped up into parcels of land called 'counties'. At the American Consul in London, he'd been shown a map of England divided up into its counties. Each county had been a different shape and a different colour. There had been no straight lines. The states in America were separated by straight lines. Some of these English counties were smaller than his white grandfather's cotton plantation. It was a mystery to him how such a small island had come to rule half the world. If ever there was a case of the tail wagging the dog … why didn't the Hindus and Moslems chuck the British out of India? What was stopping them? Americans had chucked the Brits out of America.

Under normal circumstances Jeb would have booked accommodation for himself and Henry at just such a hotel or, at the 'Station Hotel' he'd also spotted. That he did not do so was due to the fact that he and Henry – when he arrived – wished to keep a low profile. They were visiting Tyneside, incognito. The 'County' and the 'Station Hotel' were just the sort of posh hotels in which the Confederate agents would have booked accommodation. Slave owners were fond of their creature comforts.

There was nothing to be gained by a chance contretemps with the representatives of the Confederate States. A confrontation might lead to them killing each other.

A respectable public house with rooms to let was what he was after. Somewhere tucked away.

He turned left out of the Central Station for no other reason than he found himself drawn, willy-nilly, towards following a man trying to keep a bull under control. The bull had a ring through its nose. The bull wasn't happy.

A man, pulling a bull! A little man … pulling a big bull. Here was a metaphor, if ever there was one, of Britain and its Empire. A small island telling the world what to do. The limeys better not tell America what to do. The British government better keep its nose out of the American war. If it interfered, why, America would give it a bloody nose. Had these islanders learnt nothing from the American War of Independence? America had whopped Britain once and, would do it again, if it had to.

The 'limeys' were scared of America. The American eagle was clawing the back of their bulldog. The resentment felt by the British bulldog could not be overstated. Britain's neutrality in America's civil war was window dressing. It was not sincere.

****

The sky was cloudless but more black than blue. As he did every day, the god Vulcan was blessing the town with a halo of smoky air. The making of hydraulic cranes, steam ships, steam locomotives and weapons of war, came at a price. Heavy engineering was not for the faint hearted. Progress was a mixed blessing. It put sovereigns into the pockets of the bosses. Into the pockets of workers it put shillings. Its smoke congested the lungs of everyone.

The iron rimmed wheels of carts, wagons and coaches, bumping over cobbles, echoed like hammer blows in a cave. Coming out of the station and into this busy thoroughfare was as intimidating and noisy as standing too close to Niagara Falls.

Looking up at the blue-black sky and feeling a cold wind, he thought it might snow. He wasn't used to the contrariness of English weather. England's weather and the British government had much in common. Neither could be trusted to deliver what they promised. He'd heard it said that on a sunny day in England one should always carry an umbrella.

Two men carrying a tree trunk under their arms as if they were ready to use it as a battering ram, begged his pardon as they asked him to make way.

Ahead of him was a cattle market. Its pens were full of animals. Bovine bellows and snorts sounded like foghorns. If the bull knew where he was going, no wonder he was acting up.

The bull reminded him of the 'Battle of Bull Run': a Yankee defeat. A British politician who fancied himself a wag had called the battle 'Yankee Run' … damn the Limeys and their sense of humour.

Leaving the pitiful wailings of the doomed beasts he turned down a cobbled bank. The bank was steep. In the early morning light its frosted cobbles looked like penny buns dusted with icing sugar.

At the bottom of the bank, as he'd expected, he came to a river … the River Tyne. Close-to, the river was a poisonous broth. Its mud flats bubbled and plopped. In watery cul-de-sacs, spiral galaxies of rainbow-coloured oil heaved, sighed and slowly spun. Water gushing out of a green bearded sewer was the colour of ginger beer. Broken barrels and the branches of trees bobbed, unloved, under wooden quays.

In 1863 the Tyne offered five-star accommodation to typhoid and cholera. No one had stopped to ask if swapping salmon and trout for two ruthless takers of human life was a good deal. It was progress … damn it! Heavy engineering was making the 'toon' rich. Moaning keel men should shut their gobs. Salmon fishermen should gan and fish the Tweed.

Horses, wagons, carts, were everywhere. One of Sir William Armstrong's hydraulic cranes – Jeb had seen them at work on the docks at Liverpool – was lifting and letting fall a heavy weight onto a balk of wood. A new jetty? An extension to the quayside?

In the middle of the river a steam dredger – black smoke bellowing out of its top hat funnel – snorted, rattled and hooted. Its buckets were scooping out the river's bottom filth to make deep water for the safe passage of the new steam colliers.

Outside a wooden shack made out of salvaged wood, a group of men, wearing cloth caps and mufflers, sat huddled, all very convivial, round a brazier. To make themselves heard above the quayside noise, their voices were loud.

Their local accent being strong, Jeb, apart from understanding the odd word or phrase, had not a clue as to what they were saying. But he did know they sounded happy. Slaves never sounded like that.

'Howay, Michael, let's see the fire, man.'

'Billy, a divent want yuh to get burnt, that's why am hogg'n the fire. Am sufferin for yuh, Billy. It's cos am yah marraw that am not complain'n. I have nivva forgotten the time you saved me from drowning off Byker Sands.'

'Micky?'

'Yes, Billy? If you're ganna say sorry for accusing your best mate of hogging the fire … divent bother. Tell the priest you've sinned and say a couple of Hail Marys … that is, if yuh divent want to gan to hell for making false applications … for good measure, yuh nar, like wearing a belt and braces … put a bob in the sin tin your ma keeps on the mantelpiece.'

'Micky, you should wear a wig.'

'A divent need a wig. Ave got me own hair. Unlike some folk a nar, I still gan to the barbers.'

'I meant a lawyer's wig, Micky. A wig like that lawyer had on his heed when he sent me Aunty Doris to Australia for stealing a penny loaf.'

'Tell's the story again of what she did … a like that story.'

'Aye, well … when the judge telt her he was sending her to Australia she didn't faint or turn white.'

'What did she dee?'

'Yuh nar what she done.'

'Tell's again. Your story's like the tide, a like to see it come back in.'

'She hopped oot the witness box, didn't she? … Went hopp'n aal roond the court. There was hell on. "Restrain that woman, constable!' shooted the judge. When the constable collared her and escorted her back to the dock with her head under his arm and she had stopped jumping up and doon, and was able to look the judge in the eye, the judge said, leaning forward from his pulpit: "Why were you hopping round my court?" "A was gett'n used to where yuh wor sending me, wasn't a, sor?" said Doris, aal very polite because she was talking to a judge. "I beg your pardon?" said the judge. "I was a kangaroo, wasn't a? Yee been' a judge should nar a kangaroo hops." Aye, the judge wasn't impressed by me Aunt Doris's animal impersonations. Before she was departed … '

'Yuh mean "Deported". Yuh shud have said "Deported".'

'Hoy! We's tell'n the tale? Yee or me? You're like the wind when it's blarin the wrong way. You're making me tack. As I was saying, afore a was rudely interrupted … afore my Aunt Doris departed all involuntary … at least a got that reet, to the other side of the world he gave her a bag of tripe sentence.'

'What's a bag of tripe sentence?'

'Two weeks' oakum picking. He telt me Aunty Doris: "that will teach you, wench, not to make a mockery of my court".'

'A like that story, Billy, and, cos you've told it, so canny you've made me forget aal aboot the cad weather … howay and warm ya hands at the brazier. As wor laas telt's last neet, "Micky, you're not a sharing man." That's cos a never nar which side of the paillasse is hors and which is mine.'

'A love the smell of the bone yard,' said another man, by way of explaining why he was sniffing the frosty air. 'A divent nar why but it makes me feel hungry.'

'Bones make lovely broth,' said Micky.

'I can't get enough of it.'

'Sex?'

'Nar, broth.'

'If yuh have lots of sex,' said Billy, 'yuh need lots of broth. Yuh put watta in a boiler to make steam. Yuh put broth in ya belly to make sex.'

'Broth makes me fart,' said Micky.

'There's nee salmon in the river,' said an old man to anyone who might be listening, 'not like there used to be when I was a bairn. Where have aal the salmon gone? That's what a want to nar. Wor river's an open sewer. It smells of death.'

'Aye,' said his pal, sitting next to him, 'the river's a corpse … nee doubt about that.'

'Last week a deed dog floated past me barge.'

'Salmon?'

'Nar, nee salmon … just a deed dog. It was aal blown up with its legs stuck up in the air like a table turned upside doon the way bailiffs take tables out of houses. Where have aal the salmon gone? That's what I want to nar.'

'And the keel boats … divent forget the keel boats.'

'The cholera loves the river.'

'Divent forget the typhoid.'

'Aye, the cholera and the typhoid love the river the way I love wor lass's mince and dumplings. Every Thursday we have mince and dumplings. It puts a lining on me stomach for the fish I get on a Friday.'

'Yuh divent have to eat fish on a Friday. You're not a Catholic.'

'A nar … but me granny is. She has false teeth made out of wood. She inherited them from her mother. Aye, the poor inherit their mother's false teeth … the rich inherit castles. Life's not fair.'

'Man does not live by bread alone.'

'I nar that … we're not seagulls. What yuh gett'n at?'

'What 'am gett'n at, is this … me gran's false teeth were made of wood taken from the cross … yuh nar … the cross Jesus was crucified on. She said they were magic. When she drank water she tasted wine. She tasted what she fancied she was eating.'

'If her choppers were made of wood did she not get spelks in her gob?'

'Aye, she did … she said it was Jesus telling her to eat fish on a Friday.'

'If she'd spelks in her gob she couldn't eat mince and dumplings. Fish is easier to chew than meat. I think she was eating fish on a Friday because she couldn't eat owt else … that's what I think. I would have telt her straight … if you think your false teeth are made from wood taken from the cross then … you're bonkers.'

'A forgot to tell you … me granny was from Byker.'

'Oh, yuh didn't tell me that, did yuh? We aal nar yuh divent argue with a Byker granny. The last time a did that a ended up freezing aal neet in the netty.'

'A miss the keel boats.'

'A saw one the other day. It was coming doon from Dunston. To get under the bridge it put its sail doon.'

'The new steam colliers can't gan under the old stone bridge.'

'They can gan under the High Level Bridge.'

'A nar that … but they can't dee that because they canna gan any further upriver than the old stone bridge.'

'I've heard rumours that Armstrong … him that makes the guns and hydraulic cranes … is ganna knock the old bridge doon. He's ganin to build an iron bridge that'll swing open and shut like wor netty door does on a windy neet.'

'Divent be daft … neebody can build a bridge like that.'

'Sir William Armstrong can … you'll see.'

'Oh, the pan's got a handle on it now, has it? Sir William … he a pal of yours?'

'Divent be daft … he's posh. Posh folk divent tark to watermen … there gans another murderer,' pointing with his clay pipe at a steam paddle wheel tugboat.

'Aye, you're reet there, Tommy. Steam paddlers are thugs. They're as bad as 'prentices. They smash up row boats with their paddles. The fire fizzing out of their funnels sets the washing on fire. They spit out soot. They put black soot spots aal over your face. When a came home one neet, wor lass took one look at me … yuh nar what she said? She said a looked like a Dalmatian. "That's alreet, pet," a said. "A thought you were ganna say something nasty like … 'Bob, yuh look like a Sunderland waterman.' Yuh nar what she said? "Bobby, a love yuh too much to ever call yuh that." There gans another murderer,' said Bob, pointing more or less at Jeb, who, in eavesdropping and not understanding a quarter of what he was hearing, said: 'I beg your pardon. I am not a murderer. I am a musician. I play the banjo the way the Bible tells us angels play harps. I am a stranger in your town. I am from the New World. I am an American.'

Jeb's intrusion into the locals' banter shut them up the way rain stops play at a cricket match.

'Divent worry, bonny lad,' said Bob, 'a didn't mean you … a meant the steam paddler, ower there. Afore the steamers poked their funnels into me workplace, I was a keel man. The steamers have killed the keels … that's why a call them "murderers". Keel boats need wind … steamers divent … doesn't matter to a steamer whether it's windy or flat calm … or, whether the tide is ganin out or coming in, yuh see. A steam collier gans to London as fast as a bloke gans to the netty when he has the trots.'

'Where have aal the salmon gone?'

'The other day a fisherman caught a penny-farthing bike.'

'When yuh gan fish'n these days yuh never nar what you're ganna catch. It's like ganin haem and finding your lass in bed with the neighbour.'

'That happened to Arthur.'

'A nar it did.'

'That's why he went to America. You're an American, sir, yuh might have met him,' said Bob.

'America is a big country,' said Jeb smiling.

'Ah, well, a just thought you might have bumped into him, that's aal. 'am not been nosy, like, but what yuh deeing … doing in Newcastle?'

'I am here on business,' said Jeb.

'Aye, that's what the toff said when his missus caught him coming out of a brothel.'

'My business is private.'

'Aye, that's what the toff said as well. You are, sir, if I may say so, a very polite gentleman.'

'Am I?'

'You have told me to mind my own business without giving me a black eye. Should yuh … you not be at home, sir, fighting in your country's civil war?'

'A war has many kinds of warriors.'

'You'll be against slavery?'

'Because I am a black man?'

'Aye, a suppose so.'

'You are right of course. I am against slavery.'

'I think, sir … young man … that you and I have at least one thing in common.'

'And what would that be?'

'We are both mongrels, sir. What I mean, sir, is, I'm thinking you're a mixture of races … tell me, I'm wrong.'

The circumstances … the warmth of feeling the men were making him feel … mitigated any feeling Jeb might have felt of been interrogated.

'Let me explain,' continued Bob. 'Me mother is from Moffatt … that's in Scotland. Me great grandfatha … grandfather, is from Madrid … that's in Spain. I am, sir, a mixture of the kilt and the cast-a-net.'

'Cast-a-net?' said Jeb.

'Yuh nar, sir … you know, sir,' said Bob, miming a flamenco dancer clicking castanets.

'Olay!' said Jeb, entering into the spirit of the conversation. The rough waterman's pride in his family history made Jeb want to proclaim his own heritage. 'And I am the progeny of a love affair between a white woman and a black slave.'

'Get away!'

'Well, ye bugger!'

'And I,' said an old man with no front teeth and who was using a conch shell as an ear trumpet, 'caught the last salmon afore Grey's Monument was built.'

'Wardle, yuh deaf old bugger, we're not talking about fish.'

'What I want to nar,' continued the deaf old man, 'is we killed aal the salmon. In my day a keel man's clock was the tide. Did yuh nar that?'

These men were free spirits. If they had been slaves they would not have been half so free with what they had said. When you were a slave you did not just have chains around your ankles. If you didn't want to be whipped, you had to be careful what you said.

Bidding these happy belligerents 'good day' he continued his ramble along the quayside.

******

The ships in the river were a mixture of sail and steam. Lumbering square sailed colliers were being towed by paddlewheel tugboats half their size. Then there were the new screw colliers, moving up and down the river under their own steam … as if by magic … there not being a sail or paddlewheel to be seen.

There were barges and skiffs. There were cobles and the odd keel boat; as out of date now as a stone hammer would have been in the Iron Age.

Kittiwakes screeched … 'Kit-e-wake! Kit-e-wake!' There was noise. Stench. Steamers hooted. There were baritone steamers and soprano steamers and steamers, who, when they were letting off steam, roared like Niagara Falls. Signal flags, as colourful as tropical parrots, flew from the masts of ships moored three abreast.

Continuing his walk, once having to dodge into a doorway to avoid being run down by a shire-horse pulling a cart, Jeb found himself approaching a stone pier supporting a monumentally high bridge.

The bridge strode across the river on towering, tapering stone piers. It was a giant with strong legs and a mannequin's waist. If it could have spoken it would have had a baritone voice. It would have said, hands on hips … very aggressive … in a testosterone baritone: 'I am progress. I am not mediaeval. I am the Industrial Revolution.'

Looking up – arching back his head to see the top of the bridge – so high was it above the river – he saw a steam locomotive pulling a train of wagons. Slung under the railway bridge, like a bairn in a papoose, was a second bridge. Looking hard at this bridge he made out diminutive people, cabs and carriages. The size of the bridge made him feel like Tom Thumb.

He walked on, thinking: 'how could such an ancient town be so full of New World 'go?'.

In a gap between two warehouses he came to a flight of stone stairs. A nameplate told him: 'Castle Garth Stairs'. Their worn stone treads smiled at him like men and women with missing front teeth. When he heard sad music coming from somewhere hidden round a corner at their top, he did not hesitate, he went up them two at a time.

JEB MEETS WATERLOO BOB

Ok, he … Jeb Prior Phelan … was a secret agent on a mission to rid America's dyer's hand of slavery but the cause for which he was fighting never trumped the fact, that in his heart of hearts, he was a musician. When this god damned war was over, he was going to form a band … the 'Jeb Prior Phelan Band'.

He was young. Strong. The valise he was carrying and the banjo case strung across his back, did not slow him down one iota. He was so used to carrying them, he was unaware of them. Music was his safety valve. It helped him express the sorrow and rage he felt at what the owners of slaves had done to black people; at what his white mother had told him, his slave-owning white grandfather had done to his black father.

On the stairs, first landing, he ducked under a line of frozen washing. The tiny shops, on either side of the stairs, had bull's eye windows and ill-fitting doors. Somewhere, someone was cooking. He could smell hot food.

One shop was selling second hand clothes. A black and white scarf with a hole in it was on sale for a penny. Through an open doorway, he saw a blazing coal fire. In front of the fire a man, with nails in his mouth, was repairing a boot on a cobbler's last.

In contrast to the overpowering dullness of his surroundings the music he could hear was … ethereal. It was taking him to a land of milk and honey. It was taking him to a time when the North had won the civil war … to a time when black folk would no longer be slaves.

Turning a twist in the stairs he saw a castle. He'd never seen a castle before. He'd read about them, but had never actually seen one. When it had been built men had killed each other with bows and arrows, spears and swords. Now they killed each other with Colt revolvers and the Armstrong Gun.

In the shelter of a tunnel – really, a hole cut through one of the castle's metre-thick outer walls – a busker-beggar was playing an instrument he'd never seen before. The fellow looked to be in as bad a state of disrepair as the castle. He had no legs. He sat propped up playing in a coffin. The coffin did not have wings to fly its occupant to heaven, but it did have wheels.

The drone of the instrument he was playing was melancholic. Jeb knew a fellow musician when he heard one.

Waterloo Bob, for that was the busker's name, eyed Jeb up the way pirates eye unopened chests of treasure.

Not many toffs climbed Castle Garth Stairs. Not many went doon (down) them for that matter, either. The boots the tall young man had on his plates of meat must have cost a bob or two.

The young fellow was a black man. Not many of those around the 'toon', either. The cut of his overcoat looked foreign. The leather valise he was carrying looked French. Bob knew about bags like that from the time he'd spent parlez-vous, at the Battle of Waterloo. The Duke of Wellington himself had told him to aim his cannon a little more to the left. Anyone dressed as handsome as this young fellow, had to have money.

In anticipation of a donation dropping into his tin he played, improvisations on the well-known song, then going round the music halls, 'Keep Your Feet Still Geordie Hinny'.

The enthusiasm with which he played made him rock from side to side as if he was in a rowing boat in a swell instead of in a mutilated coffin on dry land. His stumps twitched to the music. A leather cushion, sprouting horse hair – like fungi growing in a damp dell – supported his back. If his coffin-bogey … his poor man's chariot, had not been braked with a brick, he'd have played himself all the way, bumpity-bump, doon (down) Castle Garth Stairs.

The social distance between Jeb and the busker was wider than the Atlantic Ocean. Jeb was a gentleman and a secret agent. He had behind him all the power of Abraham Lincoln's Union government.

'Waterloo Bob' wasn't asking for charity but he would be very grateful indeed if folk passing by, felt inclined to drop a coin or two into his tin.

The music Jeb was hearing made him forget the reason he was in Newcastle. Without thinking that he'd be drawing attention to himself – which was the last thing he wanted, his reason for being in Newcastle being of a secretive nature – Jeb, under the spell of the music he was hearing … it was as if someone was tickling his bare feet with a feather … he just had to react … throwing caution to the wind, unpacked his banjo, and after tuning it, began a musical conversation with the beggar-busker, 'Waterloo Bob'.

Their music melted icicles. It made heads pop out of windows. It stopped servants polishing boots. Two women, wearing long black dresses and with shawls over their heads, in lieu of bonnets, danced an impromptu reel.

Folk on their way down the stairs, stopped to watch and listen. On such a cold day the music warmed them up. Folk on their way up the stairs, glad of an excuse to get their breath back, stopped, to watch and listen.

Waterloo Bob threw in the towel first.

'Alreet, bonny lad,' he said, 'yee win. You're a lot younger than me, and you've got two legs.'

Jeb bowed. He eyed the audience their playing had gathered around them with suspicion. They were a shabbily dressed lot. The children were not wearing shoes.

When Jeb put his banjo back into its case, those who'd gathered to listen, drifted off as slowly as leaves fall off a tree in early autumn. The music had made them feel warm and sunny inside. They wanted more of the same. It was with reluctance that they dithered back to their hard, everyday lives.

When they were alone, Jeb said, dropping a sovereign into the busker's tin: 'You are a maestro on your instrument, sir.'

Waterloo Bob couldn't believe his luck. He pounced on the sovereign, the way a sparrow hawk pounces on a mouse. He felt the way he'd felt when grape shot at Waterloo had taken off his legs. It was aal a dream. But there were bad dreams and good dreams, wasn't there?

It would have to be spent in a shop where he knew someone he could trust would give him the right change. Just touching it warmed his hands. It was as hot as the muzzles of cannon fired a hundred times at Waterloo, Waterloo! Bloody French and their grape shot. If it hadn't been for the great Duke himself passing by on Copenhagen, he might have died. What was it the duke had said? 'There's a fellow over there with a fine pair of lungs on him hollering for his mother ... see that he is looked after.'

Life was a rum business ... saved by the great duke himself. If Old Nosey had known half of what he'd got up to, he'd have had him flogged. And now, this young whipper-snapper – a fine musician, nee doubt aboot that – had given him a sovereign. A sovereign, yuh bugger; a lot of money, that.

Only when the coin was stowed in a pocket and the pocket's flap buttoned, did Bob express his gratitude.

'That is very kind of you, sor.'

'You are a fine musician.'

'You're canny yourself, sor.'

'You play like an angel?'

'Aye! But a divent want to gan to heaven yet, thank yee very much. There's not many angels in Newcastle, I'll tell you that. Bob's me name,' pointing to the name 'Waterloo Bob' chalked on a piece of wood tied to the end of the coffin the way a name tag is tied to the big toe of a corpse in a mortuary, 'Waterloo Bob. Around here they call me Waterloo but me real name's Bob.'

'And the name of the instrument you play so well, Bob, is …?'

'The name of me instrument … do yuh not nar?'

'I beg your pardon?'

'Do-you-not-know?'

'I would not be asking if I knew.'

'Aye! That's true. The name of me instrument, young man, what can play the banjo better than an angel can play a harp but has gaps in his knowledge as big as scuppers on a whaler, is the Northumbrian Small Pipes.'

'It looks to me,' said Jeb, 'as if a Scotsman's bagpipe has had a baby.'

'Aye! The Scot's bagpipes is for the glens … the Northumbrian small pipes are for the fireside.'

'It was a pleasure to play with you, Bob. In our musical duel you bested me. If we'd been using swords instead of crotchets and quavers, I would now be strumming a harp.'

'A wouldn't say that, sor, a stopped playing afore yee did.'

'You let me win because you wanted me to feel welcome in your town.'

'Did a?'

'In America there is much prejudice against people of my colour.'

'You might be a man of colour, sir, but … you're a toff … a gentleman into the bargain as well … yuh nar how to tip.'

'If I had not tipped handsomely, would I not have been a gentleman?'

'A divent nar aboot that, sor, but a sovereign gans a lang way to help'n me think you're a canny lad. If there's more of where that came from, Waterloo Bob's your man.'

'Do you ever dream, Bob?'

'Dream?'

'Aye, Bob, dream.'

'I have nightmares, sir. A sometimes dream I have me legs back and a can chase the lasses. It's arful when a wake up.'

'I can understand that.'

'It's good of you to say so, sir but, a divent think yuh can. When you've got legs you never think aboot them. When you haven't got them you miss them aal the time. It's like me pal, Ernie … plays the spoons … married … fifty years … took his missis for granted the way I took me legs … when I had them. When she died … dropsy got her … he went to pieces. Never plays the spoons now. We used to busk together … spoons and small pipes … keeping time with him wasn't easy. I sometimes thought … between you and me like … spoons and small pipes divent mix … yuh nar, like oil and watta divent mix. It's a funny world … me, with no legs and Spoons … that's what a always called him … like, am called, Waterloo … and, Spoons with nee brains, now that his missis is up there nagging the angels to unblock the netty. Women have a thing aboot blocked netties. A divent nar why. Sometimes, you have to work an ebb tide … sometimes, a full tide … sometimes, a low tide … that's when yuh get stuck on a sandbank like Robinson Crusoe and to get by and help yuh keep ya temper yuh have to smoke three pipes or play the pipes … there's nee hurrying the flow. Hoy! You're yawn'n. That's enough of me looking in the mirror … by the cut of your jib, young man, I'd say your tide was in. Yuh divent look to me like a man stuck on a sandbank.'

'Because I look prosperous?'

'Aye! Only a toff with too much money would be daft enough … a mean, kind enough … to give a busker a sovereign.'

'All that glitters Bob, is not gold.'

'Aye! That's true. I hope, sor, you're not telling me the sovereign you've given me's a dud.'

'The sovereign is real, Bob. My tide, Bob, is not in, it is out. It is out because my country is at war. My countrymen are fighting each other. My tide is out and will stay out until no man of colour is a slave in the greatest country on Earth.'

'Australia?'

'No, Bob … the New World… America.'

'A knew you weren't from aroond here. Have you come to Newcastle to get away from the war? A wouldn't blame you if you had … war's a terrible thing. A nar about the American war because when Spoons pushes me into the Grainger Market, a bloke there … he's called Wardle … reads me the newspapers.'

'Spoons being the gentleman with whom you used to busk? He who went to pieces after his wife died?'

'Aye! But gan steady on call'n him a "gentleman". 'ave started call'n him "Pusher". He pushes me round the toon in me chariot, see. He keeps saying when his heed gets better and he stops seeing double, he'll be back, playing the spoons. If he does a hope he keeps better time than he did afore his missis joined the celestial choir … lost a lot of me pals at Waterloo … which side are you on in the war?'

'The colour of my skin should tell you that.'

'Aye! Aye! A see what yuh mean … so, you are what they call a Yankee, are you? Wardle told me when I bought him a gill … he gets thirsty reading oot loud, you see, and if you want to keep him gannin you have to tickle his tonsils. Wardle told me that Mr Palmerston … he's our Prime Minister, calls a battle called Bull Run … Yankee Run, because the Yankees ran away from the blokes what keeps slaves.'

'At the Battle of Bull Run the Union army was not at its best. We have a lot to learn about fighting … but, we will learn, and we will win the war.'

'Aye! Aye! I'm sure you will. You learn a lot aboot yourself and your mates when the fighting starts … grog helps … war's an arful business. At Waterloo I saw men shit themselves … officers, as well. When someone's ganna stick a lance in your belly button, as if he was ganna take a winkle oot of its shell, it matters not a toss whether you're a toff with a big house or a poor bugger who lives near one of them sewers that gan into the river at the Ouseburn. All men have bowels, and bowels, am telling yuh, is like wives who wants aal their own way … they dee what they want to dee.' After nodding sage like at his summation of the waywardness of bowels, he said: 'What yuh deeing here?'

'I beg your pardon?' said Jeb.

'What are yuh deeing here? Why are you in Newcastle?'

'What am I doing here?' said Jeb.

'Aye! That's what a said … what are yuh deeing here? If you're not running away from the war, what yuh deeing here?'

Jeb hesitated.

Waterloo Bob had seen officers hesitate like that at Waterloo. It was when they didn't know what to do. But, this was Newcastle on a brass monkey cold morning, not a battlefield … though, when he thought aboot it … aal of life was a battlefield … at least for him it was. If the young gentleman hadn't been so generous and tipped him a sovereign he'd have had to busk aal day to earn enough to buy a pork pie … and not a fresh one straight out of the oven, either.

It wasn't as if he was asking the young fella if the French lancers were ganna charge and they were aal ganna die … nar, his question was easy … unless the young gentleman had something to hide … in which case, when he made up his mind to reply, whatever he said would be a lie.

To earn money a busker had to be good at two things. Number one: he had to be a good musician. Number two: he had to be able to read folk's faces. He had to be able to guess the kind of music they liked … the kind of music that would make them put their hands in their pockets and give to the worthy cause, called Waterloo Bob … him, what had had has legs blown off at Waterloo.

'Why am I in Newcastle?' repeated Jeb.

'Aye, man! What yuh deeing here? A mean, yuh haven't come aal the way from America to play a duet with Waterloo Bob, have yuh?'

'I am in Newcastle,' said Jeb, inspired by the blackened stones of the Norman castle he could see a hundred yards in front of him, 'because Newcastle has a castle. I am interested in castles. We don't have many castles in America. In fact, we don't have any.'

'If I had legs,' said Waterloo, 'I'd say, "Pull the other one".'

'Would you?'

'Aye, a would.'

'Are you calling me a liar?'

'If a was, would yuh challenge me to a duel?'

'No, I would not,' laughing, 'I would tell you that in your last arpeggio you hit three wrong notes.'

'A wouldn't like that.'

'I know you wouldn't. Losing your legs at Waterloo for the British Empire has taught you discretion. You are a wise man, Bob.'

'I'm a maimed man.'

'And a wonderful piper.'

'Aye! A suppose, a am.'

'Good day to you, Waterloo Bob.'

'And, good day to you too, sir. And thank you most kindly for the sovereign.'

******

With the benefit of hindsight Jeb regretted the impulse which had made him play a duet with Waterloo Bob. But … goddam it … it had been a celebration … a celebration of musicianship … a spontaneous act of good fellowship. It had been like clinking glasses with friends.

Shaking his head at his waywardness, he told himself: 'Jeb Prior Phelan, when it comes to playing the banjo, you are a show-off.'

He walked between the stalls of an outdoor market. He looked at Newcastle's castle the way someone who has never seen an orange before looks at an orange.

It rose up in front of him like a sentry shouting 'Who goes there? Stop or I'll shoot!'. Why did it did not have battlements? He thought all castles had battlements. In lieu of banners and battle pennants, a line of frozen washing hung across a flight of steps leading to an arched doorway.

It looked like an old man who has lost his wife. Where were its knights in shining armour and heralds blowing welcome to kings on long trumpets?

As a visitor to the town, he was unaware that the castle's keep was now the town's jail. In a word, parochial practicality had usurped pageantry. Why go to the bother of building a jail for the town's criminals when the Normans had built one for you?

The noise made by a steam locomotive pulling coal wagons across the High Level Bridge – the stairs he'd climbed having brought him level with the lower deck of the bridge he'd walked under on the quayside – temporarily drowned out the noise of hawkers, carts, cabs and carriages.

On the river … sail and steam. The old and the new. On land: a castle and a steam locomotive. The past and the future. The castle had no doubt been built by 'dooks' and 'pearls' to let the peasants know who was boss.

Thank the Lord, America was a new country. To grow and prosper it had to dump slavery overboard the way it had dumped tea into Boston harbour in 1773 … that had let the Limeys know the New World meant business … that the American colonies weren't going to be taxed without representation. Americans were not feudal serfs.

Once this goddamned civil war was over and slavery was abolished the greatest country on Earth would prosper the way a desert comes to life after a cloud burst of rain. America was a land of possibilities … of opportunity. America's achievements in the years ahead would make England look like a toothless lion. To find their Empire on a map the Limeys would have to use a magnifying glass. In years to come, Jeb just knew, America would be Gulliver and Great Britain, Lilliput.

Walking on he saw a church with a lantern tower supported on flying buttresses. That was clever. The top of the lantern kept disappearing into the town's smoky air. Sometimes it was there. Sometimes it wasn't. Likewise, the top storeys of the tallest houses. At times, all were as vague as is the face of a woman behind a veil.

Jeb did not know it, but Geordies called the days when low pressure ganged up with commercial and domestic smoke, the 'Guillotine'. The reason being that when the foggy ceiling was as low as six foot, Geordies over that height had nee heeds (no heads).

Around the church, as piglets gather round the teats of a sow, there were stalls. The square buzzed and bustled with the noise of buyers and sellers.

A hawker standing on a chair in front of a stall, with a canvas awning that looked as if it might once have been a ship's sail, was shouting: 'Ves-cuts! Best gen-men's ves-cuts!' He needed a shave. His overcoat was tied with a rope belt.

A man pushing a milk churn on a hand barrow told Jeb, in a rough but friendly way: 'Oot mee way, bonny lad! A divent want me milk to freeze … me customers divent want ice borgs!'

A hawker selling potatoes from a cart harnessed to a donkey, munching from a nosebag, shouted at Jeb, through cupped hands – as if Jeb was a vessel entering the Tyne and he was the 'hailer' at Lloyd's hailing station at North Shields – 'Tatties for the pan! Tynemouth tatties. Fresh from the clamp. Nee frost on them.'

It was while he was trying to interpret the local dialect by comparing the goods the hawkers had on display with what they were hollering – 'vest-cuts' must be 'waistcoats' … 'tatties' must be 'potatoes' – that Jeb received a poke in the back. The 'pok' sent him stumbling forward.

Turning to face his assailant, his hand reaching for the butt of his Colt, Jeb found himself face-to-face with an out of breath Waterloo Bob.

On the longest of his stumps the busker had strapped a wooden leg. It was with the help of that prosthetic and two crutches he was able to stand and walk.

'You set a fast pace, Mr America. If yuh hadn't stopped to look at the castle the way a used to look at mesel in a mirror when a was a bairn, I'd niva have caught you. You'd be the fish what got away.'

'What do you want?'

'Henry Adams,' said Bob, looking Jeb straight in the eye. 'Does that name mean owt (anything) to you? I can see by the look on your face, it does. Divent start telling me lies now. You'd never get away telling a lass yuh loved her if you didn't mean it. If I may say so, sor, you're an arful bad liar.'

'How'd you know that name?' said Jeb.

'You're going to have to trust me, bonny lad, and believe me when I tell you, I am on your side. Your generous tip of a sovereign might be the best money you ever spent. Buy me a lamb chop and a pint of ale … nee floaters in it, mind … at the New Bridge, ower there … everything's new aroond here except me … and I'll let you into a few secrets. A sometimes think me and the castle are the oldest things left standing in the toon … and "Pusher Spoons" of course. I know the landlord at the Bridge … him and me were at Waterloo. I lost me legs; he lost his balls. I can't chase the lasses and he doesn't want to. He'll give us a seat where we can talk, nice and private. Away from nosy parkers and folk with big lugs. What do you say?'

'The fact you know the name "Henry Adams" has put me on my guard. I will not deny I am curious to know how you know that name.'

'I've set your tail wagg'n, have I? Like a tom cat's does when it sees a cat it doesn't like?'

'I warn you, Bob, I am not a man to be double crossed.'

'A can see that. If a did, yuh nar (you know) double cross you, what would you do? Kill me?'

'Certainly not. I'd steal your peg leg and burn your pipes.'

'You have a cruel streak in you, Mr America.'

'There are limits to the bond we forged when we played together.'

'Aye! That's true. Hi! I can't keep calling you, Mr America, can I? What's your name? Not Henry Adams, I hope.'

'Call me Phelan.'

'Would that be your real name?'

'It might be, and it might not be.'

'Would that be like me calling the River Tyne the River Thames and saying Newcastle is called London?'

'You have a way with you, Bob, that a find, infatuat'n. You know how to call a man a liar without insulting him.'

WATERLOO BOB SPILLS THE BEANS

On the short walk to the 'New Bridge' public house Jeb kept looking at the legless busker limping alongside him as if he, Waterloo Bob, was as great a mystery as the pyramids. How did a legless beggar-busker, know the name of the man he, Jeb Prior Phelan, an agent of the Northern States, was to meet off the London train that evening?

Liverpool was full of Confederate spies. Was Newcastle the same? The Confederates were using every trick in the book to get their hands on weapons. In Liverpool Jeb had paid spies to spy on Confederate agents. Confederate agents had paid spies to spy on Union agents. If you had money it was easy to buy information.

But, whose side were the Limeys on? The British, Jeb knew, did not approve of slavery. The official position of the British government was one of strict neutrality.

Confederates thought cotton was 'king' and so did the merchants of Liverpool … well, they were wrong. That all men were born free trumped all their claims; trouble was, when a man thinks he can make a lot of money through sailing close to the wind he does not see right and wrong through a clear pane of glass; greed makes him warm to the grey areas of morality. He warms to the notion that the black man is happy wearing a ball and chain. He will claim, with all sincerity: 'give the black man his freedom and he will not know what to do with it. A freed slave would be an unhappy fellow. Come on, England, hear my point of view. The bellum way of life is bucolic bliss. The bellum way of life is a pastoral bliss for all its citizens.'

******

The landlord of the New Bridge had white curly hair. He looked as if he was wearing a lawyer's wig. The end of his nose was red like the end of one of the new Lucifer safety matches.

'This is Mike,' said Waterloo Bob.

'Mike Barlow, sir, at your service,' said Mike, extending a hand, 'B for Barlow! B for banter! B for blather! B for Balls! But not for the ones between a man's legs … cos I aint got any.'

'Bob did mention your loss,' said Jeb, taking the extended hand.

Mike squeezed the blood out of Jeb's hand. He pumped it up and down the way sailors pump bilge pumps to stop their ship sinking.

'What'll you have? Any friend of Waterloo's is my friend. First drink on the house … free as the wind that used to fill a keel's sail … then you can buy me a whisky.'

****

Using a private language of nods and winks Waterloo let Mike know he wished to be seated where he and his young companion could talk in private.

'It's a long way from the fire,' said Mike, escorting them to a table in a cosy nook, 'but if you want to blather in private this is the place to dee it … unless you want to take the new steam train to Tynemouth and stand on the cliff tops and talk to seagulls. Will you be having cad-day (cold-day) broth with your ale, Bob?'

'Aye, a will … times that by two, Mike. The young fellow here isn't local … he's foreign.'

'He's not from Sunderland, is he?'

'Nar! Nar! Not that foreign. Will you be having the cad-day broth, Mr Phelan?'

'Do you recommend it?'

'A dee. It keeps out the cad better than a flannel vest smeared with chip pan fat. Divent stint on the ham, Mike. Mr Phelan, here, is a gentleman what knows how to tip.'

****

The 'cad-day' broth, full of vegetables, barley and big lumps of ham, was just what Jeb needed on such a cold day. It shovelled warmth into him the way a fireman, shovelling coal into a steam locomotive's furnace, feeds a hungry fire.

All the time they were eating – dipping slabs of bread the size of roof tiles into their broth – Jeb wanted to be told how Bob knew the name, Henry Adams. He did not want to have to ask. Having to ask would be like begging and he, Jeb Prior Phelan, was not a beggar. He was an agent of the government of the United States of America. He was young. He was not an experienced negotiator. He was pitifully inept at hiding his impatience.

To calm himself, he uncased his banjo. He strummed a petulant chord.

'Aye!' said Bob, pushing himself upright on his seat with the help of his peg leg, 'that's one way to tell me to hurry up and tell yuh what a nar.'

'If it's a question of money?'

'Aye! That will come into it … am sure aboot that, but the reason you're sitting there looking aal angry at me and wanting to throttle the information oot of me is because you think you've been rumbled at whatever it is you are up to.'

'Henry Adams?'

'Aye! Henry Adams. You're gannin at me the way the French went at me at Waterloo. Divent fret your banjo, bonny lad, am ganin to tell yuh. Newcastle is a small town, Mr Phelan. Everyone, including the beadle and the aldermen, knar me. And I nar them. I have one arm … I was ganna say leg but, I haven't got any… I have one arm in respectable Newcastle and one arm in its underworld. I nar the town's flowers and its weeds. I busk outside the new Central Station. I've nimble fingers for playing the pipes, sharp eyes and sharper lugs. I'm a nark for the police and a spy for anyone what pays me.'

'You have been paid to keep a look out for a man with an American accent called Henry Adams?' Jeb blurted out.

'You're as quick on the uptake as the run in a woollen sock, Mr Phelan … or, should I call you, Mr Adams?'

'I assure you, I am not Mr Adams, though I understand why you think I might be.'

'I'm asking mesel how many Americans are there in the toon? You're like them railways, when a was a bairn they didn't exist, now, they are all ower the place.'

'Bob?

'Aye?'

'If I was Mr Adams, would you tell whoever is paying you that you have met me?'

'Nar, I wouldn't.'

'Why not?'

'Because you tipped me a sovereign … because you are a musician … because … I don't nar … I like you.'

'Are you able to tell me who is paying you?'

'Aye, a can. Two local lads … out of work keel men. Geordie and Jackie Coxon. Everyone nars the Coxon brothers. Not many folk like them. They're not bad lads just a bit sharp, if yuh nar what a mean? If I told them I'd seen an American in the toon they'd want to nar the far end. They'd promise to pay me but, only, when they get paid. Bob's not daft. A nar, they'd never cough up.'

'Do you know who they are working for? Who is paying them?'

'They wouldn't tell me. I have me own spies in the toon. Pusher-Spoons is one of them. He has legs and when he's not bubbling his eyes out ower his deed missus, he gets around. The gossip doon the Sandgate is they're working for two Americans.'

'Do you know their names?'

'Nar, but I could find oot.'

'And that would cost?'

'A sovereign buys a lot of gossip.'

'Can I trust you?'

'Course you can.'

'But, I don't know that. Do I?'

'Nar, yuh divent.'

'Here's a sovereign, Bob, for information not yet received. I don't know why but I do trust you.'

'That's very kind of you, Mr Phelan. I'm much obliged.'

'Where will I be able to meet you?'

'I busk outside the new Central Station and outside Saint Nick's … that's the big church near the castle.'

'You're not an easy man to dupe, Bob, I'm thinking.'

'That's right, Mr Phelan … I'm not. The food that used to feed me legs now gans to feed me brain.'

'You are such a sharp fellow, Bob, I do believe your claim makes sense. I look forward to meeting you again … at the railway station or at the church perhaps or wherever I might hear your pipes. Maybe when I saunter by your pitch you might let me know you have information for me by playing something American. What about Dixie? It's a Confederate song but Mr Lincoln loves it.'

Jeb played it on his banjo.

'I only to have to hear a tune once to remember it,' said Bob, closing his eyes and humming the tune. 'Are you off?'

'I am.'

'Where are you lodging or don't you want to tell me in case I tell the Coxon brothers about you? You sure you're not Henry Adams? The Coxon brothers know a collier skipper who for a few bob will dump a body over the side when they're passing the Dogger Bank … good fishing on the Dogger … fish like a body … hard lads, the Coxon brothers.'

'I have yet to find lodgings.'

'Try the Old George. It's up the Cloth Market way. Ask anyone where the Old George is and they'll tell you. It's where Thomas Bewick used to drink.'

'And who might he be?'

'Aye! Am forgetting you're an American.'

'Will he spy for me? I have money.'

'You'll have to pay his ghost … he's deed. He drew pictures of birds and cows on blocks of wood. He did that as well as you can play the banjo.'

'Never heard of him.'

'Niva mind. It's nice to nar Americans divent nar everything. When yuh gan to the Old George divent be scared to name drop. Me and its landlord are like that,' crossing his fingers, 'I'm an old soldier. He's an old sailor … lost an arm and an eye at Trafalgar when he was eleven. Tell him Waterloo sent you and he won't watta your beer … and afore you leave … divent forget to pay for the beer and broth. If you tip Mike real handsome he'll swear on his mother's grave he's never seen you … a mean if the Coxon brothers should come knocking on his door.'

****

On his way to the Old George – following directions given him by Waterloo Bob – Jeb passed a brand new town hall. He knew it was new because the smoky air, like the Central Station and the County Hotel, had not yet had time to blacken its stone. Around it were lots of older buildings. They looked as if they had been built during the reign of that Tudor king who'd had lots of wives and, like an ogre in a fairy story, had chopped off some of their heads. Newcastle was, sometimes, Cinderella, in rags: sometimes, she was dressed to go to the ball.

He found the Old George down a cobbled lane called a 'chare'. It looked as if it had been built by a builder who did not know how to use a plumb line. Its leaning walls looked as if they'd drank too much of what they were selling.

Two wooden trap doors – bouncy when you walked over them – covered entrances to cellars.

All in all, Jeb thought the Old George just the sort of out of the way place he was after.

****

As an American who'd lived in London for less than a month and in Liverpool for less than a week, he was not overfamiliar with the idiosyncrasies of English public houses. Entering the Old George through one of its many front doors he found himself in a stone flagged tunnel. At its end he opened a door, marked: 'SNUG'.

The room was small and cosy. It was warmed by a coal fire and but dimly lit by light, coming in through a dirty window made of many small Bull's Eyes. Form seats, with green leather backs ran along three of its sides. Small tables, on iron legs with clawed feet, were available for customers (if there had been any) to place their drinks.

A notice at the side of a bell-pull said: PULL FOR A DRINK. DIVVENT BE IN A HURRY. The Old George is a sailing ship. The Old George is not one of 'em new steam piddlers. The bar is at the bow and this here snug is at the stern. If there's nee wind the Old George gets becalmed. If the wind is blow'n the rang way it takes time to tack. If it's too windy and you don't want to turn turtle like a mermaid doing a duck dive you take doon aal your sails, except a jib the size of Cushie Butterfield's bloomers. Mushy peas. 1p (small bowl) 2p (big bowl) Aal served hot.

Nelson. Landlord.

Jeb, smiling at the landlord's sweet and sour declaration of intent, rang for service. How long would he have to wait? He'd been warned to be prepared for the worst. Maybe it was a double bluff. If a customer was served within ten minutes of ringing, he'd think: 'Wow! That was quick.'

While he waited, he examined a six-foot fish in a glass case. It didn't look happy. It reminded him of slavery. On a brass plate, he read: 'Salmo salar. Caught by Col. Christopher Michael KCMG Byker Sands 1797.'

Underneath the mummified fish, a framed newspaper cutting, told the story of its demise.

'WHO CAUGHT THE FISH? In the dispute between Col Michael KCMG and his servant, Bilious, concerning who caught the salmon, the presiding justice in the case found in favour of the colonel.

Mr Justice Bell, who just happened to be a second cousin of the colonel said he could not believe – indeed he said it was impossible for him to believe – that the servant, Bilious, had caught and landed the fish unaided while the colonel was evacuating his bowels behind a rhododendron bush as a result of having eaten too heartily the night before, off a bag of prunes imported from Jamaica.

The colonel's black eye supported his story that, in a fit of angler's jealousy Bilious had launched a vicious attack on his employer who was known to all and sundry to be of an affable temperament.

A police officer called to the domestic swore under oath that he had found no sign of human excrement behind the aforesaid rhododendron bush.

The servant, Bilious, showing no sign of remorse and furthermore, by showing the true nature of his aggressive temperament by making a rude gesture with two fingers at the bench, the court had no choice but to sentence him to be transported to Australia on the first ship available.

In his concluding remarks Mr Justice Bell told Bilious that when he had inflicted GBH on the colonel he had disturbed for a full twenty minutes the peace and tranquillity of rural Byker. He was in danger of giving that stretch of the river a reputation for disorderliness which it did not deserve.'

The hatch, from which the face of a boy had been weighing him up, while he'd been reading, took Jeb by surprise. The hatch, when closed, was invisible to all but the most discerning eye.

The boy, about thirteen, had tousled blond hair and veined red cheeks like the inside of a pomegranate from sitting too close to a coal fire.

'When you've finished reading what happened five thousand years ago and if it's not too much trouble, I'll take your order … unless of course you've just come in for a warm like the cat does what lives next door at the pawn shop.'

'Are you the landlord?'

'Howay, man! If a cat had kittens would a look like its mother? I'm the cabin boy, the boots, the ostler, the rat catcher, the whistler for cabs, and Nelson, he's the landlord, says am getting better at peeling tetties, as well. I'm a rising star. Nelson says I'm rising so fast he couldn't take a reading off me with a sextant.'

'Do you do accommodation?'

'Eh?'

'Have you rooms to let?'

'I divent dee hammocks. Warm your arse in front of the fire while I whistle for Nelson. In the meantime, if you don't mind, I'll shut the gun port.'

Once again Jeb was left to contemplate the dead fish. Its dead look reminded him of why he was in Newcastle. He was here to stop the South buying weapons – weapons that would be used to support slavery – weapons that would be used to keep his people in chains … shackled to their owners the way dogs are chained to kennels.

The hatch was part of a door. Out of this – as if it were a secret entrance (like one of those doors in a gentleman's study designed to look like a bookcase) – there stepped a man whose height and bulk filled the snug the way Gulliver had filled the town square in Lilliput. One of his hands was a hook. A black and white patch covered an eye.

'Trafalgar!' said Nelson, waving the hook at Jeb, then, tapping his patch with it, by way of explaining its black and white pattern, 'Tyneside tartan. The galley tells me you're after a hammock for the neet.'

'Two hammocks, landlord, if you have them,' said Jeb, smiling at himself for calling a 'bed', a 'hammock'. 'Later this evening I will be joined by a colleague. He and I are in Newcastle to do business with your shipbuilders and makers of guns.'

'Are you, now? I can tell by your twang you're not from around these parts. You're not from Jarrow, are you? Yuh nar … from the other side of the river.'

'I'm an American,' said Jeb.

'Are you now? A thought you were. I've sailed there … aye, many a time I've sailed to the New World. After Trafalgar the navy didn't want me … sailed first mate on the Anaconda … Charleston to Liverpool.'

'A slaver?'

'Nee stomach for that. Cotton boat. Follow me, sir, and I'll show you the rooms. If you take them … two bedrooms and a sitting room. For the price of a deposit on a key, you'll have your own front door. There's an entrance from inside the pub but you don't have to use it. It's not proper for a gentleman to have to push his way through rowdies to get to his bedroom … is it? Especially when he's paid in advance.'

Taking the hint, Jeb said: 'If the rooms are to my liking, landlord, I most certainly will pay in advance.'

****

'I calls it the Collingwood Suite, sir,' said Nelson, ushering Jeb into a cold but spacious room. The beams supporting its ceiling were bowed. They were like the legs of a man who has spent more time riding a horse than walking.

'It's cad up here cos there's nee fire in the grate, sir,' said Nelson, 'soon put that reet. I calls it the Collingwood Suite, sir, after the time I spent on the Royal Sovereign with Lord Collingwood. Ten years old, I was. Told them I was older. To get on in this world it doesn't pay to tell the truth. A was a big lad for me age, see? I was a powder monkey. At Trafalgar, before the battle started, his Lordship gave me an apple. He knew I was a Tyneside lad … looked after his men, did his Lordship. Telt me the apple wouldn't stop the French killing me, but if I survived the battle it would keep away the scurvy … gas in the sitting room …

that's where yuh are now … candles in the bedrooms.'

'Like a steam ship with sails,' said Jeb.

'Aye, sir, that's very well put. I can see, like mesel, you're a poet. When the fires is lit the rooms up here is as snug as the snug, doon stairs.'

Jeb liked the rooms and after agreeing terms – all in favour of the landlord – agreed to take them for two weeks; first week paid in advance.

'You're a gentleman, sir,' said Nelson, pocketing the money Jeb had given him. 'I likes a gentleman who doesn't quibble over a bob or two. You'll be well looked after here, sir. Put your boots out on the landing before you go to bed and in the morning you'll find that in the night, the fairies have been and given them a polish. If you can't shave in their shine I won't give you your money back but I will give you a pair of boxing gloves to box the lugs of Boris whose job it is to make 'em shine. If they're not shining give Boris a "shiner". Pull that bell-rope, sir, and someone from the kitchen will be up to ask you, faster than a surfing keel boat, what you want. I recommend the hot pork sandwiches.'

'With crackling and sage and onion stuffing?'

'Is the sun hot? Is Cushie Butterfield a big lass or a splinter?'

More or less certain that he'd got the landlord's drift, Jeb nodded that he thought the sandwiches ticked all the boxes.

'They don't come cheap,' continued, Nelson,' but they are hale and hearty. They'll wet your whistle better than one o' them Indian monsoons turns a tar's pigtail into a cow's tail. You can see I keep the room ready for lodgers, sir. Nee cobwebs on the beams. A nar it's freezing up here but, as the window cleaner says when he looks at dirty windows … "we'll soon put that reet" … soon have a blaze ganin. Nee extra charge for laying fires in the bedrooms. Boris, that's the pot boy, who has aspirations … as well as hay fever … he niva stops sneezing in the summer … of becoming a landlord and prays every neet for me to die so he can jump into me clogs when I pop them, will dee the laying. He's laid so many fires a call him "Chicken" … chickens lays eggs … Boris lays fires … see?'

Jeb smiled. He was certain that if Euclid had been a student of human nature as well as a mathematician, well … he was certain the ancient Greek would have come up with the axiom: when you have found accommodation you like, laugh at your landlord's jokes.

Still smiling, he said: 'I did not come upon your public house by chance.'

'You heard of the "Old George" when you was at home in America? I knew I was famous. It's the new paddle steamers. They're making the Atlantic as small as a pond. Well! Well! Well!'

Before Jeb had time to explain who had recommended him, Boris came in with a coal scuttle, paper and sticks.

'Boris,' said Nelson, 'remember, when you're laying a fire you do not cluck. You are not a chicken laying an egg, you are a pot boy from St Peter's laying a fire what a gentleman is paying you to lay to keep him warm.'

To make sure the message was received and understood, Nelson tapped Boris's head with his hook. He tapped Boris's cranium the way a treasure hunter taps a wall, hoping an echo will tell him he has located a secret chamber.

Boris, getting the message and knowing it to be the precursor of worse to come if he didn't set to, began laying the fire as if his life depended upon it … which, it probably did.

'A bit of advice, sir,' said Nelson, pointing his hook at Boris who was making a clucking noise as he laid the fire, 'do not encourage him to talk. If he came from a wealthy family and had gone to one of them posh schools, he'd have been well on his way, by now, to being a lawyer.'

'When he answered the bell I rang in the snug,' said Jeb, 'I certainly found him to be a voluble chap.'

'Dear me, sir, don't you go telling him he's voluble … he'll want a tip. Boris,' removing the pot boy from the fire, which was now well alight, by the expedient of hooking the back of Boris's neck cloth (literally) and hauling him up and away from the fire, 'Coal! Full scuttle! The gentleman has paid in advance.'

All the way to the door Boris clucked and flapped his arms like a chicken.

'The cheeky bugger! If he doesn't become Lord Mayor of London, I'll have my hook melted down and made into a cannon ball for the next time we fight the French. Boris! Coal! Full scuttle!' shouted Nelson as he chased after the pot-boy.

******

Nelson saw Jeb as a purse full of sovereigns. If he played his cards reet he'd make a lot of money from this renter. Boris had better toe the line. When Boris was thrown the bow line … he'd best catch it. If he didn't catch it, he'd catch it round his lugs.

As a survivor of the Battle of Trafalgar, Nelson had no intention of being holed below the water line by an ambitious pot-boy.

It was with the intention of keeping his hand on the collar of his 'prize' that Nelson, therefore, personally carried a scuttle of coal aal (all) the way from the Old George's coalhouse, up two flights of stairs and into Jeb's rooms … paid for in advance.

'"O, me, name is Geordie Black, in me time I've been a crack. I've worked in the Gus and in the Betty",' he sang as he entered the Collingwood Suite. 'There you are, sir,' putting lumps of coal on the fire, 'when that takes hold you'll be able to take off your coat and not find lumps of ice under your oxters. You'll be thinking you are back in Charleston on a hot summer's day.'

'It may interest you to know, landlord, but I have never been to Charleston. I am not a slave.'

'I can see that, sir.'

'What would you say, landlord, if I told you … as I was about to do earlier … that I was recommended to your hostelry by Waterloo Bob?'

'I'd say the old rogue will be after me giving him something for him giving me a customer …yuh, nar … a couple of free pints for him bringing me trade.'

'What would you say if I told you I was employing Waterloo to spy for me?'

'If you pay as well for information as you do in advance for rooms, I'd say he's hit a seam of coal that's ganna bring him in a lot of brass … Waterloo always was lucky … that is, apart from when he lost his legs.'

'Do you drink with your customers?'

'If they are paying, I do.'

'When you have finished poking the fire with your hook, bring me a bottle of whisky and two glasses.'

'Is … one of the glasses for me?'

'Of course.'

'You are perhaps wishing to employ me in an unofficial capacity?'

'I do.'

'You wish to discuss terms … as it were?'

'I do.'

'For a young man, sir … you have aal your buttons on.'

'In the matter of worldly wisdom, landlord … may I call you Nelson? Waterloo Bob said that was your name … that was how the voluble pot-boy referred to you.'

'I've telt yuh (told you) … divent gan calling Boris, voluble … it'll gan to his heed like the pollen does in summer when he gets the hay fever. Everyone calls me Nelson. I'd be honoured, sir, if you called me Nelson.'

'In the matter of worldly wisdom, Nelson, you have more buttons on your waistcoat than any waistcoat I have ever seen. And, as we are going to be working together …'

'How'd you nar that?'

'Because, Nelson, you are a landlord and I have money. All landlords love money more than a woman loves a beau who buys her flowers. As we are going to be working together, allow me to introduce myself. Phelan's the name.'

'Phelan, eh? That's an Irish name with the O chopped off. I sailed with an O'Phelan. He told me it was Irish for wolf. I'm going to be employed by a wolf, am I?'

'But a wolf, Nelson, who will pay you in sovereigns to keep your mouth shut and your eyes and ears open. A bottle of whisky and two glasses if you please, Nelson. Over its sipping we will discuss the finer points of our bargain. No lawyers will be needed. Nothing will be written down. We will trust each other, yes?'

'Oh aye?'

****

Over more than one glass of whisky – sipped in front of a blazing coal fire – Jeb made it clear to Nelson that he wished his stay and that of the man he was meeting later that night to be hush-hush. To help Nelson understand the instruction, Jeb placed a sovereign down on the table. He placed it within touching distance of the landlord's hook.

When the hook twitched the way static electricity makes a dead frog's legs twitch, Jeb knew that he and Nelson were close to reaching a gentleman's agreement.

'Half of that is for telling no one that I and my friend, who will be arriving later tonight, are your lodgers. We do not exist.'

Nelson, scything his jowly cheeks with his hook, nodded. 'And the other half?'

'For keeping your eyes and ears open and telling me anything you hear about other Americans visiting Newcastle. Waterloo Bob was employed by the Coxon brothers to be on the look-out for the man I am meeting tonight. Note well, that I said, "was". You know the Coxons?'

'Why aye! Everyone nars those two buggers.'

'They are paying Bob to keep an eye out for the gentleman I am meeting off the London train this evening.'

'So,' said Nelson, doing his best to make sense of what Mr Phelan, the wolf, had told him, while at the same time eyeing the sovereign on the table the way a cat looks at a mouse hole, 'you are paying Waterloo to tell the Coxon brothers he's never seen any Americans ... while they are paying him to be on the look-out for Americans.'

'The Coxons have paid him in promises.'

'Aye! That sounds like them. Am thinking Waterloo is on to a good thing. He's getting paid by the game keeper and the poacher … that's clever, that is.'

'In this game of cat and mouse, Nelson, I am the game keeper.'

'I've always had a weakness for poachers.'

'You feel for the hungry man who steals a rabbit for food?'

'Aye! Something like that.'

'In that case your heart is in the right place. I assume you are against slavery?'

'Oh aye! Neebody should be a slave.'

'In that case, you are on my side. I, too, am against slavery. The colour of my skin must tell you that.'

'Aye, it does.'

'The men paying the Coxon brothers are Confederates. They do not wish slavery to be abolished. I do.'

'Should you not be back home fighting?'

'My job is to stop the South buying guns and ships.'

'Who do you work for? I mean, you're not like a waterman are you what owns one boat and when there's neebody to ferry across the river has to gan cap in hand to the poor house?'

'My boss is Abraham Lincoln.'

'That's a bit like working for the Bank of England, isn't it?'

'Mr Lincoln is determined the Union will not be split and slavery will be abolished. Are you on my side? Will you take my money?'

'Have you got a handkerchief?'

'Of course I have. I am a gentleman. I do not blow my nose on my sleeve. But, why do you ask?'

'If we have a deal we have to shake hands. As my right hand is a hook you can't shake it but you can polish it.'

To humour the landlord and seeing no harm in what he'd been asked to do, Jeb polished the proffered hook with his handkerchief as if he was a char and the hook was a doorknob in need of spit and polish.

'There,' said Nelson, 'we've shaken hands on it. You have my word on it, Mr Phelan, that as far as nosy parkers gan and them Coxon brothers, in particular, Nelson has never clapped eyes on yuh or, for that matter the gentleman you are meeting up with toneet … which in that gentleman's case is true. What is more, if anyone asks me if I've seen an American, I'll clap on full sail and tell you all about, it. I'll be on the look-out like I was when Lord Collingwood sent me to the top of the mizzen in the Royal Sovereign afore the Battle of Trafalgar. I was young, you see. I had the sharpest eyes in the fleet. Not many folk nar this, but I was the first to spy the French sails. Three hours later, I'd lost an eye and a hand,' holding up his hook and looking at it as if trying to remember what his flesh and blood hand had looked like. 'When you Americans stop killing each other there'll be lots of men … good men, on both sides … missing an arm, a leg, an eye … and them that's left dead won't know what they've missed. Talking aboot war makes me thirsty … like when I've eaten too much salted pork. If you don't mind … and I don't think you will, now we are partners and you've polished me hook, I'll have another dram. Here's the key to your front door … give's a sovereign for it … that's in case you lose it … keys are like wives, they divent come cheap. Money returned when the key is returned … undamaged. Cheers! I'll tell you something, Mr Phelan … I like deeing business with Americans.'

'Cheers!' said Jeb, raising his glass, 'but please to remember, Nelson, I am only one American. I am not all Americans.'

'Aye! Aye! But yuh nar what a meant.'

JEB EXPLORES THE TOON

J eb was keen to explore Newcastle. The town had 'go'. It was a 'can-do' kind of town. It was a town full of optimism. It was a 'covered wagon' town. It was heading west in search of new opportunities … heading west in search of new ways of doing things.

He left his rooms, via his private front door. The room's key, for the safe return of which he'd paid the costly deposit of one sovereign, he put into the deepest of his coat's pockets.

Strapped to his back in its alligator skin case, he carried his banjo. Out of choice he never went anywhere without his banjo. He was not in the least bothered that carrying it strapped to his back – like a knapsack – made him look more like a minstrel, than a gentleman. In his heart of hearts, that's what he was … a minstrel. He was much more a minstrel than a secret agent. But not so much a minstrel that he also carried with him, in its bespoke shoulder holster, his Colt revolver.

Leaving the cobbled chare into which the Old George had grown, organically – the way a wall flower grows out of a wall – he found himself in a street full of buildings in the classical style. He was in ancient Rome. Corinth and Doric columns, pilasters and architraves plunged headlong down a steep bank. Like the Central Station, the County Hotel and Town Hall they looked brand new. The town's smoky god of heavy engineering had not yet had time, like a barber with a warped sense of humour, to lather them with soot.

Blowing his nose into his handkerchief, Jeb noticed streaks of soot in his mucus. Newcastle's smoky air had turned his nose into a chimney and, his good self, by blowing his nose, into a chimney sweep.

At the top of this curving, sloping street he spied a column higher than a four storeyed building. It, too, looked brand new. Once again he was reminded of ancient Rome. The inscription on its pedestal explained that the statue of the man on its top, was one Earl Grey. It appeared the fellow had been responsible for something called the Reform Act of 1832.

Jeb had no idea what had been reformed but thought it wonderful, that dear old stuffy England with its 'dooks' and 'pearls', had been able to reform whatever it had reformed without having to resort to civil war.

He wandered under the portico of a theatre that looked like a Greek temple. A poster wrapped round one of the pillars supporting its portico advertised the last performance of: 'Ali Baba and the Forty Thieves'.

To kill the time before he was due to meet Henry and to clear his head of the whisky he'd drunk with Nelson, he made up his mind to go exploring. Slightly tipsy, he thought of himself as a bumble bee setting out on a foraging expedition for pollen.

The setting sun was at his back. He was walking east. Could he smell the sea? Less than twenty minutes into his walk bushes and trees began to replace houses and shops. Only the glow of a red furnace at the bottom of a dene reminded him he was in an industrial town.

Newcastle, he decided, was a town he had yet to get the measure of. Geordies were an independent lot. They were free spirits. They were wild horses. The town had an underworld – the Coxon brothers. It was a busy and industrious town. It had saddle bags of self-confidence. It had one foot in the past: its old, timbered buildings and one foot in the future: its brand new stone buildings.

After a short stroll, here he was, out in the country. If this had been London, an hour's walk would not have taken him to such a rural setting.

Walking kept him warm. A cold February day did not incline one to sit philosophising under a tree like Buddha. Or to sit in pastoral bliss playing the banjo. He was a secret agent. He was a minstrel. Abraham Lincoln was paying his expenses. As Blondel had wandered Europe playing his many-stringed lute in search of King Richard, he, Jeb Prior Phelan, would play his banjo to abolish slavery.

He did not know where he was going. Nor did he much care. He was clearing his head. He was killing time. As the sun set it began to turn cold. He turned up his coat collar. He adjusted his banjo case. The part of his back it had, hitherto, kept the wind off, now felt cold.

Puddles were icing over. Spying a stream at the bottom of a dene and seeing that it flowed into a big river that had to be the Tyne, he reasoned he'd do a circular walk. To get back to his lodgings at the Old George all he had to do was follow the path down to the bottom of the dene and once back on the quayside, walk up-stream to the town's bridges. When he saw the castle he would know where he was.

Before descending he admired the view. The setting sun had turned the river into the colour of a bowl of oranges and bananas.

Reaching the bottom of the dene he walked along the banks of a stinking stream. A sign told him it was called the 'Ouseburn'.

Following its putrid water, he passed a kiln. It had a broad base and tapered upwards like an enormous ship's decanter. Stencilled on a green double door in yellow paint, he read: 'Henzell's Glass Works'.

The tide was out. He wished it had been in. The stench, coming off the Tyne's mudflats, made him sniff as if he had a head cold. Upstream, looking west in the direction of the setting sun, he saw the town's ancient, many-arched stone bridge. Behind it … dwarfing it … threatening to stamp it out of existence … he saw the massive, brand new rail and road bridge he had, that morning, walked under.

The two bridges were David and Goliath. In the confrontation between the giant and the little fellow, the little fellow had come out on top. The new bridge was progress. He, Jeb Prior Phelan, was an American. He believed in progress. David and Goliath weren't real life. In real life the big fellow would have won. In real life the northern states had more industry than the break-away southern states. In the long run, the Union would win.

The old stone bridge belonged to the past. If these bridges were guests at a party, he'd ignore the old bridge and give all his attention to the brand new iron bridge standing on pillars of stone the height of which he'd never seen before.

Walking along the quay towards these bridges, he walked under a wooden pier. The balks of timber supporting it looked as if they might, at any second, collapse. If its tripod legs had belonged to humans, a policeman would have arrested them on a charge of being drunk and disorderly. On the top of this rickety looking assemblage of poles and planks, coal wagons shuddered and wobbled like tight rope walkers.

On the end of this jetty on stilts, there was a spout. The sort you see every day on a milk jug only many times bigger. Under this slippery exit there sat, lopsided on a mud bank, a steam collier waiting to be loaded with coal.

The closer Jeb got to the old, many-arched stone bridge and the brand new High Level Bridge, the heavier the traffic on the quay … people, horses, carts, carriages, repeatedly blocked his way. The setting sun, a red ball of fire in the west, had transformed the filthy river into a stage setting for an Old Testament drama … lots of blood … lots of severed heads.

He was hungry and would have made his way back to his rooms at the Old George and dined there in private; that is, if he'd not heard music coming from a public house called the Old Grey Horse.

He was tempted. He'd already drawn attention to himself playing a duet with Waterloo Bob.

Damn it! He was cold. The fiddler was playing a catchy tune. Inside it would be warm and cosy. Why shouldn't he join them if he wanted to? Damn the war. Damn the Confederates.

The inn belonged to old Newcastle. It was a pre iron and stone building. There was more ancient Briton about it than ancient Rome. It was aal wattle and daub. In fact, the way its upper storeys twisted and turned on top of each other, it looked more like an ancient oak than a building. Its higgledy-piggledy four storeys looked as if at any moment they might fall into the river.

Was there a plaque, somewhere on one of its walls claiming a king had lodged there two hundred years ago? The English and their history! One day, America would have a history, not of kings and queens but of great presidents, like Abraham Lincoln.

Damn the war! Damn the Confederates! Damn slavery! He went in.

JEB MEETS MORE TYNESIDE CHARACTERS AND RUNS INTO A SPOT OF SERIOUS TROUBLE

The Old Grey Horse's bar counter was made out of three planks of wood laid across the tops of three barrels. The gaps between the planks were caulked with wads of sail cloth.

The slabs of slate on its floor were as higgledy-piggledy as fallen headstones in a graveyard. Were the bodies of dead topers pushing them up?

In New York Jeb knew all the places to stay away from. In New York, thanks to his doting mother and stepfather's wealth – Daddy built railroads – he had money and servants to protect him. In New York he was a lion. In Newcastle he was a lamb, armed with a Colt revolver.

The topers, whose music making had drawn him in, were huddled round a coal fire. His entry put an end to their playing the way it is said an earthquake stops birds singing.

A rotund gentleman, looking up at the beamed ceiling, said, 'We's that?'

'Nowt gets past Blind Willie,' said a man with a nose like a strawberry.

'We's let the cad in, Bugle?' said Blind Willie.

'A gentleman wearing an overcoat with a red velvet collar, Willie.'

'A gentleman? Ha! Ha! What's one of them deeing in here? Do yuh nar where you are, mister?'

'In a public house called the Old Grey Horse,' said Jeb. 'I am thirsty and hungry.'

'Mutton pies and mushy peas served next door, sir,' said an elderly woman with sunken cheeks. Her white hair was tied in plaits. At intervals the two plaits were decorated with paper bows.

'Careful, Aunt Judy,' said the man called Bugle with the nose like a strawberry, 'or he'll be after you like the press gang chased me grandfatha when he was a keel man.'

'He's not after a woman,' said Aunt Judy, 'I nar men. He's a respectable young man like you was, Cull Billy when I married you … afore yuh turned to drink.'

'Nowt wrong with having a drink,' said Cull Billy, 'it helps me sing when Donald plays his squeeze box and Willie plays his fiddle.'

Whereupon, to prove his point, Cull Billy began to sing, in a fine baritone: 'She's a big lass, she's a bonny lass and she likes hor beer.'

Taking the hint Blind Willie took up the tune on his fiddle. In a trice he was joined by Donald, a tall thin man wearing a Scotch bonnet, on a concertina. Then, a big fellow wearing a top hat with a dent in it, joined in playing a penny whistle.

'Is that a banjo I hear bein' tuned?' said Blind Willie.

'Aye it is,' said Bugle.

'If he can play it, we're in for a treat.'

Jeb played, 'Marching through Georgia'. He played the 'Battle Hymn of the Republic'. He joined in with their local songs. He especially liked, 'The Waters of Tyne'. A sad song which reminded him of slavery.

He improvised … couldn't help himself. He could never resist showing off how good he was at playing the banjo … him and his banjo were a horse and carriage. Was Blind Willie on the fiddle up for it? Yes, he was. And so was Donald on the concertina. And so was the tall thin man with a dent in his top hat, on the penny whistle.

What put an end to their plucking, blowing, squeezing and strumming was the bursting into the bar of two men and two women playing, respectively – two cornets, one trombone and a tambourine.

'Oy! Oy!' said Cull Billy, 'here comes the press gang.'

The interlopers were playing fortissimo, 'Onward Christian Soldiers'. All were wearing dark blue overcoats. The men had peaked caps. The woman, playing the trombone was young. Her chestnut hair flew out the back of her dark blue poke bonnet as if under the influence of an evangelical wind. Playing the trombone involved vigorous movements of the head. To stop her bonnet falling off it was tied under her chin, with a red ribbon.

They looked like soldiers. To Jeb, their dark blue uniforms made him think they looked like Union soldiers.

When they stopped playing a woman shaking the living daylights out of a tambourine, exclaimed, 'Hallelujah!'

'Hallelujah! Hallelujah! Hallelujah!' exclaimed the cornets and trombone.

'He's at the back, Major,' said the female trombone player, extending the slide of her trombone in the direction she wished the major to look.

'Captain Starkey, show yourself,' said, the tambourine shaker, 'put your hands together, Starkey, and praise the Lord. Your wife is here to save you.'

'In the reign of Caesar Augustus,' intoned Blind Willie.

'But, Gladys,' said Captain Starkey, 'a divent want to be saved.'

'Starkey, me darling, the Lord works in mysterious ways.'

'Aye! He does that,' said Blind Willie, drawing his bow across his fiddle to make a sound like a belly ache, 'for a start he made me blind.'

'Starkey, I am here to do you good.'

'Like castor oil,' said Blind Willie.

'Blind Willie, if you don't stop interrupting the Lord when he's talking you'll go to hell when you die. Starkey, my darling, the love of my life, I am here to save you from the demon drink. And stop hogging the fire. You do that at home and I don't like it. You are in a storm. Your ship is sinking. Jesus Christ has sent me to throw you a lifebelt, Starkey. Catch it. Strap it on. Tie it tight with a Keel man's knot. Let the cork of the Lord float you above temptation. Repent! Hallelujah!'

'Hallelujah! Hallelujah! Hallelujah!' echoed the brass.

'I'd better gan,' said Captain Starkey, who, despite his military title – given to him by his cronies when, many years ago, in an explosion of exaggeration he'd claimed to have been a captain in the Grenadier Guards – was a thin little man. His area of expertise was making faces behind his wife's back. 'I'd better gan,' he repeated, 'if I divent I'll have to make me own breakfast.'

'Do you repent, Starkey? Do you repent?'

'Aye, I do,' said Starkey, 'a nar when to fly the white flag.'

'Never mind the white flag, love of my life, do you repent on the holy book, that you will never, in the name of our Lord, Jesus Christ, again touch a drop of the demon drink?'

'I do!' said Starkey, risking a wink at his cronies who, to help him not having to make his own breakfast, were keeping straight faces.

'The Lament,' said Blind Willie, 'Handel's Death March … one … two … three.'

Smiling to himself at the similarity between preachers and snake-oil salesmen, Jeb put his banjo back into its case.

'Pie and mushy peas, next door, is it?' he asked Aunty Judy.

'That's reet, darling … take me advice, gan canny on the mushy peas or you'll be farting aal neet.'

'You are speaking from experience?' said Jeb.

'Cheeky bugger! You divent ask a lady a question like that.'

'Sorry!'

'Only a gentleman would apologise. Yee take care, bonny lad.'

****

Going down a narrow passage whose ceiling was kept up by sagging beams of black oak, Jeb came to a door marked 'Victuals'.

The Old Grey Horse's menu was: Mutton pie with mushy peas …
take it or leave it.

His order was taken by a waiter with fluttering eyelids.

'Drink?' said the waiter.

'What will keep out the cold?' asked Jeb.

'For a start, sir, that overcoat you are wearing … and your hat …
and your gloves.'

'I meant …'

'I nars what yuh meant, sor, but Alfred, that's me bulldog, has got
the lumbago. It's been a long day and the tide's coming in.'

'You are fond of your dog?'

'I am, sor. If he dies I'll slit me throat.'

'But not, I hope, before you've brought me a gill of rum and a jug
of hot water.'

'The hot water, sir, will cost extra … but, as you've got a red velvet
collar on your overcoat, I expect you can afford it.'

'One M and M, Minnie,' the dog-loving waiter with fluttering eyelids
shouted through a hatch. 'As hot as you can make it … genl'man feeling
the cold. And put the pot on the fire … he wants hot watta with his rum.'

While he waited for his food and drink to be served, Jeb checked
his watch. He'd a good three hours before he'd to meet Henry off the
London train. When he'd finished his mutton pie and mushy peas – his
'M and M' as the barman with the fluttering eyelids had called it – he'd
put his feet up for an hour in the privacy of his rooms at the Old George.

Jeb nicknamed the waiter 'Flutters'. 'Flutters' was good at his
job. The 'M and M', the gill of rum, the jug of hot water were served
promptly and, Jeb had to admit, with a certain flourish.

Paying the bill, Jeb said: 'Keep the change …' and in an attempt to
sound local, added, after a pause to make sure he'd get the phrase right,
'bonny lad'.

'That's very generous, sir,' said 'Flutters', quick at subtracting the
difference between the bill and the handful of coins Jeb had given him.
'You are an American, sor?'

'I am from the New World.'

'When a tell yuh what am ganna tell yuh, divent turn around … just pretend you've got eyes in the back of your heed. The two blokes by the door … you'll have to pass them on your way out, sir … have been asking about you. They know you are an American. When they asked me, I had to tell them. If I hadn't they'd have given me two black eyes. The Coxon brothers are well known around here, sir, and for aal the wrong reasons. A tip like what you've just given me deserves more than a knuckle to the forehead. Do you get what I'm trying to tell yuh, sir?'

'You think I might be in danger?'

'Waiter! There's a worm in me pie.'

'I'll have to gan, sir. He's a regular. If he didn't find a worm in his pie the tide wouldn't come in. Just watch out … that's aal am saying.'

The warning reminded Jeb of why he was on Tyneside. Abraham Lincoln was paying his expenses. Liverpool was full of spies. Waterloo Bob had alerted him to the fact that Newcastle was the same. And the two men who'd been asking about him were the Coxons, were they? Because he was an American, might they be thinking he was Henry Adams? Did they know Henry was not a man of colour? How much were the Confederate agents paying them to be their eyes and ears? Could he offer them more?

He took his time getting ready to leave. He refused to be rushed. He prepared for action. He made sure the buttons on his overcoat were done up. If push came to shove there must be nothing loose for an assailant to grab. He feared for the safety of his banjo. To keep it safe he slung it across his back as if he was a mountain man and the cased banjo was a rifle. He pulled on his hat so tight, a force eight gale would not blow it off.

The buttoned up greatcoat would make drawing the Colt difficult … fingers crossed, it would not come to that.

He looked hard at the men to whom 'Flutters' had drawn his attention. His 'staring' made them 'stare' back. If they'd been playing poker, Jeb had raised the stakes.

His curiosity was practical. If they attacked him, it was important he knew their strengths and weaknesses.

They were of average height. They had broad shoulders. Big hands. They would be formidable opponents.

No doubt about it, they were making it clear to him that they were interested in him.

The table at which they were sitting was close to the door … too close. Unless he turned tail and found another way out, he'd have to pass them.

He was an American. He did not take kindly to … intimidation … to being provoked. He also had in his make-up – though he'd have hated to have admitted it – a dash of 'Louisiana Lip' … a streak of the bellum southerner who would fight a duel to save his reputation.

It was a trait he'd inherited from his white slave-owning grandfather … the man, his mother had told him, had made his black slave father, disappear … had had him killed.

The Coxons were talking in loud voices. They wanted Jeb to hear what they were saying.

'What yuh deeing, Jackie?'

'Stretching me legs, Geordie.'

'Think I'll dee the same.'

'You've aalways got to dee what I dee.'

'That's cos we're brothers.'

'Aye but we're not Siamese twins.'

Proud of their banter the two brothers looked at each other and smirked.

What was this young black man ganin to dee aboot the fact that their plates of meat were blocking his way oot?

In the name of Abraham Lincoln, who did these louts think they were? Did they not know they were blocking the egress of a representative of the United States of America?

No doubt about it … the legs blocking his way were a provocation. Pride was involved. No way was he going to high-step over them. No way was he going to be polite and ask them to move. His boots were size ten … handmade by his stepfather's shoemaker in New York. They had thick leather soles and pointed toes in the American cowboy style.

The poor fellows were not wearing socks. Between their broken shoes and nankeen trousers he could see flesh.

The thug farthest away was rocking back on his chair to the extent that only two of its four legs were touching the ground. He further showed his nonchalance by cracking his finger joints.

The thug closest had stretched out his legs and crossed them at the ankles. Did he think he was at home, lounging in front of his very own fireside?

Boy! Were they relaxed! They were the sort of guys who'd free a bumble bee trapped in a conservatory.

Jeb kicked the ankles of the closest provocateur with a force incremental to its provocation.

To stop himself falling, Jackie Coxon, arms wind-milling, grabbed his brother … he who was using a chair with four legs as a rocking chair.

Jeb sidled past them when they were a knotted rope of arms and legs; sprawled, like jam, all over the Old Grey Horse's slate floor. Their language? Unprintable.

In New York Jeb played skittles. He'd call that a 'number one, strike'!

JEB THE FUGITIVE

Outside the Old Grey Horse Jeb knew he'd have to move fast. The Coxons were not the sort who'd take a beating lying down. His pre-emptive strike had bought him time; that was all.

He began to feel the way he imagined a runaway slave must feel. If he was caught he'd be beaten up … maybe, even lynched.

The quayside was but dimly lit by whale oil lamps tied to posts. Which way to go? To stiffen his resolve, he reminded himself of his pedigree. He was not a runaway slave. He was Jeb Prior Phelan, an employee of President Abraham Lincoln. In a shoulder holster he carried a Colt revolver. It was loaded. He knew how to use it.

The air was smoky and foggy. The oil lamps no more than hinted at where the quay ended and the river began. How easy it would be for the thugs to push him into the Tyne's stinking, freezing water. Death by misadventure. Who would meet Henry? Fast moving clouds kept blotting out a full moon.

He made out ships' masts, bobbing up and down. Was the tide coming in? He could smell the sea. He was sure he could. There was salt in the air. Sparks flying out of the funnel of one of the new steamers, was like watching a firework display.

Gas lamps lit the top of the old, many-arched stone bridge. Behind it, the brand new High Level Bridge was a silhouette. Flaring pricks of gas light lit its pedestrian level.

Dodging into a dark corner and looking round to make sure he was not being followed, he unbuttoned his overcoat. From the fob pocket of his waistcoat he took out the gold watch given to him by his mother and stepfather as a twenty-first birthday present.

By the light … more of a glow, actually … of an oil lamp, he checked the time: nine-thirty. In two hours, he'd to be in Newcastle's Central Railway Station to meet Henry.

In the meantime, he planned to put as much distance between himself and the thugs he'd assaulted as possible.

Which way back to the Old George? He didn't know. Find the big church with the lantern tower and he'd know he was close.

He was at the bottom of an escarpment. The landmark church, the castle, the railway station were all somewhere, on top. The lanes, stairs and chares he passed, all led upwards.

When clouds blotted out the moon areas of the quay were plunged into an impenetrable blackness. There were people around but not in the great numbers he'd seen earlier in the day.

Moving out from behind a passing cart and at the same time as clouds removed their curtain over the full moon, he heard: 'There he gans!'

He'd no intention of letting the Coxons get close enough to bash out his brains. In a fist fight the odds were all in their favour.

He unbuttoned his overcoat. He took out the Colt revolver. Could he outrun them?

Turning a corner, he found himself in a busy, gas lit street. Off this main thoroughfare, an unlit cobbled lane spiralled upwards like a staircase inside a lighthouse.

He did not want to have to use the Colt in a crowded street. He did not wish to wound or, worse, kill, by accident, an innocent bystander. His pursuers were hard on his heels. They weren't breathing down his neck, but they were close … too damn close!

Being on the run was making him angry. It was getting his gander up. If he did not manage to shake them off, he'd teach them a lesson they'd remember until the day they went to hell. With retribution in mind, he sprinted into the black void of the upward spiralling cobbled lane.

As long as he was going up he knew he was going, more or less, in the right direction. Somewhere up there was the Old George and the railway station.

The Coxons were hard on his heels. They were getting altogether too close. He could hear them:

'Can you see him?'

'Where's the bugger gone?'

The lane corkscrewed up from the quayside at an angle of fifty degrees. Its cobbles were slippery. His banjo was bumping up and down on his back as if it had come to life and was playing a tune on his spine.

As the lane levelled out it ran parallel with a stone wall topped with iron railings. Looking through its bars he made out the shapes of crosses. He saw obelisks. He saw vertical slabs of stone at crazy angles. Behind this gallimaufry of silhouettes there rose the black shape of a church with a spire. He was looking at a graveyard. Had he come here to die?

He came to a gate. Pushing it open it squeaked, as if the bodies of those therein entombed had come to life and were bidding Jeb welcome.

'He's in the graveyard.'

'At least he's in the reet place for what we're ganna dee to him.'

Entering the graveyard and closing the squeaking gate, it occurred to Jeb that while its noise had told his pursuers where he was, the same noise would tell him when they were in the graveyard. When he heard the gate 'sing' he'd know exactly where they were.

It was time to make a stand. Damn it! He was not a fugitive seeking sanctuary. He was Jeb Prior Phelan, an employee of Abraham Lincoln.

He sat on the marble plinth of an angel reading a marble book. The angel's legs made a snug back rest. His Colt revolver slept in his lap like a cat. He kept his hands warm by keeping them in the pockets of his overcoat. Cold hands were not best suited for firing a Colt revolver. When he fired the Colt he wanted … needed … a warm trigger finger.

The gate squeaked. So, they were in the churchyard, were they? Clouds parted. A sudden, splurge of moonlight turned the graveyard into a stage … a stage, set for a Gothic melodrama. Moonlight was fairy light. It changed stone crosses and marble angels into spectral, phosphorescent shapes.

Jeb felt disconnected from this transformation. He was a man concentrating hard on saving his skin.

The Coxons came into the graveyard, making a lot of noise. They were soldiers going into battle to the music of fife and drum. They whacked gravestones with their cudgels as if the former were drums and the latter, drumsticks.

'We nar you're in there!'

'We're coming to get yuh.'

They were coming closer. They were sticking close together. They were not going to be picked off, one by one. For what he had in mind, that suited Jeb, just fine. When they stopped under an urn on a pillar, he stood up.

'Over here!' he shouted.

'You're in for it now, mista!'

'Neebody takes on the Coxon brothers and gets away with it.'

Jeb took careful aim. He kept his hand steady by resting it on the marble prayer book the marble angel was holding in her clasped marble hands.

He had no wish to kill or maim. He did not wish to hang for murder. He did, however, wish to scare them. He wished to make them so frightened they'd shit themselves.

His bravado at showing himself had made them cautious. For a second they dithered close to a marble urn on a marble pillar.

Jeb took aim at the urn. Bang!

Shrapnel from the shattered urn shredded the Coxons' hats, tore holes in their thin coats and cut their faces. Confused, bleeding and bewildered they tumbled … fell, in a daze onto a tombstone.

While they were checking they still had ears and noses … that they were still alive … that they still had arms and legs, Jeb appeared in front of them.

Threatening them with the Colt, he told them to take off their boots.

'Eh?'

'Take off your shoes.'

'Eh?'

'What if I divent?'

'I am pointing a loaded Colt revolver at you. If you wish to die in a cemetery that is your choice.'

'Do as he says, Geordie. I divent want to die, 'ave got a wife and bairns to feed.'

'You're reet there, Jackie … a was forgetting aboot Mary. A can't see … not proper a can't.'

'Rub your eyes with ya spit.'

'Aye, that's better.'

'Take of your shoes,' repeated Jeb.

While the two thugs – all the time muttering oaths – took off their shoes, Jeb stood well back. Shoes were weapons. Might they be carrying knives? Where were their cudgels?

He knew they'd removed their shoes when, in the moonlight, their naked feet glowed as white as the white marble feet of a nearby statue.

'Lie down on the tombstone.'

'Eh?'

'Lie on the tombstone … cross your hands … pretend you are dead … which, you will be if you don't do as you are told. Hurry up! My gun is cocked. My hands are cold. I would hate to kill you by accident.'

Not wishing to prematurely join the angels, Geordie and Jackie did as they were told. Muttering obscene oaths they stretched out, side by side on the flat tombstone. As they lay flat on their backs, glowering at him, Jeb saw the shrapnel from the urn his bullet had smashed had done terrible damage to their faces.

'Close your eyes … cross your hands.'

On their backs on the tombstone they looked like effigies. The sculptor who'd carved their faces being clearly better at carving gargoyles than angels.

Jeb threw their shoes, this way and that.

Their heads were close together. To make them shit themselves he fired the Colt into the freezing grass a centimetre from their lolling heads.

The noise of the shot deafened them. Why couldn't they hear? Were they alive?

Jeb … dear Jeb brought up in New York by a loving mother and doting stepfather, had never known what it was like to go barefoot. He'd always had shoes. The Coxon brothers, on the other hand, were used to going barefoot. They didn't like it. But they were used to it.

Seconds after he ran out of the churchyard Jeb knew they were hard on his heels. For the first time in his pampered life, he began to feel anxious.

He was running to save his life. The Coxons were corks. Just when you thought you had drowned them … up they popped … madder than ever … hellbent on revenge.

He was no murderer. To put a stop to their harassment he did not wish to have to kill them. He was a musician who just happened to be a secret agent. He was not a secret agent who just happened to be a musician.

He would only ever get mad enough to kill them if they threatened his banjo. If they burst its drum, he'd waste more than their ear drums. 'Hallelujah!' as the tambourine evangelist had exclaimed in the Old Grey Horse. 'Hallelujah!' for the cause of ending slavery in America.

Where was he? He was lost.

INTRODUCING THE SINGER, SONGWRITER, COMEDIAN AND LOCAL CELEBRITY: ROWLAND HARRISON

On the stage of the Theatre Royal, the cast of the pantomime, 'Abdullah and the Forty Thieves' were taking their fourth or was it their fifth curtain call.

It was the show's final performance. Tomorrow, those in the line-up would be looking for work. Most of the lasses would be going back into service. Most of the blokes would be going back to shovelling coal. For a lucky few, the coming months might mean walk-on parts in Shakespeare … the odd part in a farce or melodrama … or, with those with the stomach for it … the music hall.

Centre stage in the line-up of performers taking their umpteenth curtain call and loving every minute of it and holding hands with Abdullah and bowing to say thank you to the audience for their applause … which was much appreciated … thank you very much … was 'Witty-Watty, the donkey man' played by the local singer, songwriter and comedian, Rowland Harrison: stage name 'Geordie Black'.

Rowley (everyone called him 'Rowley') had stolen the show. 'Esmeralda', his donkey – a real donkey – had pissed on stage.

A donkey does not piss in a thimble.

'It's "Paddy's Pant",' Rowley had exclaimed.

His ad lib had brought the house down.

In the wings, Albert, the Royal's stage manager, was making signs to the theatricals on stage, with egos as big as melons (in his opinion) that this was positively … definitely … their last curtain call … take it or leave it. He was thirsty. He was desperate for a pint at the theatre's Dress Circle bar. He wanted his free pint for all the hard work he'd put in to making the show a success.

****

The world of the theatre is brutal. A player, playing a king, comes off stage to find a practical joker has put a dead wasp in his cup of tea. When the curtain closes, the 'elephant' reality, sits on players and squashes the living daylights out of them.

Because it was the show's last performance, Rowley and his fellow performers were feeling particularly squashed by the 'elephant'. Rowley wondered where he'd find a new booking. On stage he was dressed as a ne'er-do-well out of the world of Scheherazade. His costume camouflaged his foreboding that if he didn't find work, he'd starve. If he didn't find work he'd not be able to marry Annie, the love of his life. Why, oh why, had she become an evangelical Salvationist? Why had she taken to learning to play the trombone? Why had she taken to hating booze?

The life of an itinerant singer, songwriter and comedian was not an easy way to earn a living. Joe Public was unpredictable. One minute they liked you, the next, you'd find yourself singing to an empty hall or, worse still, some cheeky bugger would throw a tomato at you. The fashion in music hall acts was no different to the fashion … now ganin round the toon for bowler hats … which reminded him …

'Albert,' said Rowley, 'as this is the show's last night and I might not see you for a while, would you mind if I asked you why, when you are at work, you wear a top hat? I mean … I divent mean this unkindly but you are not a toff.'

'I am when I'm a stage manager, Rowley. I'm in charge, see? In that respect I am a toff, see?' Lifting his topper and taking out from inside its tunnel, a soiled white handkerchief. 'I needs somewhere to keep me hanky. When you lot are up front prancing, I sweat for yuh, see? I sweats with worry as much water out of me pores as your donkey pissed on stage, toneet. When it started pissing I didn't nar what to dee. I nearly pulled the curtain shut.'

'I'm glad you didn't.'

'So am I. Your ad-lib brought the house down.'

'Four encores or was it five, for a pissing donkey? I owe a lot to that donkey.'

'Give him a carrot.'

'I'm wondering, Albert, where I will find, not a carrot for the donkey who so obligingly helped me to an abundance of encores, but where me next money-earning "carrot" will be coming from.'

'Your next booking?'

Rowley nodded. 'I have a booking tomorrow neet at Sir William Armstrong's house in Jesmond.'

'Soiree?'

'Aye! Pays well … after that … nee bookings.'

'Divent worry, Rowley, I see lots of acts. You are very popular. You have the ability, Rowley, to make folk either laugh or cry. That's a gift, that is. Me? I don't have that gift but I likes to be theatrical … that's another reason why I wear an out of character top hat. When you gans to a funeral you wears black. When you are looking after theatrical folk, you dress theatrical. There's front of house … there's them what's on the stage and there's backstage. I'm backstage but I likes to think I have a bit of "stage" in me. A top hat makes me look tall. I am of the opinion, Rowley, that a stage manager should be tall, like a policeman. Think of your encores, Rowley. They loved you toneet. Will you be celebrating with a drink across the road?'

'If I do, divent tell Annie.'

'She still learning to play the trombone?'

'Aye.'

'Still against the booze?'

'Aye.'

'It takes aal sorts, Rowley.'

'It does indeed, Albert.'

'I suppose to a performer like yourself, Rowley, applause is an alcoholic drink.'

'Me encores,' said Rowley, patting Albert on the back, 'make me feel as if I've been aal day on the brandy.'

WHAT FOUR MEMBERS OF THE AUDIENCE (UPPER CIRCLE) THOUGHT OF 'ABDULLAH AND THE FORTY THIEVES'. THE COXONS USE THE 'OLD GEORGE' AS A SHOE SHOP.

Dress Circle, Gods, Stalls, the Pit and those who'd sneaked in without paying, all agreed that Abdullah and the Forty Thieves was the best pantomime the Theatre Royal had ever put on.

The rowdies in the pit had laughed so much they'd dropped the orange peel they'd kept to throw at any performer they disliked.

Big watermen, used to shouting 'Hoy!' for a rope, had put two fingers in their gobs and, in lieu of clapping their approval had whistled. They'd played their mouths with two fingers the way players of the French horn nuance that instrument's notes by putting a hand down its bell.

For the rest of their lives they'd remember the neet they went to the Theatre Royal and with their own eyes had seen Witty-Watty's donkey piss on the stage.

The show had made them feel warm inside. It had made them forget the long hours they worked.

******

The elephant 'Reality' sitting on the performers backstage in their dressing rooms, now sat on the audience leaving the theatre. It sat on the departing theatre goers in the form of a north east wind.

'Bugger, it's cad toneet.'

'Brass monkey weather.'

The gas lights in the theatre's portico hissed. Flakes of snow drifted down out of a black sky. The moon and stars appeared and disappeared. Clouds scudded across the face of the moon faster than the old mail coaches had travelled to London.

'Bugger, it's cad toneet.'

'Brass monkey weather.'

'We'll have to cuddle up close toneet.'

'Mind, a divent want bairns.'

****

On their way to the Old George for a post-show drink, a group of Upper Circle friends argued about whether or not the donkey really had pissed.

The unshakeable view of Billy, the group's sceptic, was that there had been a bag of water under the donkey's tail.

'I'm telling yuh,' said Billy, 'it's the show's last neet … the theatricals were trying to dee something special … so we'd talk about the show. It's like advertising … it's to make us want to come back next year.'

'Witty-Watty took out a plug when he lifted up the donkey's tail,' said Edna, the sceptic's girlfriend.

Edna always took Billy's side. If Billy said the Earth was flat she'd say he was right and that aal the professors of geography were idiots. She loved Billy. She wanted to marry him.

'I'm telling yuh, that was real piss,' said John, the sceptic's pal.

John was proud to call himself a mechanic. He worked at Sir William Armstrong's factory at Elswick. He helped make machinery that did a job in a day that in the old days would have taken an army of men a week to do. He belonged to the new age of steam power. Sir William

Armstrong was his hero. As a teenager he'd attended one of Sir William's lectures at the Lit and Phil on how the electrical telegraph worked.

He'd only got into the lecture – they were always sold out – because his 'fatha' knew the doorman.

He had learnt to read and write at a charity school. He knew about Charles Darwin. He'd heard that, a long time ago, Man's great-great-great … there were a lot of 'greats' before you got there … had been apes. In truth he didn't like to think about this and wasn't at all sure if it was true but, thought it might be when he looked at his pal Billy, who at that moment was licking a snowflake off the end of his nose with a tongue long enough to have belonged to an anteater. John had seen drawings of an anteater in Mr Dickens' magazine, All the Year Round.

'Am telling you,' said John, 'that was real piss.'

'How'd yuh nar that? Howay, clever bugger, tell's.'

'It came out hot … at least, ninety psi.'

'Eh? What yuh on about? How'd yuh nar it was hot? And what yuh on about pie-in-the-sky for?'

'Were you not watching?'

'Billy was eating an apple when the donkey did its wee,' said Edna.

'It was hot because when it came out it made the air shimmer, yuh nar, like the way air does above a brazier … remember? When a used to work with yuh on the river we had a brazier in wor shack …remember? Where we used to sit to keep warm while waiting for the tide to turn.'

'Aye! Good days them,' said Billy, 'William was king of England and the keel men were kings of the Tyne.'

'Are yuh not curious?'

'Aboot what?'

'Why the air shimmers above a brazier?'

'Nar, am not … but, a think you are ganna tell me. When you get on your hobby horse, you're like the tide coming in … nee, matter what you dee you can't stop it. Howay then … get it off your chest … tell's why air shimmers ower a brazier … if yuh divent, it'll be stuck in your throat and when we get to the Old George, you'll choke on your pint

… and that, bonny lad, would put us aal off wor beer.'

'When light moves through layers of air at different temperatures it is refracted.'

'What's that mean? A nivva knew light could fart. Ha! Ha!'

'You are a wag, Billy,' said Edna.

'It means, the changes in air temperature have bent the rays of light,' said John.

'Oh aye! And what aboot pie-in-the-sky?'

'Psi, stands for … pounds per square inch. Only a real donkey's bladder could have kept squirting out water at that pressure for such a long time. If the water had been in a bag tied under the donkey's tail the bag would have had to be bigger than the donkey. If you want to work at Armstrong's you've got to know about things like water pressure. When the iron comes out the furnace yuh have to nar when it's ready to pour … it's the same as know'n when it's the reet time to ask your girlfriend if she'll marry yuh,' winking at Edna.

'Aye! Aye! Divent start turning the mangle. A divent want to talk about that. A nar when the tide's in and when it's out. And a nar when its ganna rain cos a nar about clouds. I divent nar their names … I expect you do … but a nar when not to gan out in a boat.'

'Aye, so you do, Billy … but if you want to get a job at Armstrong's and make good money, you've got to be able to read instructions and dee fractions. You must nar that half an inch is the same as four-eighths. I'm making good money … better than a did when a was a waterman. I'm on piece work.'

'How can yuh be on peace work when you're making guns?'

'You tell him, Billy,' said Edna.

'If there were nee wars and the world was aal peaceful like wor river is on a foggy neet, when the steam hammers are sleeping in their hammocks, there'd be nee need for guns.'

'You tell him, Billy.'

'See that,' said John, picking his nose, 'that's a "piece" of snot. When the guns stopped firing at Waterloo that was "peace" … "Piece" and

"Peace", yuh see, Billy, are two different words … sound the same but mean different things. And I'll tell you this … when the lads is negotiating the going rate for their piece work, it's not at aal peaceful.'

'Oh aye!' said Billy. 'Can a tell you a secret? This'll knock you off your high horse.'

'Go on, tell him,' said Edna, 'am proud of yuh.'

'You've been poaching and sold a brace of game to a butcher in the Grainger Market?' suggested John.

'Nar! Nar! Nowt like that.'

'You've found a bag of sovereigns.'

'Nar! Nar! Am learning to read.'

'My Billy's ambitious,' said Edna, grabbing hold of Billy's hand the way a keel man grabs hold of a rope thrown him by the first mate of a collier in a hurry to take on coal. 'I've told him if he wants to marry me, he'll have to leave the watta. We aal nar the "Waters of Tyne" kept the lovers apart … well, that's what the river's deeing to me and Billy.'

'I'm up to F,' said Billy. 'I'm looking forward to G the way a collier captain waits for a high tide to get him off a sandbank.'

'Billy doesn't see why there should be a G in "enough".'

'When a can read as well as a used to handle a keel boat, I'm ganna write a letter to Sir William in me own hand asking for a job where I have to read instructions and measure things not with me elbows and hands but with a proper ruler, aal notched in feet and inches.'

'Am pleased for you,' said John, 'but, whatever yuh dee, divent say yuh can dee something if yuh can't. Sir William knows aal about everything. Last week he passed me when a was struggling to sharpen a chisel … you'll never believe this, but he showed me how to do it … am telling you, Sir William is as good with his hands as he is with his heed.'

'You've got to leave the river, Billy,' said Edna. 'Nearly aal the keel men have gone to "Fiddler's Green". The new steamers can work when there's nee wind. And, Sir William is talking about pulling doon the old stone bridge ower the river … so I've heard … it's been there an awful long time but that doesn't bother him. He's ganna build a bridge what opens and shuts like a door. When he does that, steamers will be able to gan aal the way upriver to Dunston staithes.'

'He'll never dee that,' said Billy, 'neebody can build a bridge what opens and shuts like a door.'

'He will,' said John. 'I've heard that rumour. The Duke of Wellington said steam trains would never catch on … now, they're like measles … they're everywhere. Who'd ever have thought you could gan on a day trip to Tynemouth? And look at the High Level Bridge, who'd have thought wor River Tyne would ever have a big iron bridge like that ganin over it? Steam engines on the top, horses and coaches and folk underneath.'

'And cats,' said Billy, 'yesterday a saw a cat walk across the bridge. It wasn't scared of heights.'

'How'd you know it wasn't scared?'

'How'd you know the Duke of Wellington didn't think trains would ever spread like measles?'

'Read it in the newspaper, didn't I? When you can read you get to know things. How'd you know the cat had a head for heights?'

'It was walking on the parapet … wasn't it? It wouldn't dee that, would it, if it was scared? It was after them kittiwakes. If it had fallen in the river it wouldn't have drowned.'

'Now you're telling me yuh nar the cat can swim? And yuh call me a "clever bugger".'

'Nar! Nar! What am say'n is the river would have poisoned it. The river's dirty. It doesn't smell clean like it used to dee. When a was ten it aalways smelt of seaweed like them rocks dee, at low tide, at Cullercoats. At the Ouseburn the other day the stink was so bad a had to put a peg on me nose … and them steamers ganin up and doon … hoot'n and toot'n … and another thing … there's nee fish in the river … where's aal the salmon gone? That's what a want to nar. Where have aal the salmon gone?'

'Just make sure … when we get to the Old George, Billy, you're a steam ship and not a sailing ship.'

'What duh yuh mean?'

'A mean a divent want yuh getting becalmed halfway to the bar when you're buying the drinks.'

'Cheeky bugger … yuh calling me tight?'

'Would I?'

'Aye! Yuh would.'

'If I have to pick between steam ships and salmon, Billy, I'll pick steam ships every time. Billy, bonny lad, you know as well as I do, when we were bairns we were sick of salmon. Remember when we used to ask wor mothers, "What's for tea, Ma?" And if she didn't have any tripe in the pantry she'd cut a bit of rope off the washing line, tie a hook on its end and tell us, "Gan and catch a salmon." If you caught anything under five foot … why, man, it was a tiddler! Howay, man, Billy, put your thinking hat on. We were sick of salmon. Everyone went doon sick, sometime or other with the salmonella. Eating salmon saved me from drowning.'

'You on aboot that again, are yuh? When yuh got oot of your depth at Byker Sands?'

'Aye! I am. I never knew a could swim until me feet couldn't touch the bottom. You see, I'd eaten so much salmon I thought I was a fish.'

'You divent look much like a mermaid to me.'

'I was a merman … wasn't I?'

'Nivva heard of one of them.'

'Think about it, Billy, when you're ordering the first round … it'll take your mind off the pain of having to put your hand in your pocket.'

From somewhere down on the river, a steam ship hooted.

'Did you hear that?' said Billy, shaking his head in disbelief that one of the new steam ships was able to make a sound loud enough to travel from the river, aal the way up Dean Street and aal the way up Grey Street and still make yuh want to put your fingers in your ears. 'That's a steam ship farting, that is.'

'That, bonny lad, is the sound of progress,' said John.

'Aye! Well, I divent like it. Rivers should be quiet places … not like me Auntie Doris tell'n us not to eat peas off me knife. The only place a can hear mesell sing a shanty, now, is when am up at Dunston.'

'Progress is a girl that eggs you on/ tells you things will be better, anon,' sang John.

'But where have aal the salmon gone,' sang Billy. 'I'm telling yuh, John, there's as many keel men left now as there are salmon left in the river… am tell'n yuh … and that's not many … and soon there'll be none … nee keel men … nee salmon … just a river full of steamers, belching smoke and hooting and deein me heed in. I'm telling yuh, if I had a magic lamp like that bloke Abdullah, I'd rub it and tell the genii, "Nee more steam paddlers … get rid of aal of them". If the genii comes from the Sandgate he'll nar what a mean … plenty of genies doon there … they make the clothes on your washing line disappear and empty your coal house.'

'Billy,' said Edna, squeezing her beloved's hand to stop his blather, 'what letter comes after F?'

'Eh?'

'What letter comes after F?'

'Give's time to think … am like the tide on the turn … am ganin up river and doon river aal at the same time … give's a clue.'

'Where are we going?'

'The Old George … a nar that.'

'And, George begins with …?'

'G … you've thrown me a rope, bonny lass and Billy has caught it and thrown it roond a cleat … making aal firm and fast … after F comes G. G for George and g for genii.'

'Aye!' said John. 'And G is for Gallowgate where they used to hang people who didn't buy their round.'

'John, howay, man, a can't be learning me letters and thinking about getting me round in aal at the same time, can a?'

'In you get, bonny lad … M is for money … P is for pint.'

'He's only up to F,' said Edna, 'you'll confuse him. I was keeping M … for marriage. If he thinks M is for money, he'll never marry me.'

****

In the 'Old George', Billy and his girlfriend Edna, John and his wife Brenda (a quiet lass who since leaving the theatre had said nothing) supped their drinks in an alcove close to a coal fire.

Over the first round, Billy, put the world to rights by telling his captive audience about the 'specials' he'd sculled upriver that morning.

'There was two of them … a French-American and an American-American.'

'How do you nar that?' said John.

'Because a was counting. A nar when I've got two people in me boat, a nar aal aboot the Plimsoll line and overloading a boat … there was two of them.'

'I meant, how'd yuh nar one was a French-American and one was an American-American?'

'Because, Billy's not daft, that's how he knew,' said Edna.

'I heard them talking, didn't I?' said Billy.

'Billy's got big lugs and he knows how to use them,' said Edna. 'I like a man with big ears and ear lobes.'

'Billy's got no ear lobes,' said Brenda.

'A girl can't expect to find everything she likes in one man,' said Edna. 'Yuh divent gan into a fish shop if you want a leg of lamb.'

'Hoy!' exploded Billy. 'Will yuh stop talking aboot me as if I wasn't here … I am not a bairn, yuh nar … I knew the French-American wasn't from Howdon because he talked funny. He kept calling me, "Monsieur". He was worried me boat was ganna sink. He kept saying … am not good at deeing accents like Witty-Watty we saw toneet … but he kept saying: "Monsieur, ze but … it vill not sink?" When a sculled a bit too close to a sewer he put a silk handkerchief ower his gob and said, "Mon dew". I'll tell yuh this … the smell of the scent coming off his snotrag and the stink coming off the river had me nose ganin like a lurcher's at a lump of shite … beggin your pardon, ladies … that's when the other guy opened his gob … couldn't believe me lugs when he said: "Know what that stink reminds me of, Francois?". So, I said to myself … in me heed, like … starting to build up a picture of me clients, like … while pretending to do nowt else but me sculling … the Frenchman's name is, Francois, is it? "That stink reminds me of the smell a slave makes afore he's whipped." Then, he looks at me the way the coalman does when he's wondering if a nar he's ganna charge me for ten bags when he's only given me nine. He was a big bloke. Too old to work a keel. I didn't like him.'

'The coalman?' said John.

'Nar! Nar! The American … will yuh listen to what am saying … you might be able to read and write but yuh divent nar how to listen … to show him … the American … not the coalman … that I wasn't cocking me lugs at what him and the Frenchy were blathering on about a started to sing, Witty-Watty's song. "O, me, name is Geordie Black" … a very catchy tune that … doesn't matter what part he's playing, Rowley Harrison aalways sings it when he comes on stage … it's to let the audience nar who he is, see? A seen him at the Empire last year … he made's laugh … then, he made's cry … anyway, there I was singing … not loud like a dog, barking … more quiet … like an owl, hooting … when the Frenchie says to his pal: "My slaves sing when they're pick'n cotton. When I hear their singing, I know they're happy." That's when I forgot aal about pretending not to be listening to what they were saying and blurted out … a couldn't help mesel … "Ye one of those Americans what owns slaves?" a asked him … straight out. He didn't bat an eyelid … just looked me in the eye and told me: "The only thing you need to worry about, Mr Boatman," he said, "is that I have a sovereign in my pocket … row me and my friend to Sir William Armstrong's works at Elswick and back to Noo-castle and it's yours to spend on women and drink".'

'And did you?' asked John.

'Aye! I did … rowed them aal the way there and back.'

'A meant, did you spend the sovereign on women and drink?'

'No … a did not.'

'He bought me a bunch of flowers,' said Edna.

'There's nee flowers out at this time of year,' said John.

'There are if you've got enough money in your pocket to buy them,' said Billy, 'and you're in love,' giving Edna a kiss.

'Billy bought me daffodils,' said, Edna. 'They are aal the way from the Scilly Isles. Steam ships built on the Tyne ferry the daffs aal the way from the Scilly Isles to Falmouth … where, one of Stephenson's steam engines takes them to Lundon where another steam engine puffs them aal the way to Newcastle … aye, without Tyneside steam and coal there'd be nee daffs in the toon in February.'

'How much did you pay for them,' asked John, 'just out of interest, like?'

When Billy told John how much he'd paid for the flowers, John said, 'Eh! You're kidding, aren't you?'

Feeling embarrassed that his private extravagance was now public knowledges Billy looked hard at a Maling's ware jug on a shelf above the bar.

'Daffodils from the Scilly Isles,' said John, shaking his head, 'bought at a silly price by me old pal Billy who must be silly in the heed to have paid that much for a bunch of flowers.'

'Billy's not silly in the heed,' said Edna, 'are you, my darling? He's in love. When we get to L, Billy, you'll find that letter easy to remember … L is for love.'

'Billy,' said John, 'a seen a bull the other day … reminded me of you.'

'Was it in a field with a lot of cows?' asked Billy, striking a pose as he imagined himself the proud possessor of a harem. 'In the pantomime, Abdullah had ten wives.'

'No, it had a ring through its nose and a little fat wife was taking it to the knacker's yard.'

'If you don't mind, I'll have another gin and water,' said Edna. 'And stop putting ideas into Billy's heed. If it gets filled up with your notions, John, there'll be nee room for aal the other letters he has to learn; there's a lot of letters after F, Billy.'

'If you say so, pet.'

'Billy?'

'What now?'

'A think I've got a fly in me eye … can you have a look and see if you can see it? I know you'll be gentle, cos I've seen you tie a reef knot.'

******

Over a second round of drinks, bought by John – despite him telling Billy that if someone had tipped him a sovereign he'd have bought aal the drinks – they found themselves once again talking about the two Americans.

'When he got going, the old American did aal the talking,' said Billy. 'He kept asking as many questions as me mother did that neet a came haem with a black eye.'

'What sort of questions?' said John.

'He wanted to nar if you could get a steam boat up to Elswick. A told him, the old stone bridge stopped the steamers getting that far up the river … but, when they dropped their sails, keels could gan up and doon, nee bother. Then, he wanted to know what a keel boat was … so, a pointed one out to him. Bell's keel, full of coal, coming from Dunston … so full it looked like a mole hill on the wata. Then he wanted to know how much a keel could carry. "How many tons, my man?" he said. A didn't like it … him calling me, his 'man'. A thought he's talking to me as if I was one of his slaves. To put him in his place a rocked the boat. Me antics made him grab the gunnels. Heh! Heh! His knuckles was white. I've seen white knuckles afore when drowning men clutch a rope that's been thrown them. When we'd stopped rocking I told him a keel could carry twenty-one ton of coal … then, he wanted to nar if a keel could carry any cargo. I said I supposed it could … then he wanted to nar if a keel could be loaded from the quay we could see at Armstrong's works … a said that if the tide was reet, a supposed it could.'

When an outside door close to the snug in which the friends were sitting, opened and shut, it puffed into their cosy corner – as if it was a pair of bellows – wafts of freezing air. Looking up to see who was responsible for giving them the 'shivers', the friends saw two men.

'They look the worse for wear,' said John.

'Shut the door, after yuh, gen'lmen,' Nelson shouted at the newcomers.

'It's the Coxon brothers,' whispered Billy. 'They're working for the two Americans a told yuh about. It was them what booked me to take the Americans upriver.'

'A hope they divent cause trouble,' said John.

'I think they've been in trouble by the looks of them,' said Brenda; a gin and hot watta having loosened her tongue.

'They're not wearing boots,' said Edna.

'They're not getting mine,' said Billy.

'Billy, darling, if they try to take your boots, I'll scratch their eyes out.'

'Thank yuh, pet.'

'Their faces are aal cut the way me mother scores belly pork to make crackling.'

'I'll bet they've been poaching,' said John. 'That's gamekeeper's acne, that is. Whenever we had rabbits, me dad looked like that.'

To show Geordie and Jackie (well known to Nelson) that he was in nee mood to stand any of their nonsense, Nelson showed the bruised and battered ruffians, a blackthorn shillelagh.

'Now, bonny lads,' he said, banging the cudgel on the bar's counter, 'wht'll yuh be having … booze or bandages? Yee two been in the wars? You've as many cuts on your faces as I've seen on the back of a matelot after twenty strokes of the cat.'

'Blunt razor, Nelson,' said Jackie Carson.

'Aye, blunt razor,' said Geordie Carson.

'Pull the other one, me hearties. I'm not as gullible as that carpenter Joseph when he believed Gabriel was the father of the bairn in Mrs Joseph's belly. With cuts like that you'll be wanting bandages not booze. This is a public house, not the keel man's hospital.'

'Two rums and watta, Nelson … like Colly gave yuh on the Royal Sovereign, after Trafalgar,' said Geordie Coxon.

'Divent set him off tarkin aboot Trafalgar,' said Jackie Coxon, 'start Nelson off aboot how him and Admiral Collingwood shot doon the foremast of a French man o'war and we'll need a shave afore we get wor rum.'

'Nelson?' said Geordie, leaning over the counter and whispering. 'Have yuh got any shoes … boots, yuh can let's have?'

'Eh?'

'Boots … have yuh got any?'

'Aye, a have … they're on me plates of meat.'

'Spare boots, Nelson … size ten for me and size nine for me brother.'

'We nar yuh sometimes take boots instead of sovereigns,' said Jackie.

'If a gentleman can't pay with money he has to pay with something … and paying with your boots is better than paying with your trousers … especially if you're not wearing drawers. What you two been up to?'

'Divent tell him,' said Jackie.

'We was robbed,' said Geordie.

'The Coxon brothers … robbed? Pull the other one … that'll be the day!'

'There was ten of them,' said Geordie.

'I counted more than that,' said Jackie.

'Now, a nar you're joking,' said Nelson, 'trying to make on yuh can count to ten. That's a good'n … that is … the Coxon brothers been able to count to ten.'

'Two rums and water, Nelson, and two pairs of boots, size ten and nine … and we divent want Dutch clogs either … we want proper boots … or shoes,' said Jackie.

'And we divent want brown boots, either. We want black boots. Black suits wor mood. When we get wor hands on the fellah stole wor boots, he'll be black and blue aal over. He'll look like me hands look after I've been blackberry picking.'

'So,' said Nelson, 'there was only one bloke stole your boots?'

'Nivva ye mind, Nelson,' said Geordie.

'We've put wor order in,' said Jackie.

'Let's see the Queen's face, first,' said Nelson. 'If you think you can pay with rabbit skins … think again. I've got enough boots under the counter to start a boot shop and enough rabbit skins to keep aal of the navy warm if every man jack of them was sent to the South Pole.'

'Are yuh ready for a shock, Nelson?' said Geordie.

'Gan on, dee it,' said Jackie, who could read his brother's mind.

'Me and me brother want to buy you a drink,' said Geordie.

'As a thank you,' said Jackie, 'for aal the good times we've had at the George.'

'Like that time yuh put a plate of tripe on the counter and said we could help worselves.'

'A nearly got killed in the crush.'

After pretending to corkscrew wax out of an ear with his hook – to make sure he'd heard right – Nelson said: 'I'll have a whisky and water … lots of water. When you two come in here I like to keep a clear heed. If I had daughters … I'd lock them up.'

'Put it on the bill, Nelson,' said Jackie.

'You see, bonny lad,' said Geordie, 'we're in the money.'

'Robbed a bank, have you?' said Nelson. 'If you had, I wouldn't be surprised. Let's see your money. I can't buy myself a whisky with fresh air … never mind serving you rum and letting you rummage through me collection of boots. I warn yuhs now … afore yuh gan rummaging … me collection's not in apple pie order. Sometimes a customer paid with one boot. You'd have a bigger choice if you had a peg leg.'

'It's American money,' said Geordie.

'Am not taking foreign money. This is the Old George, not the Baltic Exchange.'

'You're too quick to hoist the top sails after a storm, Nelson.'

'Like wor old man,' said Jackie, keen to underwrite his brother's meaning with an example drawn from his own library of family history, 'that time he jumped ashore with a keel's mooring rope between his teeth. When fatha landed in the watta he pulled out aal his front teeth.'

'What a meant was,' said Geordie, dropping a sovereign onto the bar counter, 'is, it's English money paid to me and me brother by our American employers for services rendered. An English sovereign, Nelson, to buy two rums and watta, a whisky and watta for a landlord with as many locks on his cash box as that miser in that bloke Dickens's Christmas Carol and boots or shoes to fit.'

'Black!' said Jackie.

'Aye, black boots or shoes … what fit. And when yuh give's me, me change, a divent want it dropped into me hand like coal gannin doon a chute into a keel. A want you to count out the coins you give me, one by one. A wouldn't trust you, Nelson, as far as a could throw a cauldron.'

'Gan to the seat with the lift up lid, in the corner, ower there,' Nelson told the brothers, 'that's where you'll find the boots … nee socks, mind … just boots. A tanner a boot … a bob the pair.'

He gave them time to try on their new footwear … time for them to stamp around in their new boots … time for them to make sure they were comfortable.

He served them their rum and himself a whisky.

He dropped Geordie's change – as he'd been instructed to do – coin by coin, into the latter's outstretched palm.

'Correct to the farthing, bonny lad,' said Nelson. 'Am not being nosy, like …'

'Not much!' said Geordie.

'Nelson,' said Jackie, 'yuh sound just like me mother when she used to ask me dad … "Am not been nosy, like, but how much money have yuh made this week?" … remember that, Jackie?'

'Aye, a dee.'

'Alreet! Alreet!' said Nelson, lifting up the patch covering his missing eye to scratch the scarred socket. 'I'll cut to the quick … what yee two bonny lads deeing for these Americans that they pays yuh in sovereigns?'

'We're local knowledge,' said Geordie. 'Aren't we, Jackie?'

'Aye! Local knowledge … we tell him when the tide's in and when it's out.'

'Has he not got eyes in his heed?' said Nelson. 'Neebody gets paid in sovereigns for telling somebody the tide is out or in.'

'We dee other things as well,' said Jackie.

'Like … cleaning their boots and carrying their bags?' suggested Nelson. 'A niva thought I'd see the day when the Coxon brothers wore livery … you'll be coming in here next with powdered wigs on ya heeds. You've aalready got knuckle marks on your foreheeds. Everyone in the navy, had one of those. "Yes, sir!" knuckle to the foreheed. "No, sir!" Knuckle to the foreheed.'

'You're seeing things, Nelson,' said Geordie.

'It's cos you've only got one eye,' said Jackie.

'What I'm saying,' said Nelson, 'is, I'm seeing red marks on your clocks, like them Hindu women had on their foreheeds … what a saw, when a sailed into Bombay … they got them to show they were married … you two have got them from knuckling to these Americans. If you're not careful you'll let the gangrene in … gangrene's aalways wanting to be let in. If you two bonny lads aren't knuckling to the Americans, I'll burn me shellaleigh and fight the pair of you with me good hand tied behind me back.'

'Divent push your luck, Nelson,' warned Jackie.

'We're keel men, on hard times,' said Geordie.

'We're not in livery.'

'Shall a tell him?'

'Why not!'

'We're spies.'

'Oh aye!' said Nelson.

Nelson knew men. He'd sailed twice round the world. He hated lemons because he'd had to suck them to stop the scurvy. Under fire, he'd seen braggarts turn into cowards and quiet men … men who'd run five fathoms to avoid a brawl … turn into heroes.

He'd seen officers drink rum to give them courage. With his one good eye he knew, from experience, when a customer … aggravated and emboldened by booze … was going to hit him … experience, enabling him … most of the time … to land the first punch … his speciality being jabbing forked fingers into his would-be attacker's eyes. Whereupon, having weakened his opponent – as bulls are weakened in a bull fight by barbs in their necks – he was in the habit of administering a rabbit punch to the fellow's neck, followed by the homily: 'Sir, you are a sinner and a bully … picking on a poor fellow with one arm and one eye … say sorry, or, I'll put my hook up your nose.'

Locals always said: 'Sorry, Nelson,' well knowing that if they did not eat humble pie, Nelson would order Boris, the pot boy, to empty a piss pot over them.

A local man knew the hook threat was aal blather but the piss pot wasn't. Ganning haem with a black eye was one thing … ganning haem smelling like a netty … well … yuh had your pride … didn't yuh?

Men were like lemons. To get the juice out of them you had to cut them open and squeeze them. Someone had already cut the brothers open. Who? With a bit of squeezing – what he called the 'Nelson touch' – he'd get them to tell him aal their secrets. He wanted to know more about the Americans who were paying them in sovereigns. Did aal Americans pay in sovereigns?

He relished his secret that upstairs he had an American guest who had paid him in sovereigns.

To help him think, he tapped a wart on his cheek with his hook. It crossed his mind that Newcastle was filling up with Americans faster than the tide covered the sandbank opposite Armstrong's engineering works at Elswick.

'He's playing with his wart,' said Geordie.

'That means he's thinking,' said Jackie.

'When yuh see a crocus yuh nar spring's on its way.'

'When Nelson plays with his wart yuh nar he's thinking.'

'What yuh thinking, Nelson?'

'Am thinking about Americans with too much money.'

'Showing Nelson a sovereign,' said Geordie, 'is like showing a rabbit a lettuce.'

'If I nar Nelson, he wants a finger in the pie,' said Jackie.

'Do you want a finger in the pie, Nelson?' said Geordie.

'I might do,' said Nelson.

'Might dee!' said Geordie.

'He'll be telling us next he doesn't watta his beer,' said Jackie.

'If you are spies,' said Nelson, 'who are you spying on? Not, I hopes, on poor old Nelson who served as a powder monkey on the Royal Sovereign and lost an arm and an eye in the service of his country.'

'For god's sake, Nelson, divent start on again aboot that … nar, we're not spying on you … yuh nar that,' said Geordie.

'But we are here to let you put your finger …' said Jackie.

'His little finger,' said Geordie.

'In the gravy …'

'In the American pie.'

'Oh aye!' said Nelson, 'that's very kind of you. When you two are kind to people like me, a start to worry. You haven't got religion, have you?'

'Nar! Nar! Divent be daft,' said Geordie. 'Me and my brother came in here to cut a deal, like.'

'And to buy boots,' Nelson reminded them.

'Aye! Alreet then … and to buy boots.'

'What's the deal?'

'He's interested,' said Jackie. 'He's taken the bait … now, aal you've got to dee is get him to the shore and bash him on the heed with his walking stick.'

'It's called a shellaleigh,' said Nelson. 'I divent need a walking stick, I've got legs. I'm not like me old pal, Waterloo Bob. What's the deal?'

'If you hear about any other Americans in the toon, send a carrier pigeon doon to the Sandgate to tell me and Jackie,' said Geordie.

'We nearly had him in the Old Grey Horse,' said Jackie.

'Aye!' said Geordie. 'He was ordering a mutton pie with his rum … soon as he opened his gob a knew he was the American wor paymaster wants to nar about. He stood out like a kipper in a basket of herring. You haven't seen him, have yuh? You nar everything that gans on in the toon.'

'We're gannin roond aal the pubs,' said Jackie. 'Putting the word out. If yuh see a black American … tell Geordie and Jackie.'

'If a tell yuh I might have seen a black man with an American accent, div a get to dip me finger in the gravy?' asked Nelson.

'What did this bloke, you might have seen, look like? Was he short or tall?' said Jackie.

'Middle height,' said Nelson.

'Oh aye! He wasn't a lascar, was he?'

'Nar! Nar! I've sailed with lascars … very good seamen … lots of them live doon at South Shields … Nar! Nar! This bloke a might have seen wasn't a lascar.'

'Was he carrying a banjo in a case?'

'A what?'

'Yee ganin deaf, Nelson? A banjo in a case?'

'Not that a noticed,' said Nelson.

No doubt about it … the American to whom he was renting rooms was the American they were after.

Mr Phelan had paid in advance. He was a good tipper. Nelson was his 'eyes and ears'. They'd struck a bargain. You couldn't trust the Coxons. If he told them the American they were after was renting the rooms above their heads he'd be lucky if they gave him a farthing. The gulf between what they promised and what they did was as wide as the Pacific Ocean … and he knew how wide that was … he'd sailed across it

… three times. Mr Phelan was a gentleman. With his own eyes Nelson had seen the ugly side of slavery. The folk who said it had a good side, were wrong. They hadn't seen it, not with their own eyes, they hadn't.

He liked Mr Phelan. There was no way he was going to let on to the Coxons that the man they were after was lodging upstairs.

SOME DRESS CIRCLE CHARACTERS

Dress Circle ladies were never in a hurry to quit, the cosy warmth of the Theatre Royal. Scurrying and hurrying was for the poor. It took time for one's servant to collect one's coat from the cloakroom. It took time to find the right coin with which to tip. Not too much, not too little. It paid to tip. A well-known non-tipper had once found a dead mouse in her pocket.

A trip to the powder room to check one's face was part of the night out. After laughing so much at Witty-Watty's urinating donkey, mascara needed to be checked. A fur stole could not be flung over a shoulder as if it was a bag of coal. Stoles were like flowers – to look their best they needed to be arranged.

And then, there was the carriage problem. One did not wish to go out on such a cold night, unless one's carriage was there, ready, and waiting for one.

For some of the above reasons, Lady Armstrong, with her maid Emma, and Doris – a relative up from London – were among the last to leave the theatre. Outside a north-east wind scoured their cheeks.

'William said we were to meet him in his office at Hood Street,' said Lady Armstrong.

'Is it far?' asked Doris.

Doris was not used to the Newcastle way of doing things. Surely, Meggie, as Lady Armstrong's friends called her, would not expect a lady to walk miles on a night like this? There had been times during her visit to the Armstrong home in Jesmond, when Doris had felt she'd have been more at home with Hottentots, than with Geordies.

'Meggie,' said Doris, 'I don't wish to sound squeamish but I must remind you … I am dressed for the theatre … not for a grouse shoot on a Scottish moor.'

'Two miles,' said Lady Armstrong, 'but don't worry, the streets are gas-lit, all the way. It will be perfectly safe. It is years since the keel men caused trouble.'

'You are joking?'

'Of course I am.'

'Meggie, you are a tease.'

'Excuse me, ma'am,' said Emma, 'but would you mind if I popped across the road and put a penny in Waterloo Bob's tin? He's in his chariot.'

'Where is the veteran?'

'In that doorway, over there, ma'am.'

'A beggar in a chariot!' said Doris.

'It's not a chariot, ma'am, like what folk with money travel around in,' explained Emma. 'It's a coffin on wooden wheels. Its end has been chopped off, so Bob, can slide in and out, easy, like. You see, ma'am, Bob has nee legs. When he's not using his peg leg he gans about the town in a buggy. The folk what knows him calls it his chariot. He is a musician, ma'am. He plays the Northumbrian small pipes.'

'Never heard of them. And I am musical. I play the piano and the balalaika. What are they?'

'The Northumbrian small pipes, ma'am?'

'Yes, Emma, the Northumbrian small pipes. What are they? I wish to be enlightened.'

'They are like miniature bagpipes, ma'am. You don't blow air into them with your gob, you use bellows, like a blacksmith uses. Not big bellows like a blacksmith uses, but little ones like what a fairy or goblin might use to puff a spider off a plate of tripe.'

'Think of a Scotsman playing the bagpipes,' said Lady Armstrong who enjoyed teasing her London relative. 'The fellow is walking to Newcastle from Inverness. Every mile he walks takes an inch off his height. By the time he reaches the Tyne he is a wee fellow and so are his bagpipes. As Emma said, Doris, the Northumbrian small pipes are small bagpipes. William is fond of their drone. In them you hear the sad sound of Northumberland's bloody history. Everyone in Newcastle knows Waterloo Bob.'

'Heaven above, Meggie,' expostulated Doris, 'do you know the name of every busker in Newcastle? London is so full of them, I wouldn't know where to start.'

'Newcastle, Doris, is an intimate town. While I would not go so far as to claim Newcastle folk are all on first name terms with each other, the town has a handful of characters with whom everyone is familiar. Emma, put this in Bob's tin–' taking money out of a purse and handing it to the maid.

'Thank you, ma'am,' said Emma, dropping a curtsey in appreciation of the high value coin her mistress had handed her.

'Ask him to play something for me,' said Lady Armstrong, 'something cheerful … something that will make me think I am back in the theatre. Off you go. Doris and I will wait here.'

Returning from her errand, Emma said: 'Bob sends his regards, ma'am and thanks you kindly. If it's aalreet with you, ma'am, he's going to play Bobby Shafto.'

'That quite cheers me up,' said Lady Armstrong on hearing the familiar tune. 'Sometimes, Doris, I need cheering up. Do you know, it is fifteen years since William and I had a holiday?'

'At least you still have a husband, Meggie; mine is dead. And as for the tune, I agree it is very cheering. It makes me forget my woes.'

To show his gratitude for Meggie's generous contribution, Bob improvised. He put the simple tune into a First Class railway carriage and took it on a musical journey. He dressed up the folk tune in a variety of styles.

If these styles had been costumes, they'd have ranged from brocaded Elizabethan tunics to powder blue Regency waistcoats. It was after going through many variations that the tune changed … merged …

hiccupped … into 'Dixie'.

'I know that tune,' said Doris, 'it's a Confederate song. How does a Tyneside busker know a Confederate song? Newcastle is a long way from America and its civil war. Meggie, you and William may not have had a holiday in fifteen years but at least William is not a soldier fighting in a brutal civil war.'

'I don't recognise it,' said Lady Armstrong, 'though it is a foot tapper.'

'It's a new one to me as well, ma'am,' said Emma.

'I'm afraid,' said Doris, 'the American Civil War is creeping into all our lives. I only know the tune because I heard it played at the Adelphi Theatre, last year. An American owns the Adelphi. The poor dear didn't know which side to support. Outside his theatre he flew the Stars and Stripes and the Confederate flag. At the time there was a lot of ill feeling, in London, against the North.'

'I read about it in the Times,' said Lady Armstrong. 'I believe the North had the audacity to stop one of our mail ships. "Brother Jonathan" as I believe we call our American cousins reminds me of a Sandgate teenager. He is rather too full of himself. He has yet to learn how to hold his drink. I fear affluence is making Brother Jonathan think he can take on the British Empire.'

'Talking of the British Empire, Meggie, makes me think of India. I do hope Hood Street is not as far as Madras.'

'Don't fret, Hood Street is around this corner.'

'And … gas-lit, all the way?'

'Of course.'

'I'm sure it's not far, but I'm equally sure that on such a cold night the nobility would have taken a coach. I know they would.'

'William is a knight of the realm, Doris, but my husband and I do not belong to the nobility. In British society we are the jam in the middle of a sponge cake.'

'But, Meggie, William has met the queen. Tell me again, what she said to him.'

'When she knighted him, he said she smiled at him and was most gracious.'

'It is a great honour to be knighted.'

'William is of course pleased and conscious of the honour her majesty has done him, but my dear husband is not a natural courtier. The honour has not gone to his head. Indeed, I don't think there is room for it, so full is it already of ideas about how to use water to turn wheels and lift enormous weights. He says he is now a pan with two handles. One handle is cast iron. One handle is silver. The cast iron handle he calls, William. The silver handle he calls, Sir William. I keep teasing him that to keep its shine silver must be polished; that he should insist those who are not his equals call him "Sir William".'

'I know William, Meggie, and so do you. We both know he'd care not a jot if his silver handle tarnished. He is not in awe of dukes and lords. I know he has met many on his business visits to London. I would not say he knows more people in high society than my good self but, like the battle of Waterloo, it is a close-run thing.'

'Only one thing awes my dear William and that is water power. If England's nobility was a hydraulic crane, I do believe he'd be more than happy to spend months at a stately home. William is in love with nuts and bolts and pulley wheels.'

'Excuse me, ma'am,' said Emma, 'I knows you've already given very generous to charity … Waterloo Bob was ever so grateful … but I'm seeing the Sally Bashers coming our way. If I know anything about them, I knows they'll be shaking their collection boxes under our noses.'

'Sally Bashers?' said Doris.

'It's a new organisation, ma'am. They are called the Salvation Army but everyone I know calls them the "Sally Bashers". They're temperance … yuh know, ma'am, against … boozing.'

'If they are an army,' said Doris, eyeing with apprehension the fifteen or so men and women marching towards her, 'will they attack me?'

'Divent be daft, ma'am … begging your pardon, ma'am … they're temperance. As long as we … you know? All of us put a few pence in their collecting box, we'll be safer than we would be doon at Sandgate at two o'clock in the morning when the tide's high and there's nee moon.'

'Emma,' said Doris, 'why have they stopped?'

'They have stopped, ma'am, for a "repentance". They wish to give a soldier a chance to repent.'

'A soldier!'

'They call members of their congregation, soldiers, ma'am. Instead of having deacons and bishops, they have majors and colonels.'

Under a gas lamp, in the centre of a circle of men and women armed with cornets, trombones, euphoniums and tambourines, there stood a man who looked as if he was about to be hung.

'Starkey!' shouted Major Starkey. 'Are you ready to say your testament? Have you seen the light?'

Looking up at a hissing gas lamp, as if that was what his wife had meant, Starkey nodded.

'Hallelujah!' hallooed the Major, shaking her tambourine. When the tambourine failed to jingle, she glared at it the way a Byker granny glares at a shopkeeper who has given her the wrong change.

'Major,' said a fellow evangelist, 'the Lord has frozen your jingles. It is a very cold night.'

'Without my tambourine I cannot Hallelujah with conviction,' said Major Starkey.

'Does that mean, Gladys,' said Captain Starkey, 'I'm off the hook … at least for toneet?' And, looking up at the gas lamp, like a Labrador begging for a biscuit, 'I've seen the light, Gladys.'

'Certainly not … down on your knees, Starkey. Pray the Lord will give you strength never to touch another drop of the hard stuff for as long as you live.'

'Gladys, the cobbles is cad and damp.'

'And Hell is hot and sulphurous … down, Starkey, and move into the light. I want you where I can see you … hands together, Starkey.'

'I'm not a bairn, Gladys. You're me wife, not me mother.'

'The angel of the Lord has sent me to look after you, Starkey.'

'I wish he hadn't bothered.'

'Starkey! Pray! Let the Lord fill your sails with love.'

******

'What a humiliation for the poor man,' said Doris.

'Excuse me, ma'am,' said Emma, 'but he's used to it. The major knows what she's doing. She won't let him start saying he believes in Jesus until she's got a bigger crowd … then, out will come the collecting boxes. She calls him the "Magnet". It happens every week. Even when it's cold, like tonight, she'll not let him off the hook. He repents as regular as the tide … well, not that regular. The tide's twice a day … Captain Starkey's once a week. He'll repent tonight and be back on the booze on Monday.'

'I believe in the Lord Jesus Christ,' boomed out Captain Starkey, down on his knees under the gas lamp in the middle of a circle made up of men and women threatening him with trumpets, cornets, trombones and tambourines.

'The tide's coming in,' said Emma. 'Here come the collecting boxes.'

'May the Lord bless you,' said a Salvationist, when Lady Armstrong, Doris and Emma dropped coins into the collection box she was holding. 'May the Lord bless you. Hallelujah!'

Continuing their way down Hood Street to Sir William's office, Lady Armstrong, musing, said: 'Do you know, Doris, I exaggerate only a little when I say, that every day a new public house opens on Scotswood Road. It's all because of William's Elswick factory. It would seem that making guns and hydraulic cranes is thirsty work.'

'Repenting one's sins to gawpers, it seems to me, is also thirsty work,' said Doris. 'I don't object to going down on my knees on a hassock, in a church, but I certainly would not go down to pray on damp cobbles. It would play havoc … absolute havoc … with my arthritis. And it would appear from what Emma has told us that this fellow's repentance is not sincere … is that the case, Emma?'

'When it comes to booze, ma'am, everyone in the toon knows Captain Starkey is weak. I sympathise. My weakness is for gloves. I can't stop buying them. I can't walk past a glove shop without looking in the window. I buy on tick. I'm paying two pence a week for six months for me last pair.'

'But, Emma, if you are so fond of gloves why are you not wearing them tonight? Meggie and I have our muffs. Your hands must be frozen.'

'That's another, thing, ma'am. When I buy them, I don't wear them. I don't want them to get dirty, see; and all worn out. I keeps them snug in a drawer. When it takes me fancy I takes them out and admires them. I treat them, ma'am, like the way I suppose a miser treats his sovereigns. I suppose Captain Starkey is a bit like me when I buys gloves. I mean to wear them to keep me hands warm but, I never do. When the Captain's on his knees praying I'm sure he means well … it's just that, like me, with gloves, he's weak.'

'Quite!' said Doris, looking at Emma the way an Englishman in Australia must have looked when he saw his first black swan.

'In a way,' said Lady Armstrong, 'I admire Captain Starkey's preparedness to go down on his knees …'

'On cobbles as well, ma'am,' said Emma.

'Yes, Emma … on cobbles as well. I do admire his willingness to bare his soul in public. I would never do it … nor, would William. The Salvation Army is a new organisation. I suppose it is the modern way of doing, things. William and I prefer to keep our thoughts about religion private.'

'I do hope you are not having doubts, Meggie?' said Doris. 'There is nothing wrong in professing one's faith in our Lord Jesus Christ. The gossip in London is that where St Paul's now stands there was, a long time ago, a tropical forest … imagine, wet, foggy London being a tropical forest … ridiculous … quite ridiculous. It gets worse. The same gossip … scientific in nature … says huge reptiles … some bigger than elephants … roamed there the way cats and dogs do now … ridiculous. A member of the House of Lords told me that. And he meant it. I mean, he wasn't joking. I sometimes don't get jokes but I knew, he meant it when he said Genesis wasn't true. The Bible wrong? God made everything we know; including that brow-beaten drunkard down on his knees on the cobbles asking God to forgive his waywardness … and all by gas light … which I'm sure the good Lord made too … though I can't remember gas light being mentioned in Genesis.'

'Wouldn't it have been wonderful, ma'am,' said Emma, 'if, when Starkey had been doon on his knees, repenting, an angel had flown oot of the gas lamp and landed on Starkey's head.'

'That would have been a miracle,' said Doris. 'I stopped believing in them when Palmerston came back as Prime Minister. He dyes his hair, you know. At a dinner party he squeezed my hand and gave me, what I believe is called … "the eye".'

'If I saw an angel,' said Lady Armstrong, laughing at Doris's thumbnail description of Britain's Prime Minister, 'I do believe I would need smelling salts and my dear William would take out a notebook and log the incident as a possible natural phenomena … like a cloud sometimes looks like a blacksmith's anvil. He'd start asking himself questions about how light refracts on a cold night … had he drank too many glasses of port? He'd keep asking questions until he'd worked out a rational explanation to explain an angel, popping out of a gaslight.'

'Is William not a true believer in our Lord?' asked Doris. 'Does he not believe in angels?'

'William believes in science, Doris. He is not, in the least, metaphysical. Remember when you screamed last year in Jesmond Dene? On one of our moonlight walks? You thought you'd been touched by a ghost.'

'And William showed me I'd walked through a spider's web.'

'Yes … William is a great one for taking the "super" out of supernatural. He likes nothing better than removing the petals off a flower and showing how it is made. The lecture he is attending tonight at the Lit and Phil will have had him on the edge of his seat. It is being given by a man called Huxley. He is here to champion the views of Mr

Charles Darwin. Have you heard of him?'

'I have, ma'am,' said Emma. 'When you and Sir William are finished reading The Times and Mr Phillips (Sir William and Lady Armstrong's butler) has no more use for it, he is kind enough to give it to me and when I've finished with it I give it to Mary (a chamber maid) who uses it to light the fires. Mary can't read, but I can. Sometimes Mary doesn't believe what I read to her. When I told her about the civil war in America and that black people were slaves … she wouldn't believe me.'

'If it's in The Times or in the Bible,' said Doris, 'then I say, it must be true.'

'Begging your pardon, ma'am, Mr Darwin doesn't believe what's in the Bible. That's what I read in The Times. He says a long time ago we looked like monkeys.'

'Mr Darwin, Emma, is a gentleman with too much imagination. I am coming round to the opinion that The Times is not as truthful as the Bible.'

'I think Mr Darwin's right, ma'am,' said Emma, 'we do come from monkeys. You knows why? I looks at the evidence … just like Sir William does. You go doon to the Sandgate toneet and you'll see men, women and bairns eating baked potatoes the way monkeys eat nuts … nee knives and forks … that's why I think Mr Darwin's right when he says a long time ago we were apes.'

'Emma!' said Doris.

'Yes, ma'am?'

'Know your place. I find the idea that my ancestors were apes … absurd … quite absurd! I'll have you know, Emma, I have taken tea with his Grace, the Archbishop of Canterbury. I was with my friend Lady Elizabeth. Meggie, you know who I mean? You met her at Kensington Palace. I'm afraid, Meggie, Lady Elizabeth is an advanced thinker. She thinks women should have the vote. She was halfway through a custard slice when his grace coughed to remind her that before we tuck in, we say grace.'

'Does that mean, ma'am,' said Emma, 'that if I say grace before tucking into a ham sandwich the pig feels better about been eaten?'

'Emma, I am not a philosopher. I am a Christian. Grace is our way of saying thank you to God for making England a green and pleasant land.'

'Meggie! Meggie!' shouted a voice from behind them.

'William!' said Lady Armstrong.

'I am quite out of breath,' said Sir William catching up with them. 'I must be getting old, or, is Grey Street getting longer and steeper?'

'From what Meggie has been telling me, William, it is because you work too hard and don't say your prayers,' said Doris.

'Working too hard … yes … but, not saying my prayers … of that, I am far from certain. Has anyone, I wonder, carried out a scientific investigation into the efficacy of praying? Doris, the world is changing. Science is the new religion. To get the new railway across the Tyne we engineers did not pray. We paid Mr Stephenson to build the High Level Bridge. To get the railway to Edinburgh engineers with vision knocked down the walls of a Norman castle. In one fell swoop engineers brought Newcastle, kicking and screaming, into the nineteenth century.'

'William,' said Doris, 'I have never heard you sound so passionate. Your fervour scares me.'

'William is often like that,' said Lady Armstrong, linking her husband. 'When my dear William has been to a Lit and Phil lecture, he never fails to be passionate about the subject of the lecture.'

'You sounded, William, if I may say so,' said Doris, 'but, hopefully with more sincerity … as passionate as that Salvationist I saw swearing allegiance to our Lord, Jesus Christ. Did you see him … on his knees, kneeling, in prayer, on the cobbles?'

'I did. I do believe he was crying.'

'Guilt was making him weep. Guilt!'

'I thought he was crying because the cobbles on which he was kneeling were hurting his knees.'

'You are saying, William, he was weeping because his knees were hurting?'

'Yes.'

'William … you are a sophist vandal. I must remember never to introduce you to the Archbishop of Canterbury. His cook does a heavenly Angel Cake but, then again, with his employer being the "Bish" he should be able to, shouldn't he?'

'My ancestry, Doris, helps me keep my feet on the ground. I hail not from dukes and earls but from the border reivers … men who wore steel bonnets and stole cattle … men who wiped their noses on the sleeves of their leather jerkins … men who pulled meat off bones with their bare hands …'

'William!' said Lady Armstrong.

'Excuse me, sir,' said Emma, 'was that when we was more like monkeys than we are now?'

'In the lecture I attended this evening, Emma, Mr Huxley did make that claim. Yes, a long time ago – a very long time ago – our distant ancestors were apes. It is Mr Darwin's theory of evolution. Huxley is its champion.'

'Of course,' said Doris, 'Mr Huxley excluded the upper classes from this preposterous assertion?'

'No, Doris, he did not. Mother Nature is quite immune to the nuances of class. When typhoid took the life of Prince Albert it did not know it was taking the life of a prince.'

'You believe … this … gossip, William? A man of science like you … believing in … gossip. Next thing you will be reading tea cups to help you design your hydraulic cranes. Before you go to bed tonight, William, I suggest you read your Bible.'

'Do you know the poetry of Matthew Arnold?'

'Know his poetry? I have had tea with him. In London I have had tea with everyone of importance. Mr Arnold is a sad man. He is losing faith faster than horses pull a mail coach.'

'"Dover Beach" … do you know it?'

'I refuse to read modern poetry.'

'In his poem, "Dover Beach", Doris, Doctor Arnold tells us the "sea of faith" is running an ebb current … that, we are here, as on a "darkling plain".'

'If everyone lost their faith as easily as Doctor Arnold, William, I fear the Archbishop of Canterbury would be reduced to begging for bread off a beadle … weeds would grow out of pulpits and I, for one, am not having that.'

'He could busk, like Waterloo Bob,' suggested Emma.

'Ah!' said Sir William, 'but, what instrument would he play?'

'His Grace plays the pianoforte, badly,' said Doris. 'At Lambeth he murdered a Mozart sonata.'

'A pianoforte is not so easy to carry around as the Northumbrian small pipes,' said Lady Armstrong, laughing.

'Doris,' said Sir William, 'you have made me feel creative.'

'Dear me, I do hope you are not going to turn water into wine.'

'I envisage a pianoforte on wheels. I will lay a railway line up Grey Street. A steam locomotive will pull the pianoforte up and down. Every shop doorway will be … not a railway station, but a busking station.'

'Ridiculous! Your flight of imagination, William, reminds me of a grouse on the "Glorious Twelfth". Bang! Bang! And there'd you be dead as a door nail in the heather.'

'Plain song,' said Emma.

'I beg your pardon?' said Doris.

'Plain song, ma'am,' repeated Emma. 'As a man of the church the archbishop will be used to singing. I'm thinking his busking instrument could be his voice. Let him do plain song … railway lines would spoil Grey Street.'

'Emma,' said Sir William, 'well done. Mr Ruskin would be proud of you. You have used aesthetics to blow up pragmatism. Well done.'

'Thank you, sir.'

'After you, ladies, we are here,' said Sir William, beckoning his wife, Emma and Doris towards a double door, sporting a brass plate with his name on it.

The door opened before Sir William had pulled its bell chain. This impressed Doris.

'You have your servants well trained, William; that, at least, is something in your favour.'

'Good evening, Richard,' said Sir William to the smiling young man holding the door open for them.

'Good evening, sir.'

'Good evening, Richard,' said Lady Armstrong.

'Good evening, ma'am.'

Why was Meggie winking at her maid? Why was this good looking young man winking at the maid? Had everyone become infected with the 'wink'? Was the 'wink' on Tyneside an infectious disease?

'I suppose, like you, William,' said Doris, watching, wide eyed, as Richard semaphored 'I love you' to Emma in a lover's code of winks, 'your man, Richard …'

'Richard is my chief clerk,' explained Sir William.

'He is also,' said Doris (a river in spate), 'a premature opener of doors. Such a man, I do verily believe, will be a true believer in the malicious gossip that Adam and Eve were apes? He is the sort of fellow who will cut his toenails on Sunday. Richard, do you cut your toenails on the Sabbath?'

'No, ma'am.'

'Would you swear that on the Bible?'

'No, ma'am.'

'Your answer shows, at least, some respect for the Good Book. Do you believe Jesus rose from the dead? Pray … do not answer. But … miracle of miracles, you can see through solid oak doors so you know when to open them before anyone has rung … Geordies are amazing!'

'While I agree with you, Doris, that Geordies are amazing,' said Sir William, 'the reason the door was opened so promptly is because the office has windows. Richard was expecting us. He was looking out for us.'

'The street may be gas-lit, William, but it is not as well lit as Regent Street. You will be telling me next that this young whipper-snapper,' glaring at Richard, 'can see in the dark … like a cat!'

'Richard was probably using my nyctoscope,' said Sir William.

'Your what?'

'It's a device William has invented to see in the dark,' said Lady Armstrong.

'It turns night into day, ma'am,' said Emma.

'Does it indeed! Meggie, you have married a magician. William, are you going to walk into your office or fly?'

'I think I will walk, but … I do predict that one day men will fly through the air like birds.'

'Ridiculous!'

'Ladies, after you.'

Doris knew nothing about William's world of science. But, she did know about love. To a woman of her experience, it was as obvious as gooseberries are tart that Richard and Emma were head over heels in love.

She knew a lot about love. Charlie, her dear Charlie, had been killed in the Crimean War. Her trip to Newcastle to see Meggie and William was by way of letting society know she was no longer obliged to wear 'weeds'.

When friends asked if Charlie had died in the charge of the Light Brigade, to avoid answering, she'd gotten into the habit of pulling out a handkerchief and weeping.

Charlie … dear, stupid, silly Charlie, hadn't died on the field of battle. He'd died in a stable. He'd been kicked to death by a horse.

In church, her knees comfy on a hassock, she asked God's forgiveness for encouraging the rumour that her beloved had died a noble death.

When servants fell in love, floorboards squeaked in the middle of the night. A coal scuttle designed to be carried by one person, suddenly needed two people to carry it. One's dinner was served late, cold and burnt.

Doris made a mental note to tell Meggie to keep an eye on Emma and Richard.

Before going inside out of the cold, all paused to watch the Salvationists march past.

Captain Starkey, having sworn his testament, was, for the time being, at least, a mufti member of the club.

They marched up Hood Street in battle order. They were marching to war. Their bandsmen and bandswomen were full cheeked and red cheeked with blowing cornets, euphoniums and trombones.

The tambourine shakers, at least those whose jingles had not frozen, exclaimed – every so often – while shaking their tambourines above their bonneted heads: 'Halleluiah!' They were God's town criers. They marched to the tune: 'Gems from Haydn's Creation'.

When a real army is on the march skirmishers protect its flanks. The Salvationists' 'skirmishers' were armed with collecting boxes.

As an excuse to better observe the spectacle, Richard sidled up to Emma.

As soon as Doris saw them holding hands she knew the hot-beef sandwiches Meggie had promised, would be served up cold. That's what happened when servants fell in love. Cupid did not care if a pan boiled dry. On top of all of that, the music made her want to cry. It made her miss Charlie. In bed Charlie had been a great farter. She missed his farts.

'The Salvationists are on the march,' observed Richard.

'The devil better watch out,' said Emma, squeezing Richard's hand.

'Is that the penitent holding the banner?' said Doris.

'I do believe it is, Captain Starkey, ma'am,' said Emma.

'What does the banner say? Since Charlie died in the … in the Crimea, my eyes are not what they were.'

'It says, ma'am,' said Emma, '"Temperance leads to Jesus". Look out, ma'am, here come the collecting boxes.'

'Richard, put that,' said Sir William, handing Richard half-a-crown, 'in a box for me.'

'I'll go with you,' said Emma.

'Meggie, your servants are holding hands,' exclaimed Doris.

'They are in love.'

'You allow your servants to fall in love, Meggie?'

'Richard has the makings of an excellent draughtsman,' said Sir William, 'he can draw.'

'What has that, William, to do with falling in love?'

'It is my experience, Doris, that a happy employee makes a better worker than an employee who is unhappy. Would you have me flog him for falling in love? The late Lord Nelson was not a flogger; likewise our local hero, Lord Collingwood. They looked after their men. and their men, in return, did their duty and looked after them. Dear me! A brass band is as noisy as a steam hammer.'

'It's the trombone player,' said Lady Armstrong, 'she is improvising.'

'Musicians should not deviate when playing religious music,' said Doris, 'they should stick to the notes. Playing around with hymns is sacrilege. It's like our Prime Minister. He has mistresses, you know.'

'What if the trombone player is in love?' said Lady Armstrong. 'Love is a great liberator, Doris. It allows the soul to fly. See how it has put a glow on the faces of Emma and Richard.'

'I would not trust those two in the coalhouse. Meggie, put your foot down.'

'Doris, dear Doris, I am no more able to stop my servants falling in love than Canute was able to stop the tide coming in.'

'I'm telling you, Meggie, when servants fall in love … beware the Ides of March! Look what happened to Samson when he fell in love with Delilah.'

'He brought the house down,' said Lady Armstrong, 'like Witty-Watty's donkey did tonight. William,' she explained, to her husband, 'on stage tonight Geordie Black's donkey … he was playing the part of Witty-Watty – urinated on stage. I don't think it was planned.'

'I shouldn't think it was,' said Sir William, laughing. 'Sometimes my hydraulic cranes have a mind of their own. Did Geordie Black have a repartee? He has a reputation for quick thinking. At Elswick last week

I overheard a foreman encouraging the men in his team to know the names of the pieces of machinery they were dealing with by telling them: "If Geordie Black nars the name of every pebble on the beach at Tynemooth, it should be easy for yee bonny lads to learn the names of a few bits of machinery!" There then followed a delightful bit of banter. I quote: "Think you are draughtsmen," said the foreman. "What duh we draw?" said an apprentice. "The bogey roond the yard!" said the foreman. Whereupon, all laughing, they fell to work, full of enthusiasm, reassembling the hydraulic crane they had taken apart. Laughing makes you strong, Doris. It makes it easier for you to tighten a nut … to fit a bolt into a hole.'

'Ridiculous! Meggie, I am being serious. When one's servants fall in love they serve you burnt toast. They polish one shoe and forget you have two feet.'

'Doris, dear Doris,' said Lady Armstrong, 'Richard and Emma are not Samson and Delilah. They are two young people who are fond of each other. They are good servants. They work hard. Richard has already proved to you, he is an excellent servant.'

'Has he?'

'Who opened the door to us before we knocked? Richard! He was doing his duty. He was looking out for us.'

'He was looking out for Emma. If he'd not known Emma was with us, he might have taken half an hour to open the door.'

'And we poor souls would have turned to blocks of ice,' said Sir William, signalling to Richard and Emma, who, having put his contribution to the Salvationists in a collecting box, had taken French leave and were shadows in a doorway across the road.

'Are they kissing!' said Doris.

'Overcoats, Richard!' shouted Sir William. 'In you go, ladies. Richard will have a roaring fire going. It will thaw you out, Doris.'

'What do you mean, William? "Thaw me out". Do you mean my views on servants falling in love or my hands? Feel them! My fingers are icicles.'

'They are cold,' said Sir William, patting Doris's proffered hands, 'now, if you were one of my hydraulic cranes …'

'Me? A relation of your wife … through marriage … who has a third cousin married to a duke … a hydraulic crane! Whatever next?'

'Doris, I speak metaphorically. If you were one of my hydraulic cranes I fear that when it thawed after such a cold night, its watertight seals would be dripping like an orphan's nose in a parish poor house.'

'Your metaphor … what is it supposed to mean? Are you trying to tell me something unpalatable?'

'William,' said Lady Armstrong, 'stop teasing.'

'William, it will serve you right if the hot beef sandwiches Meggie promised are served cold. Servants falling in love, William, is a lunar eclipse. It is a singular event. Eclipses burn toast. I speak from experience.'

Machines, thought Sir William, as he followed the ladies into the warmth of his Hood Street office, were so much easier to look after than people. When a hydraulic crane leaked water you tightened a nut. Hosting a middle-aged, Bible-punching widow was not for the faint hearted.

A PEAK INTO A MAGICIAN'S INCUBATOR

Sir William's Hood Street office was where clients from all over the world came to sign contracts worth, in today's money, millions of pounds.

The office was furnished to let clients know they were doing business with a firm of solid worth.

Doris was impressed. She fancied she was in an ante-room in the Houses of Parliament. Emma and Richard helped everyone take their coats off. She liked being fussed over. Her opinion of the love birds went up a notch.

'You've a nice fire going, Richard,' said Sir William.

'Thank you, sir.'

'Sandwiches?'

'As ready to bite into, sir, as the flies I make for you when you gan fishing.'

'I wish I had the time to go fishing, Richard. The business of heavy engineering is fascinating but also time consuming. Making guns and cranes and going fishing, is like mixing oil and water … it doesn't work! If I was a sorcerer, I might do it but, I'm not … so, I can't. Ah! Richard, the Tyne is not the river it used to be.'

'No, sir.'

'The Coquet is still a good river to fish but not the coaly Tyne. I fear the dye works, the pottery works, the lead works and, though I hate to think it, let alone say it … my works at Elswick, are killing the fish in the Tyne. Do you know, Richard, if you had been my apprentice fifty years ago your indentures would have stated I was not allowed to feed you salmon more than three times a week?'

'Salmon were that plentiful, sir?'

'They were so plentiful, Richard, that in their season they clogged up our Tyne the way I have seen Regent Street brought to a standstill with omnibuses. A five-foot salmon was the norm … a six-footer, nothing exceptional.

'Sad, sir.'

'It is indeed, Richard. I fear it is the price we must pay for progress. Meggie, Doris … shall we eat picnic style, by the fire?'

'There will be napkins?' said Doris.

'Richard?'

'Doilies under the hot beef sandwiches, sir, and napkins folded in the shape of cranes, sir.'

'Hydraulic cranes?'

'No, sir. The bird. It's called origami, sir. A Japanese art form, sir. The gentleman from Tokyo who bought twenty of our guns and five hydraulic cranes, taught me. It's wonderful what you can make, sir, just by folding paper.'

'A bit like how a trickle of water can be made to lift a heavy weight,' said Sir William.

****

The picnic-style meal, served by Emma and Richard, appealed to what remained of the hunter-gatherer in Doris's nature.

The napkins folded into the shape of a bird, called a crane, were such a novelty. She demanded Richard show her how it was done. When she returned to London she would instruct her butler to fold napkins into the shape of a crane. She would show him, crease by crease, how it was done. Since he'd read Pickwick Papers, he thought he was Sam Weller. He kept telling everyone he was from Dulwich; that he wished he'd never left the village of his birth. Doris often wished he'd stayed there. Servants!

Should she show the Archbishop of Canterbury how to fold a napkin into the shape of a crane? If 'horrid-thingummy' or whatever folding paper into the shape of a bird was called became a craze in ecclesiastical circles – like 'transubstantiation' – and she could claim to be its originator, she might be given a stained glass window in Westminster Abbey.

Throughout the British Empire she would be known as the woman who introduced London to the Japanese art of paper folding. She might … heaven forbid … what dress would she wear? … be asked to demonstrate to the Queen how to fold a napkin into the shape of a crane. She envisaged a table at Buckingham Palace decorated with napkins, in the shape of cranes. She saw origami cranes nesting in the middle of Meissen plates.

'The beef sandwiches are really nice,' Sir William told Richard.

'Thank you, sir. I will tell Mavis.'

'Mavis! That's a bird, isn't it?' said Doris. 'Can you make a Mavis out of a napkin? A crane and a Mavis! Richard, show me how to fold a napkin to look like a Mavis.'

'Mavis is William's cook here, in Hood Street,' explained Lady Armstrong.

'So, that is why the beef sandwiches are hot,' said Doris, raising her lorgnette to get a better look at Emma and Richard. 'I do verily believe, Meggie, if Mavis had been a bird, instead of a cook, our hot beef sandwiches would have been served cold. In my London circle it is universally accepted that when employees fall in love, hot meals are served cold. Furthermore,' glaring at Emma and Richard through her lorgnette, 'that their infatuation is measurable by the coldness of the gravy they serve. Richard, do stop looking at Emma as if she was a glass of water and you were thirsty.'

'Yes, ma'am.'

'Show me again how to fold a napkin into the shape of a crane. When I return to London I wish to impress the Archbishop of Canterbury.'

'May I help, ma'am?' said Emma.

'You know how to fold paper into the shape of a crane?'

'Yes, ma'am, Richard showed me. Richard, ma'am, is a very good teacher.'

'I'm sure he is! Men always are when they are after something.'

'Richard,' said Sir William, 'if Emma is able to teach Doris origami …'

'Emma is a quick learner, sir,' said Richard.

'See how they pat each other on the back,' said Doris. 'Once, a long time ago, one of my coachmen fell in love with one of my maids. Surname of "Darling" and so was the horse he was always kissing … until, she bit him.'

'The horse or the maid?' asked Lady Armstrong.

'The horse, of course. Men, Meggie, are the opposite of knives … you don't want them too sharp. Men need to be kept in their place. When I was nine and my brother Bob was ten, he drank my lemonade. I've never forgotten that.'

'Richard,' said Sir William, 'come with me. I need you in the "incubator".'

Sir William never stopped working. Only that morning, over breakfast, Meggie had chided him for making dams with his porridge in an experiment to see how much milk they would store before bursting.

****

To get to the 'incubator', Sir William and Richard walked down a short corridor and up three stairs.

Sir William had heard the tale of the misappropriated lemonade many times. Doris was a 'repeater'. When Meggie had had enough, she would shut her relative up by broaching the subject of the charge of the Light Brigade. Meggie called it, the 'Stopper'. Mentioning the charge of the Light Brigade to Doris made her cough into a handkerchief.

'Thank you for rescuing me, sir,' said Richard as he stood back from the open office door to allow Sir William to enter the 'incubator' first.

'It was not altruism, Richard,' said Sir William. 'I was rescuing myself.'

'Begging your pardon, sir … but, what's "altruism"?'

Sir William explained.

'I'll remember that, sir. I'm keen to build up my vocabulary.'

'As keen as I am to invent new ways of using water to lift heavy weights.'

'If I was as keen as that, sir, I'd know every word in the dictionary.'

He liked Sir William and Sir William liked him. He thought his boss, super-clever. Behind his back, workmen called Sir William: 'Master of the Draulickers'. Sir William knew everything there was to know about hydraulic cranes.

In his engineering works at Elswick, Sir William employed hundreds of men. Sir William's family and friends had invested huge sums into getting the business started.

To keep it at the forefront of technology it needed men with brains and ability across a wide range of skills. Sir William had a good eye for talent. He'd been quick to spot Richard's talent for draughtsmanship. In the twinkling of an eye Richard could draw to scale the breech loading mechanism of an Armstrong Gun.

The 'incubator' had a fire and a long table upon which rolls of paper were scattered. William called the room the 'incubator'. because it was where he breathed life into his latest ideas. Richard's drawing skills enabled him to see (as a computer generated image does today) what he had imagined.

One of his latest ideas was for a swing bridge. He wished to build ships at Elswick. The eighteenth century stone bridge stopped the movement of anything bigger than a keel, going upriver. There had been a crossing there since Roman times.

His plan was to pull down the old bridge and replace it with a bridge that swung open and shut like a door. When a vessel wanted to go upriver to Elswick you swung it open. When the vessel had passed through, you swung it shut. Sir William played around with heavy engineering the way the Japanese folded paper.

Sir William handed Richard an architect's drawing of a house built on the side of a hill. It grew out of the hillside, the way a chimney grows out of a gable roof.

'To keep me busy in my old age, Richard.'

'Cragside, sir?'

'Yes, Richard, Cragside. Mr Shaw, my architect, has great plans for the house. When I'm thinking up new ways of improving breech loading guns and making hydraulic cranes lift ever greater weights, at the back of my mind, like a fairy castle, seen through a London Peculiar, I am building Cragside. In this troubled world, Richard, I am of the opinion, dreaming is not a luxury, it is a necessity. Our American cousins' dream of keeping their country united.'

'Their civil war, sir?'

'Yes. I suppose they have a point. Imagine if Scotland or Wales wished to secede from the United Kingdom. The break-up of our union would be a disaster. What are your dreams, Richard?'

'I think you know, sir … with respect, sir, I have heard it said a lawyer never asks a question to which he does not already know the answer.'

'Richard, you are not only a fine draughtsman but, as you get older, you are becoming a fine dissector of human nature. What is your answer to my question? Your answer might prove me wrong.'

'I don't think so, sir. I dream of marrying Emma.'

'And why should you not? I approve and so does Meggie.'

'Lady Armstrong, sir?'

'Yes, are you surprised?'

'I don't know, sir. I don't understand women. I only know, I like them.'

'It may surprise you to know, Richard, that while I love Meggie, I do not understand her. I understand mathematical formula. When it tells me how much water pressure I need to lift a ton, I believe it. When Meggie tells me not to work too hard, she puts me between the devil and the deep blue sea. I know she is right, but my inner demon won't let me stop working. To whom do I owe allegiance?'

'I don't know, sir.'

'Nor do I, Richard.'

'Are we in the "incubator", sir, to escape, or are we here to work, sir?'

'Primarily to escape. I can stand the noise of steam hammers knocking hot iron into parabolas, but Doris's monologues quite do my head in.'

'Yes, sir.'

'A word of advice, before you ask Emma for her hand, find out if she has relatives, in London. Beware! They will invite themselves for a week and stay a month.'

'Talking of London, sir, while you were out at the Lit and Phil the last post brought a letter from London. It came by express mail, sir. Its frank tells me it is from the government.'

'Where is it?'

'In the "Signing Room", sir, where I always put the mail.'

'I wonder if they want to buy the Armstrong Gun?'

''That would be good news, sir.'

'It would, indeed. I will go to the "Signing Room" through the kitchen; that way I will avoid Doris.'

'Shall I come with you, sir?'

'No, no need. You may re-join the ladies. As I recued you from, Doris you must now go and rescue Emma. If she is teaching the relative from London origami, she will be exhausted.'

****

'Good evening, Mavis,' said Sir William.

He spoke to Mavis the way a poacher talks to a gamekeeper.

'What can I get you, sir?'

He was trespassing. When this short, stocky woman folded her roly-poly arms it reminded him of a man-o-war opening its gun ports. The phrase: 'Out of the frying pan and into the fire' crossed his mind. Mavis was as much a force of nature as Doris.

'Passing through, Mavis.'

'Like a draught, I'll be bound.'

He and Mavis went back a long way. She'd been a servant in his father's house. She'd known him when he'd been young enough for her to pinch his cheeks and give him an apple. She'd mothered him and spoilt him because she liked him.

'As usual, Mavis,' said Sir William, 'the hot beef sandwiches were delicious.'

'And, pray, why shouldn't they be?'

'Because, Mrs Coxon …'

'Oooo! I'm Mrs Coxon now, am I? That means am ganin to get a lecture. If I was a soldier or a keel man, waiting for the tide to turn, I'd be standing to attention. Carry on, Sir William … I'm ready for me lashing.'

'Mavis, if you were a man, I'd employ you at Elswick.'

'In what position, sir? High or low?'

'High, of course. You'd be management.'

'My job?'

'A settler of industrial disputes. You know how to intimidate.'

'When you was a lad, Sir William, I never dreamed when I gave you apples to make you big and strong, you'd grow up a flatterer.'

'Mavis, you are making me blush.'

'And, so you should, sir. I nars why you are taking a short cut through my kitchen.'

'I am going to my office.'

'The long way round? That's like living in Newcastle and ganin to Hexham, via North Shields. I have good hearing, Sir William. I wasn't eavesdropping … divent gan calling me "Key-Hole Mavis". I heard what you told young Richard. It's the relative from London what's making you gan the long way round.'

'Mavis,' said Sir William, putting a shush-finger to his lips, 'you must learn discretion.'

'You mean, sir … keep me gob shut? That if I see a rat enjoying a beef sandwich, I should sing "Keep your feet still, Geordie hinny" instead of throwing a brick at it?'

'Yes. The expression, "keep me gob shut",' said Sir William, smiling, 'is indelicate. You are using a sledgehammer to crack a nut. If you were one of my hydraulic cranes, Mavis, you would lift weights way beyond my expectations.'

'Is that a compliment, sir?'

'Yes.'

'Do I get a pay rise?'

'No.'

'So, sir, it's a wait for the wind compliment.'

'No one waits for the wind to blow these days, Mavis … or, for the tide. Steam ships do not need wind to blow them to London. The Tyne is being dredged. Soon the new steamers will be able to come and go regardless of whether the tide is high or low.'

'The tide is low, sir, for the keel men. A keel man out of work, sir, is a sad sight, sir. He sits looking at the river aal day like a fisherman what never gets a bite. Take me nephews, Geordie and Jackie … I keeps telling them to learn to read and write. If they did, sir, I knows you'd give them work … wouldn't you, sir?'

'Yes, I would. A man who tries to better himself deserves a helping hand. But, Mavis, if I may make so bold, your nephews have a reputation. As Yorkshire men know about Dick Turpin; Geordies know about the Coxon brothers.'

'I hasten to add, sir, not that I'm disowning them, like what Peter did to Jesus but, they are not my blood. I inherited them when I married Isaac. Some folk when they marry inherit castles and jewels; I inherited the Coxon brothers. Life's not fair, is it, sir? They might be scoundrels, sir, but they are not lazy … and they are versatile … turn their hands to anything … mischief included. At the moment they are working for two Americans. Geordie told me, the Americans don't like our warm beer. They drinks wine and spirits, sir. I shouldn't tell you this, sir …

but, I'm going to … we go back a long way, you and me. And, Geordie and Jackie are blabbers. When they've got a few bob in their pockets they are as full of themselves as the river is when the tide's in. They keep telling me to put the kettle on for when the Americans come to Hood Street to see Mr Rendel to buy guns.'

'The Americans are coming here?'

'To see Mr Rendel, sir.'

'Rendel is in Paris.'

'I wouldn't know about that, sir. Geordie and Jackie told me … they can't stop their blabbing when they've had a drink … they don't know when to stop … unlike me, sir, who knows when to put the brake on 'cos I was brought up when nobody went faster than a ten mile an hour mail coach … Geordie and Jackie have told me … well, I overheard them talking … they have loud voices … and I have sharp ears … that the Americans is here to buy the guns, sir, what you makes at Elswick.'

'Mavis, you are an incorrigible gossip. Please do not repeat to anyone what you have just told me.'

'Am I doing it again, sir? What do you call it?'

'"Indiscretion". In business, Mavis, we have a rule. If you do not tell me what is going on because you know I know what is going on, then I will be able to say: "I know nothing about that!".'

'Them's a jumble of words, sir, but, blowing away the commas and capital letters I think I knows what you are telling me. It's like when Isaac, me better half, has been to the pub. When he swears blind he's been working late loading a collier, he nars I nar he's been to the pub … because he nars I nar he doesn't feel he has to tell me the truth. If anybody asks me, "Where's Isaac?" I'll say, "He's loading coal" and they'll nar I'm lying and that I know I'm lying, and that I know Isaac is at the pub, boozing.'

'Mavis …' began Sir William.

'Yes, sir?'

'Mavis, when you make one of your excellent cakes you have a list of ingredients?'

'I do, sir.'

'There is an order in which you mix them?'

'There is, sir. You take the egg out of its shell afore you drop it in the flour.'

'Quite! Mavis, you have taken my point too much to heart.'

'Have I, sir?'

'What I am trying to say is …'

'Like the way you are going to the "Signing Room", sir … the long way round … through MY kitchen?'

'What I am trying to say, Mavis, is that, making guns and cranes is like baking a cake.'

'Is it? When I've been making a sponge cake I've never thought I was making an Armstrong Gun.'

'There is an order in which the necessary ingredients are brought together … that is the common thread, Mavis. The engineering takes place at Elswick … that is ingredient number one. Mr Rendel sells them and signs contracts off for them in the "Signing Room" … that is ingredient number two. And you, Mavis, are ingredient number three … you make the tea and coffee and hot beef sandwiches for the gentlemen signing contracts worth many thousands of pounds. It makes them feel they are getting value for their money … which, I know, they are. If and when these Americans show up to see Mr Rendel, it will be your job to show them that we on Tyneside know how to make a good cup of coffee as well as a good cup of tea. And, Mavis …'

'Yes, sir?'

'Would it surprise you to know that this very evening at the lecture I attended at the Lit and Phil, I was told that our ancestors were monkeys?'

'Wouldn't surprise me, sir. You live in Jesmond, sir. If you lived, like what I do, doon on the Sandgate, it wouldn't surprise you, either.'

******

Before making a career for himself in engineering, Sir William had been a solicitor. He knew about contracts. He knew, before you had your client's money in your pocket you could never be sure he'd pay. In the armaments business the sums involved were vast. You were dealing with individuals who were not spending their own money. They were the representatives of governments. They were spending other people's money. The governments they represented might, at any moment, collapse.

It was all too easy for Sir William's employees to assume the pieces of iron they were hammering into cleats and bending into right angles were easy to sell. They were not. Contracts had to be fought for and won against, not only other British firms but from firms all over the world. Competition was fierce.

His sales manager, Rendel, was on commission. He was good at his job. The 'Signing Room', which Sir William now entered, was his office. A wood panelled room. An austere room. A room devoid of distracting fripperies. No ornaments. No paintings. A room designed to focus minds on pounds, shillings and pence.

Thinking all the while about what Mavis had told him, Sir William poked the room's fire. Sparks flew. Flames flared.

Was Rendel selling guns to the Americans? If so, to which side? The Union or to the slave states? Businessmen had always made money out of wars. When it came to making money … money trounced morals.

From his reading of 'The Times' he knew Union and Confederate spies were active in Liverpool. Lairds of Liverpool had been accused of building warships for the South. A judge had reached the verdict that the vessels were not warships because they were not armed … the judge's summation failing to explain why merchant ships needed gun ports!

The 'Signing Room's' visitor's book, the commercial equivalent of a ship's log, lay open on a lectern. Flipping through its pages Sir William found no mention of the Americans, who Mavis claimed, were employing the Coxons.

Sir William was not by nature a salesman. His energy and imagination went, not into selling, but into understanding how things worked. He loved pulleys and wheels and steam hammers. He saw a babbling brook as a source of power. Harnessed in the right way a trickle of water could be made to lift heavy weights.

The smoke and furnaces of his business were upriver, at Elswick. The men who came to Hood Street did not wish to get their hands dirty. When they signed contracts for hundreds of thousands of pounds, they wanted brandy and cigars. They wished to be constantly reminded that they were important. The sight of an oil can might well have made them faint.

The letter Sir William had come looking for was in a wicker basket, stencilled 'IN'. Taking the envelope to a gas lamp, he read 'Foreign Office' on its seal.

He'd met Lord Russell, Britain's Foreign Secretary, on numerous occasions. They were well known to each other. The letter was marked 'Private and Personal'.

Sir William hoped the letter was not an invitation to an official dinner. He could hold his own at such functions, but he did find them a trial.

Opening the letter: 'Dear Sir William, It would be a pleasure to be writing to you if only I was doing so as your personal acquaintance and not as Foreign Secretary. My wife and I so much enjoyed hosting your good self and Meggie last year at Pembroke Lodge.

I have heard from inside sources that Her Majesty has spoken of the pleasure it gave her to make you a knight of the realm. It appears she found the musicality of your accent much to her liking.

The Prince of Wales continues to be fascinated by the technological advances you are making; especially, with artillery. England needs you, Sir William!

The mention of artillery brings me to the reason I am writing. I have been informed that, sometime soon, an American or Americans – it is my experience they travel in posses – will be knocking on your door. They will present to you a letter of introduction from Her Majesty's Government, signed by, myself.

The name of the fellow diplomacy has forced me to recommend is Henry Adams. He is the son of Charles Adams, the head of the American Legation in London.

Henry is a pleasant enough young man, but quite out of his depth in English society. He does not hunt, shoot or fish. To make him feel welcome and put him at his ease, you will – as the saying goes – have to bend over backwards.

I am of the sincere opinion that neither he nor his father like us very much. I do not mean personally, of course. I mean the English in general. They are jealous of our Empire.

Americans have a high opinion of themselves. I think of them as puppies. They bark a lot. They have sharp teeth and can give you a nasty bite. On more than one occasion I have had to remind Mr Adams senior that GB has the most powerful navy in the world. We are not to be, and will not be, taunted. To be blunt, Sir William – I put it to you, colloquially – who do these Americans think they are?

You will, no doubt, have read in 'The Times' of the sabre rattling between our two countries. The North's audacity in stopping and boarding one of our mail ships was, quite simply, an act of piracy; there is no other word for it.

By the time this letter reaches your good self, you will be pleased to learn that diplomacy and common sense, has resolved this matter. Britain and America will not be going to war. Thank God!

The purpose of young Mr Adam's visit is to remind you that in their civil war, England is neutral. If Americans wish to kill each other, what can we do about it?

It is well known, in official circles, that, in the Crimean War, the Americans sold guns to the Russians. Did American guns kill the Light Brigade when they charged – as Tennyson so eloquently puts it – "into the valley of death"?

In their civil war we must turn the other cheek. We must do our best not to aggravate either side. The South is quite happy to aid and abet British manufacturers to break the law. To get their hands on the weapons you make on Tyneside both sides are quite unscrupulous in employing what they call "Shysters" – what we call "Conmen".

We must do our best – difficult as it is – to forget and, indeed, forgive, our American friends for selling guns to the Russians to be used against us in our Crimean War.

The sooner someone comes out on top in the American conflict, the better. I am quite worn out trying to placate Adams. He reminds me of Hood's poem, "November". Do you know it? Every line begins with a negative. I warn you now, the son is a chip off the same block.

The FO is hosting a party in July. All the big-wigs will be there. It would be beneficial to your business if you could find time to attend. I will, in the course of time, be sending you an invitation. Something for you to look forward to.

Lord John Russell.

Were the Americans employing the Coxons, the Americans to whom Lord Russell had given a letter of accreditation? If they were, why had they not introduced themselves? Was their way of doing business, the New World way of doing business? Should he telegraph Rendel? Would his sales manager be able to shed light on what was going on?

'Excuse me, sir,' said Richard, coming into the room, 'Lady Margaret has sent me to ask when you might be going home?'

'Our carriage is ready and waiting?'

'Yes, sir. Shall I tell Lady Margaret, sir, you are on your way?'

'Is it safe to return?'

'If I may make so bold, sir, your guest from London has stopped chatting. If she was a steam engine, sir, I'd be telling you, she's run out of coal and water. She is a miracle, sir. She is able to talk while eating one of Mavis's beef sandwiches. Only, the origami keeps her quiet, sir.'

'In that case, Richard, we must encourage Doris to study that art. You are sure the lady in question has run out of water and coal? What is her psi?'

'When I left, sir, I'd say it was zero. She is finding the making of an origami frog, difficult, sir.'

'Before I re-join the ladies, Richard?'

'Sir?'

'I believe Mr Rendel is in Paris.'

'That's right, sir. He's there on business.'

'Do you know if his business in Paris has anything to do with Brother Jonathan?'

'The Americans, sir?'

'Yes.'

'No, sir.'

'If any Americans should call at Hood Street, Richard, and I am not here, give them my card. Invite them to dine with me at Jesmond. They are, Richard, according to this letter from London–' pointing to the letter from Lord Russell– 'important fellows. They must be wooed as you are wooing Emma.'

'Sir, you are making me blush. Am I that obvious?'

'Yes, you are. Meggie thinks you and Emma were made for each other. Please do not let infatuation mar your draughtsmanship. When you draw my swing bridge, I want it to open and shut smoothly ... you know, I do believe it will amuse Meggie to entertain Americans.'

'And your London relative, sir, can teach them origami.'

'I wonder,' said Sir William, tapping his chin with Lord Russell's letter, 'could one make an origami Armstrong Gun. Do you know, Richard, Lairds of Liverpool are in the law courts for selling warships to the Confederacy? I have no wish for my works at Elswick to be the cause of members of parliament asking questions. When politicians interfere with engineering, Richard, gun barrels end up looking like cucumbers.'

'The bent ones, sir?'

'Yes, Richard, the bent, ones. Is cotton king, Richard? That is the question everyone keeps asking. Liverpool depends on cotton. Is cotton king, Richard?'

'I don't know, sir. The Americans we are to woo ... are they from the North or the South?'

'They will be Abraham Lincoln's representatives. They will be against slavery.'

'That's good, sir. There's no one I know agrees with slavery.'

'I agree, Richard. It is an abominable practice. I was reading in 'The Times' the owners of slaves call the owning of slaves the "Peculiar Institution". Euphemisms, Richard, are masks behind which unpalatable truths hide like cowards.'

'Sir, what is a euphemism?'

Sir William explained.

'Every day I talk to you, sir, my vocabulary gets bigger and bigger.'

'And, every day, your draughtsmanship gets better and better. You have a natural talent for drawing, Richard. Our relationship is symbiotic. In simple terms that means we are useful to each other. Your drawings make what I envisage in my head as real as a daguerreotype. Which reminds me,' taking a folded piece of paper out of a trouser pocket and handing it to Richard, 'more details of my plan to build a swing bridge across the river. When I demolish the old stone bridge and replace it with a swinging bridge, I will be able to build ships at Elswick. Big ships.'

'The keel men won't like it, sir. Steamers have already taken their downstream work. The only work they have left is carrying coal from Dunston.'

'I'm afraid, Richard, the keel man's sun has set. We will never see his like again. When progress challenges something which has been there forever ... why, it is like when the North Tyne joins the South Tyne ...'

'Their confluence at Hexham, sir?'

'Just so, Richard. A confluence. When two rivers come together, they make white water. They become angry with each other. Before they settle down and are once again able to flow smoothly on, they have to get to know each other ... as you and Emma will have to get to know each other, if you ever marry. Let us call the North Tyne "Old Father Tyne". Let us call the South Tyne "Change". Let us call the new, enlarged river, their marriage makes, "Progress".'

'"Progress", sir, is a dead river.'

'Sadly, yes, it is. Whenever something is made, Richard, there will be a waste product.'

'Like, sir, when a carpenter planes wood he makes shavings?'

'Exactly, Richard.'

'And if we burn the shavings to keep us warm, sir?'

'We make smoke.'

'Which makes us cough and splutter and hurts wor eyes.'

'If the old river is dead, sir, no one has given it a Christian funeral.'

'And at the old Tyne's funeral, Richard, what sermon might a vicar preach?'

'If he was an old vicar, sir, he'd say how he remembered the river when it was full of salmon and didn't smell of rotten eggs. That's what the vicar did at me grandpa's funeral. When me grandpa died he was a bag of bones. Age, sir, and life's wear and tear had turned a big fellow into a midget. In his prime, sir, he'd rowed with Harry Clasper. On Ascension Day he was in charge of the Lord Mayor's barge.'

'I fear, Richard, that what we call progress is a two-edged sword.'

'Like falling in love, sir, and getting married?'

'How so?'

'If I was married, sir, the missus would want me home and not here working at the office.'

'Marriage and work, Richard, is a see-saw difficult to keep balanced. Lady Margaret understands my passion to understand the natural world. But I also know she sometimes wishes I show as much interest in a new dress she has bought, as I do in hydraulics. She finds it frustrating, that I am not interested in fashion.'

'Is that because you are a scientist, sir, and science is about facts?'

'Some facts, Richard, are more factual than others. Often, what we now take to be factual, was born … came into the world … as a theory. Think of Galileo claiming the Earth goes round the Sun. A theory once ridiculed by the Catholic Church but now accepted as a fact.'

'Will Mr Darwin's theory, sir, that our ancestors were apes, ever become a fact?'

'Who knows. To turn that theory into a fact, scientists will have to become detectives. They will have to look for evidence to support their claim. Mavis is already a believer. She says the Sandgate is full of monkeys. Mavis is a philosopher. Her books are her pots and pans. Her sharp eye is her quill pen. When I am in her kitchen, I feel our roles are reversed. She is my employer and I am her employee.'

'Does she scare you, sir?'

'Is anyone listening?' said Sir William, making a show of scanning for eavesdroppers, before answering. 'Yes. Mavis is a trickling stream. You'd think she'd be easy to dam … wrong.'

'Never forget, sir, to stop the "press" getting their men the Sandgate lasses took up arms. The "press" thought the wives would be easy to handle, but they were wrong, sir, weren't they? The wives were like waves going over the groyne at South Shields when she's a-blowing hard from the north-east.'

'You have a gift, Richard for finding similes in everyday life.'

'Begging your pardon, sir, but what's a simile?'

Sir William explained.

'That's one for the notebook, sir.'

'You and I, Richard, are autodidacts.'

'Are we, sir?'

'Yes, we are. Before you ask me, I will tell you what "autodidact" means. An "autodidact", Richard, is a fellow who is self-taught. As you know, by profession, I am a solicitor. In my teens I was apprenticed to the law.'

'You are not a solicitor, now, sir. You are an engineer. You make things out of iron. You use iron to make things the way the Japanese use their origami skills to make birds and animals out of paper.'

'It is amazing the shapes hot iron can be turned into. My heart was never in the law, Richard. My inborn inclination was ever toward natural philosophy. I do not know why that should be so, Richard. Was it something I was born with, along with my five senses?'

Richard raised his eyebrows. He loved talking to Sir William. Talking to Sir William was like going to school without you knowing you were sitting behind a desk, looking at a blackboard, in front of which, stood a teacher wielding a cane.

'Anyway, Richard, whether I was born with it or not, my inclination, for as long as I can remember, has been to study natural philosophy. It is in the study of that subject, Richard, that I am an "autodidact". I am self-taught. When I look at a stream, I see a baby who I know will meander and flow, and will, in maturity, become a river. A river, Richard, with awesome power. It is almost impossible to stop the smallest stream from flowing its own sweet way. As with Doris … dare I say it … you have little choice but to follow its flow and, by so doing, harness its energy. Think, Richard, of how water, channelled through a sluice, turns a waterwheel.

You, Richard, were born with a gift for draughtsmanship. You are self-taught. In that respect you are an "autodidact". Your simile of Tyneside women scaring the living daylights out of the "press" makes me think of what I have read about Abraham Lincoln. He is a master of the "simile".

'As you, sir, are master of the "hydraulics".'

RICHARD CHATS WITH A MEMBER OF THE TOON'S CONSTABULARY

Richard waved goodbye to the carriage taking Sir William and the ladies to Jesmond. He waved it goodbye until it turned into Pilgrim Street. He waved it goodbye as if his arms were the sails of a windmill blown by a gale. His heart was full of longing to be inside the coach with Emma. He waved the coach goodbye as if it was taking his love to the antipodes, rather than on a mile jaunt to Jesmond.

Doris forbade Emma to look out of the coach's window.

'Do not let Richard see you are enthusiastic,' she coached Emma. 'And another thing … stick your head out too far and a gas lamppost might decapitate you. Richard is not Henry the eighth and you are not Anne Boleyn. You are Meggie's maid and my instructor in horrid-thingummy.'

A passing policeman, with a bull's eye strapped to his belt, pausing, on his round, told Richard: 'When yuh stop star gazing, young fella, and gan back inside, make sure you bolt your door.'

'The keel men?' said Richard.

'I hope not, sir. If it is them, and I don't think it is, they've got guns. There's reports, there's gun shots been heard doon Sandgate. I know the town, sir, the ways I knows my own helmet when I sees it hanging up at the station with all the other helmets. To a stranger the helmets aall look the same but not to me they don't. I knows my own helmet. I can smell trouble, sir the way I know it's not going to snow tonight. At the station they are taking bets it's going to snow.'

'I think it's going to snow tonight,' said Richard.

'You're wrong, sir. Where were you born?'

'Slaley.'

'Slaley, eh? A Hexham lad. I'm Warkworth. Me mother used to tell me, when I was toasting bread on a toasting fork in front of a good fire, Hexham folk nar nowt about weather. They're good with sheep but divent ask them if it's ganna rain. You're not by any chance, sir–' shining his bull's eye onto Richard's face– 'a Rutherford?'

'As a matter of fact, I am,' said Richard. 'How'd you know that?'

'Because, sir, I'm a policeman. I'm trained to know a Warkworth face from a Hexham face. I knows faces the way I knows my helmet hanging up amongst all those other helmets at the station. You look like a Rutherford.'

'But, not a murderer, I hope?'

'Definitely not one of them, sir. You do not have to answer my question, sir, which I've been thinking about asking, if you don't wish to. It is not an official question, sir. You do not have to swear an oath. It is by way of giving me evidence my observational skills are up to the mark. I have ambition, sir, to become a detective. Are you in love?'

'You mean, with the work I do for Sir William?'

'That's interesting, that is, if I may say so, sir. I mean, you answering my question with a question. In a way, sir, your manner of answering has answered my question. When a suspect answers a question with a question I have it written down in my little black book: suspect is ducking and weaving. Now, I'm pretty certain you are in love, as my observational skills suspected. You are in love with the pretty lassie you couldn't stop waving goodbye to in the coach. You was waving so hard I thought your arms might drop off. Am I right or am I wrong? You don't have to answer if you don't want to. But if you do and your answer is the affirmative, it will give me confidence in my observational skills. When I apply to become a detective, I will cite it as evidence of my suitability to be promoted to that position. Give me an honest answer and you will be helping an officer of the law, sir.'

'As a matter of fact …'

'Yes or no, sir. Are you in love with the lassie I saw you waving off in the phaeton with the rich folk? You don't have to answer if you don't want to.'

'Yes! Yes!'

'Thank you, sir. You've helped me and, if I may say so, sir, helped yourself. I'd expect nothing less from a Rutherford. I'm a Warkworth "Bell". At the station they used to call me "Ding-Dong". When they knew I knew about weather, they changed me moniker to "Weather Bell". It's their fault if they won't believe me it's not ganin to snow toneet. When they lose their bets, they'll be buying me drinks at the "Old George" … you'll see. I'd best be getting along. Afore I go, best check my whistle. Hold me bull's eye will yuh, there's a bonny lad.'

While Richard held the bull's eye the policeman explained how if a pigeon's feather – he was a breeder of pigeons, he told Richard – got caught in the whistle's air vent, it wouldn't blow.

'When you are chasing villains, sir, every second counts. And if you don't catch the villain, sir, it's nee good telling the desk sergeant "me whistle didn't work, Sarge … it was bunged up with pigeon feather". Sarge knows I keep pigeons. You've got to be prepared, Mr Rutherford … give's me bull's eye. Thankee. Bolt your door. Caretaker, are you?'

'Among other things.'

'Take my word for it, sir, there's villainy in the air toneet. Them what says they heard gun shots is telling the truth. I knows about the weather. It wasn't thunder they heard. It was gun shots.'

'But, no snow?'

'A flake or two. It won't lie.'

Behind a bolted front door, by the light of a candle, Richard looked at his face in a mirror. Did he look like a Rutherford? What did a Rutherford look like? What should a Rutherford look like? He had a cousin who, apart from having the same number of arms and legs and eyes, as him, looked nothing like him.

Taking off his jacket he read, on the body of an origami elephant: 'Richard Rutherford I love you.'

The policeman wasn't a gifted interpreter of human physiognomy, after all … he just had bloody good eyesight.

ROWLEY HARRISON: SINGER, SONGWRITER AND COMEDIAN ENTERTAINS AN UNINVITED GUEST

Rowley sat in his dressing room with his eyes closed. Four curtain calls … or, was it five? His ad-lib, 'Cuddy's Pant', had brought the house doon.

A woman in the box, stage left, had blown him kisses. He'd caught them and blown them back. Such a pity it was the show's last neet. If only he could train a donkey to piss on the stage every neet. Oh, to bring the house down every neet by having the ability to control a donkey's bladder.

He did not hear his dressing room door open but he did hear it being locked. Turning to see who'd barged in without knocking, he saw a black man pointing a gun at him.

'If you are one of the forty thieves, young man, your dressing room is second on the left down the corridor. It is, I am told, communal.'

'Why are you holding up your hands?' said Jeb.

'You are pointing a gun at me.'

'You are American?'

'My accent?'

'Why aye, man! Am not Mutton Jeff.'

'What does that mean? In my short time on Tyneside I have learnt to understand, "Why aye man!" but not, "Mutton Jeff". "Mutton Jeff", sir, has taken me up the Mississippi and left me high and dry on a levee without a paddle.'

'M – i – ss – i - ss –i – pp – i,' rattled off Rowley.

To show his rapid-fire spelling of the river's name was meant to amuse, he attempted to pull a funny face. Fear had frozen his face muscles. Instead of pulling a funny face his effort produced a spasm of out-of-control twitches.

'Mutton-Jeff, sir,' he continued, determined not to 'die' … possibly, literally if the black man shot him … 'is Geordie rhyming slang. It's the verbal ballast the sailors on the colliers bring back from London. Let me explain.'

'Keep talking.'

'I'm deeing … doing, my best. When Tyneside colliers take coal to the "Big Smoke" they steam back to canny Newcastle with ballast in their holds. The sailors come back with Cockney rhyming slang in their heeds. Like ballast, see? "Mutton-Jeff", sir … I wish you wouldn't keep pointing that gun at me … is, Cockney rhyming slang for "deaf". Like, "Apples and pears" means "stairs". Like, "Peggy's waistcoat" means "Gateshead". Yuh nar … you know, the toon, the town, across the coaly Tyne. South bank of the river. Rhyming slang, see. I wish you wouldn't point that gun at me. It makes me want to gan … to go, to the netty.'

'The "netty"? The police?'

'Nar! Nar! No! No! Because you are pointing a gun at me you are making me want to empty my e, a, i, o, u's.'

'E, a, i, o, u?' repeated the American.

'My vowel sounds. My bowels! Your pointing that gun at me is making me in danger of losing control of my bowels. Yuh nar? You know? Go to the toilet.'

'You are saying fear is making you shit?'

'Aye! Yes!'

'I apologise,' said Jeb, lowering the revolver. 'I am desperate.'

'Aye and so am I.'

During this break in hostilities, the two men looked at each other the way a grocer looks at his scales when he is weighing a pound of butter. Should he take a little bit off and make the pound a little bit under or, be generous and give a bit extra as you might to a loyal customer or to a lass you fancied?

Jeb, was asking himself: Can I trust this chatter-box dressed up as a turbaned toff from somewhere exotic in the Middle East? What manner of man was hiding behind the make-up and fancy dress?

Rowley, as a man of the theatre, looked for a solution to the dilemma he was facing, of being summarily executed, by drawing on his theatrical experience. Cat-calls and boos and orange peel left you free to fight another day. A bullet through the heart was … was terminal. When the audience gave you the 'bird', you gritted your teeth and carried on. You had to believe in yourself. And he did believe in himself. He was Rowley Harrison, stage name, Geordie Black … four curtain calls … or, was it five?

'As I was saying,' continued Rowley, his resolve stiffened by the knowledge that if he could handle the Byker Grande on a Friday night, he could handle a man pointing a gun at him, 'Tyneside slang comes from London. Yuh nar … you know, like the plague did in the seventeenth century. We export coal. We import rhyme. Rhyme to Tyneside is like what cotton is to Liverpool.'

'Cotton!' exploded Jeb. 'A crop picked by slaves. A crop picked by the blood of my people.'

When someone bursts into your private dressing room and points a gun at you, you look more at the gun than at the person holding it. Rowley had, of course, registered the fact that the man pointing a gun at him was a black man but only at a subliminal level.

Rowley was against slavery. Of course he was. Everyone he knew was against slavery. But, no doubt about it, a black man had more right to be angry about slavery than a white man. With the black man, it would be personal. Rowley could understand that. But, what was the fellow doing on Tyneside? Was he an escaped slave? If he was, he had no need to worry. This was England. Not America. There was no slavery in England. Long hours of hard work for too little pay … but not slavery. If his owners were on Tyneside, English law would not allow them to treat him as if he was an artefact. English law would make sure he was treated as a human being.

The black man pointing a gun at him was a contradiction. His behaviour was that of a man on the run … a man, almost but not quite, at the end of his tether. Yet, he was dressed like a gentleman. He was Dress Circle. He'd have looked at Witty-Watty's pissing donkey through enamelled opera glasses with an ivory focussing wheel.

The black man needed calming down. He needed to be given time for his breathing to be allowed to return to normal. Winning over an audience was not a matter of life and death. If he failed to win the fellow's confidence, he … Rowley Harrison … stage name Geordie Black … in a few minutes … seconds … might be playing a harp.

'I have read recently, sir,' Rowley began as he scratched an imaginary spot on his nose, 'in my local newspaper, the good news that England will not be going to war with America. Yet, here I am, in my dressing room, with an American pointing a gun at me. Have you perhaps not heard the good news?'

Jeb was well aware that relations between America and England were strained. The Limeys were up in arms about the North stopping a British mail ship.

'That is indeed good news,' said Jeb. Then, pointing the revolver at the violin case he could see lying on top of pots of face paint, 'What's in there?'

'Please don't shoot my violin,' said Rowley, grabbing the case in a theatrical way. 'I need it for my act. Without my violin I will be Tyneside without coal.'

'You play?' said Jeb.

'I do.'

'I play the banjo.'

'You are a musician?'

'I am.'

'Heave-to! Bonny lad. Drop anchor. Put down the gun. Musicians are brothers. They don't shoot each other. I'm thinking … you're a canny lad.'

'God damn it!' said Jeb. 'What does that mean?'

On hearing footsteps stop outside the door, Jeb pointed the Colt at Rowley's head. Rowley put up his hands. To warn Rowley not to shout for help, Jeb put a warning finger to his lips. His eyes begged Rowley not to give him away.

'Rowley!' shouted a voice through the door. 'Are yuh at haem?'

'Aye,' shouted Rowley.

'Can I come in?'

Jeb shook his head.

'No.'

'Why not?' The door handle turned. 'Why have you locked ya door?'

'I'm counting me money.'

'Are yuh alreet?'

'Aye! Aye!'

'A hope those encores haven't gone to ya heed.'

'I'm counting me money so I can get me round in.'

'That's more like it. We're aal meeting at the Turk's. Coming?'

'See you there.'

'Sure you're alreet?'

'Aye!'

'Divent be long.'

'I'll be there.'

'Good lad.'

'Rowley in one of his moods?' said a woman in a loud, shrill voice. 'Comics is the same the world ower. Sad buggers. They give all their inner happiness away in jokes. Leave nowt for themselves.'

The footsteps died away. A sad comic, was he? If he didn't play his cards reet with the black man pointing a gun at him, in the next few seconds he might be a deed comic, as well.

'You on the run? Is the polis after you? Yuh nar, the police?'

'I am not on the run from the police. I am not a thief.'

'You might not be a thief, bonny lad, but if that gun gans bang and you kill me, you will be a murderer.'

Jeb lowered the gun.

'Drink? I've only got ginger beer. Me girlfriend, Annie … plays the trombone in the "Sally Bashers" …'

'"Sally Bashers"?'

'"Salvation Army …'

Jeb nodded but did not mention that he'd already made the acquaintance of the organisation.

'An evangelical temperance movement. Annie doesn't believe in the medicinal properties of alcohol. She wants everyone to abstain. I keep telling her: "Pet, telling Geordies not to drink is like telling foxes not to eat chickens." Yee can have the goblet. … stage-prop. Whatever you do, divent … don't press that lever there' (pointing at a spur on the goblet's handle). 'If you do, a cuckoo will pop out. Brought the house down when I used it in Sunderland. I'll drink out the bottle. I wouldn't drink out the bottle if Annie was here. Annie, has standards, see. She's from a posh family in Gateshead. Her brother makes clocks. He owns jewellery shops. One in Gateshead, one in Newcastle. But, when there's not enough glasses to go round, needs must as the keel skipper said when he told his crew to use their hands as paddles when there was nee … no wind. To get by in life, yuh have to improvise, haven't yuh? A hide me ginger beer under this ginger wig. I'm an artiste, see. I likes to be colour co-ordinated. If Annie comes in and sees it, she'll pour it doon … down the sink.'

'Annie has it in for ginger beer?'

'I'm not talking about ginger beer, bonny lad–' lifting up the ginger wig to reveal a bottle of whisky. 'Say when. Hang on–' taking the goblet off Jeb– 'Annie wouldn't like that.'

'What's wrong?'

'Grease paint on the rim. As Annie would say, "cleanliness is next to godliness" or, as the big toe said to the verruca, "you shouldn't be there". Allow me–' removing the offending smudge with a tassel on the end of his oriental cummerbund.

'There–' holding up the goblet to inspect it– 'that's better. Say when.'

'When,' said Jeb.

'There you are, bonny lad–' handing Jeb the goblet. 'Am thinking you need that.'

Jeb sipped the whisky. He was back stage in the land of make-believe. To show he thought the whisky to be a bit of alright, he smacked his lips in an over-the-top way; like an actor in a farce. When in Rome do as the Romans do.

In a theatre, nothing was what it seemed. Close to it was obvious the jewels on the theatrical's turban were bits of coloured glass. The actor looked like something out of the Arabian Nights, but he wasn't. The fellow was a Geordie. He was not exotic. He was local. He was more pit heap than pyramid.

'Name's Rowley. Stage name, Geordie Black,' said Rowley, extending a hand. 'I had four encores toneet … tonight, or was it five? Here's to the keel men … what's left of them and to the abolition of slavery.'

'I'll drink to that,' said Jeb, raising the goblet. 'I know nothing about keel men but, I'm damn certain about the last. To the abolition of slavery!'

'The abolition of slavery,' said Rowley, saluting the American with the whisky bottle. 'Careful yuh divent touch the lever I told you about. We divent want yuh sharing your dram with a cuckoo. To the abolition of slavery.'

'To the abolition of slavery.'

In the ensuing silence, after the toast, Jeb made up his mind to take Rowley a little bit into his confidence.

'You were right, Rowley, 'he said. 'I am on the run. But, not from the police. I am on the run from two local thugs. I believe them to be called the Coxon brothers. I fear my parlous state is more evident than I thought. To you I must look as out of breath as one of your foxes when it is being chased by men on horseback wearing red coats.'

'Fox hunting! That's for the toffs. Don't do it, bonny lad! Divent dee it!'

'What?' said Jeb.

'Blow your brains out.'

'I'm not going to blow my brains out, Rowley, I'm putting my gun back into its holster. The holster is under my arm. To reach it I have to stretch up. See?' opening his coat to show off the bespoke leather holster. 'Sorry if I scared you. At least I've managed to shut you up. Do you always talk a lot?'

'When you pointed that gun at me you gave me a verbal enema. Wee gans there, friend or enema?'

'I beg your pardon?'

'Nivva mind.'

'Sorry.'

'Are yuh ganna … going to tell me what's going on?'

Rowley listened to Jeb's tale with the impatient patience of a chatterbox, more used to talking than to listening.

'I thought I'd shaken the Coxons off. In running away from them I lost my bearings.'

'Like the keel man in the fog who ended up in Jarrow when he thought he was in South Shields. A hope yuh divent mind me asking, but what's your name?'

'Jeb.'

'Pleased to meet you, Jeb; especially now you are not pointing that gun at me. Would you have shot me?'

'Yes.'

'I don't believe you. You're not a cold blooded killer.'

'How'd you know?'

'Because I'm still breathing. I'm still talking. I'm still alive. I'm doing it again, aren't I?'

For the umpteenth time Jeb wondered what manner of man lay under the make-up. Could he trust him? When Rowley had said he was against slavery, Jeb had believed him. But slavery was not part of Rowley's world. He was a white Englishman. Slavery was not his fight. When push came to shove how many folk would fight to the death for a foreign cause?

Did the Coxon brothers know where he'd sought sanctuary? How close behind him had they been?

As a Union agent he was not short of English pounds, shillings and pence. Rowley would be biddable. He was also a musician. In different circumstances would he have played a duet with him as he'd done with Waterloo Bob?

If memory served him right, the Old George was not far from the theatre. Should he bid Rowley good night and find his own way there? To get there, would he have to go down unlit alleyways, called 'chares'? From the Coxons' point of view, a 'chare' was the perfect killing ground.

To find his way back to the Old George common sense told him he needed help. He needed someone with local knowledge.

In under an hour he'd to be in the town's railway station to meet Henry. He had a choice. He could bid Rowley good night, apologise for his intrusion, give him a good tip and walk out, or trust him.

His dithering ceased when Rowley bowed the opening bars of a sad song on his violin. In the tune's sadness Jeb heard his people rage against slavery. It made him take Rowley one hundred per cent into his confidence.

He told him why he was in Newcastle. He told him where he was lodging. He told him about having to meet, in under an hour, Henry Adams, a man of importance in diplomatic circles, off the express train from London.

Rowley found it difficult to put himself in the American's boots. They lived in different societies. Rowley knew about hardship … about being out of work … about being short of money but, he knew nothing about slavery. If he wasn't happy about the fee he had been paid for playing a part he could walk away and find something better. Easier said than done, but he did have that choice. He was a free man. No one could force him to stay. If he fancied going on a trip to London on one of the new express trains, no one could stop him. He was a free man.

'I am on the run, Rowley,' continued Jeb, 'because I believe no man should be the property and chattel of another man.'

Rowley knew right from wrong. The American was a canny bloke. If he wanted help, he'd come to the right place.

To avoid being misunderstood, Rowley now did his best to speak English as it was spoken in London and not doon on the Sandgate.

'Do not shoot me when I take out my scimitar. It's wood. It's not a real sword. It's not real, like your gun.'

Ever so slowly Rowley drew the wooden scimitar from out of the red sash wound round his waist.

'Jeb,' he said, putting the scimitar out of harm's way, 'you are not wearing fustian. I have a thing about fustian. You are dressed like a gentleman. If I may say so, an affluent gentleman. Your boots are polished and that overcoat you are wearing didn't come from Paddy's Market. In theatrical terms, sir, you are, Dress Circle. If you'd sat in the Gods or the pit, while the lasses squeezed your lemons, the lads would have been picking your pockets. As a man of the theatre' (all the while undressing) 'I think of life as a play. It has acts and scenes. Intervals. A final curtain. And, if one is fortunate, curtain calls. Tonight, I had four or, was it five? The melodrama you and I have played out in this dressing room … the magic room in which Rowley Harrison, stage name Geordie Black, is changed by theatrical magic … help me with this button please … into a Middle Eastern toff complete with a gold turban and a wooden scimitar, is, I put it to you, in need of a scene change.'

'You are saying, Rowley, in your round-about way, that you and I cannot stay cooped up in this cupboard, all night?'

'How dare you, sir! Call my dressing room a cupboard. I live, sir, in a world of illusion. It is my illusion that this is a large room. It is a dressing room worthy of a dying gladiator. Here, Rowley, shivers under a gas lamp. Here, Rowley hears applause. The draught coming under the door reminds Rowley he has chilblains. It is cold outside?'

'Bitter.'

'Snow?'

'A few flakes.'

'Jeb, you are a fugitive. The Theatre Royal is not Durham Cathedral. It does not boast a sanctuary knocker. But it does have me, Rowley Harrison, stage name "Geordie Black". You need help. I need work. Tonight was the last night of the Forty Thieves … four encores or was it five? As the hungry horse said to the cart full of potatoes, feed me and I will pull you. Where duh yuh want to gan? Where do you want to go? We cannot stay here all night.'

'To the railway station,' said Jeb, pulling out his watch and realising that if he was to be on time to meet Henry, he'd best be getting a move on. 'How far is it?'

'A fifteen-minute walk … a ten-minute trot … forever and ever, amen, if you get knocked doon … down by a cab.'

'Can we take a cab?'

'Quicker to walk.'

'What if the Coxon brothers are waiting outside for me?'

'After the punishment you dished out to them, I'm thinking they'll be in a public house licking their wounds.'

'What if their thirst for revenge is greater than their thirst for a recuperative glass of ale?'

'Not to worry, bonny lad … they won't recognise you.'

'Will they not?'

'They won't recognise you, bonny lad, because you'll be dressed as a woman.'

'I beg your pardon!'

'Jeb, my would-be assassin and fellow musician, I ask you to stop for a moment and think. Your dark complexion makes you easy to recognise. The Coxon brothers will have told their narks to be on the look-out for you. Grey Street is gas lit.'

'I'm tall.'

'Plenty of tall Geordie lasses.'

'I don't feel … I don't walk like a woman.'

'When we go outside, take a deep breath. Watch how the lasses walk. But divent … do not copy prostitutes. Copy respectable women … ladies … the sort who live in Jesmond. You know … I'm thinking … when we are outside, it might help your disguise, if you and I linked. You know … as if we were man and wife. We can have a signal system … like the watermen have on their ropes when it's so foggy, you can't see your feet. One tug on the rope means one thing. Two tugs on the rope means something else. When I squeeze your elbow once, that means you are doing canny … two squeezes means you are mincing … that you are walking like a tart … and a divent mean … and I do not mean, a tart in a pastry case.'

'I'm not happy.'

'Nor am I, bonny lad. I should be home in Gateshead by now. As far as I'm concerned, aal roads lead to Gateshead. Annie, that's the love of my life, lives in Gateshead. Her brother, Edwin, makes clocks. He's posh. He's on the council. He nars … he knows aal the big-wigs.'

'Rowley, I am a Union agent. Union agents … representatives of the government of Abraham Lincoln, do not skulk around dressed as lasses. I have a Colt revolver. I know how to use it. I am more than capable of looking after myself.'

'Shoot someone dead, sir, and you'll end up in jail. What good would that do your cause? If the Coxons catch yuh, they'll break every bone in your body. What good would that do your cause? I know the Coxons. They will have told aal their narks in the town to be on the look-out for a black man with an American accent. You can keep your gob shut but you cannot hide the colour of your skin.'

'I am not ashamed of the colour of my skin.'

'I never said you were … and nar should you be. Mr Jeb, sir, I am a practical chap.'

'Are theatre folk "practical", I would not have thought so. You live in a world of make-believe. My Colt is real. It fires real bullets. Your scimitar is made of wood. It wouldn't cut butter.'

'To make, make-believe, real, Jeb, you have to be … practical. You have to make sure your props look real. You have to know how long it takes you to change costumes. If you go on stage with your turban back to front … there's always a heckler waiting to tell you. Nar! Nar! No! No! Jeb, I'm telling you … theatre folk are practical. To hide your good looks you'll need to wear a veil.'

'Men do not wear veils.'

'I know they don't … but wives do. Think about it, bonny lad. Dressing up as a wife is better than getting beaten up by the Coxons. Bob, he plays "Widow Twanky", has a black woman's coat with a built-in bustle. You can have a choice of bonnets, just so long as you pick one with a veil. The coat's long … it will hide your bloke's boots. I'm not an undertaker but if I was eye-measuring you for a coffin, I'd say "Widow-Twanky's" coat will be a good fit … not as good as made-to-measure … but it will cover your bits and bobs. It will fit you better than the coat a seen on a scarecrow in a field in Heaton. Comedy and undertaking have a lot in common … did you know that?'

'No,' said Jeb. What a chatter box this fellow was.

'When an audience dies on you, they are, in a manner of speaking, putting you in a coffin. Keeping a stiff upper lip you call the fuzzy shapes you can see through the footlights "Lazarus" and kid yourself you are Jesus … as Cleopatra said to the asp before it bit her tit … nil desperandum.'

'And what did Mark Anthony say?'

'I divent nar … a wasn't there.'

'Rowley, in New York we have pie eating competitions.'

'Pies? Pies give me heartburn … rich pastry.'

'I was thinking, Rowley, you'd win a chatterbox competition, hands down.'

'Aye … if pies were words, a suppose a would. Will you dress up as a wife?'

'Agents of the Union government do not dress up as women. We do not hide from thugs.'

'Or,' said Rowley, 'in your case, run away and seek sanctuary in a theatre.'

'I was outnumbered.'

'Like me, every night. There's always more of them out there sucking oranges than there are actors on stage. If the Coxons spot you and it comes to a fight, I have to tell you, I'm a coward. My cudgels are words, bonny lad. If you want to meet this bloke off the London train and not have two black eyes and your arms in plaster, may I suggest … I'm not going down on my knees begging you to see reason, but I am humbly imploring you to see my suggestion of a disguise as, well, sensible.'

'I'm not taking off my trousers.'

'Now, you're talking. You won't have to. It's a long coat. Have I not told you, it'll be long enough to hide your boots. I don't nar, know, if you know this, but Bonnie Prince Charlie escaped the red coats by dressing up as a woman.'

'Republicans do not copy royalty.'

'Ah well, please yourself. What about the wolf in Little Red Riding Hood? He dressed up as an old woman.'

'And look what happened to him.'

'But, you'll do it.'

'Do I have a choice?'

'Can I tell you a story?'

'Will it take long?'

'I'll tell it while I'm changing out of my costume and into mufti. If I went down Grey Street dressed as "Witty-Watty", I'd be signing autographs aal night. When we leave the theatre, we don't want to draw attention to ourselves, do we?'

'We are leaving together?'

'You've hired me, haven't you? I'm your "local knowledge". We'll discuss terms later.'

'You are going to be my Good Samaritan?'

'If the money's reet, right, I will be.'

'My boss is fond of telling stories to get his point across.'

'And who would he be?'

'Abraham Lincoln.'

'Plenty of money, has he?'

'He is President of the United States of America. In America we don't have a queen, we have a president. Your Queen Victoria is titular head of the Old World. Mr Lincoln is chief executive of the New World. To get his way, he doesn't bully, threaten or flog, he tells stories … like you, Rowley.'

'You are telling me I am like Abraham Lincoln, the President of the United States of America?'

'First, tell me your story, then I will tell you if you are as good as Mr Lincoln. My judgement will be, I assure you, fair but fearless.'

'Well,' said Rowley, 'aal I was going to say was, you are like a bairn making sand-pies on a sandbank when the tide is coming in. You are so busy making sand-pies you haven't noticed the tide is coming in. When you do notice you dither. The longer you dither the deeper the water threatening to wash you away. If you go now, you can plodge home.'

'Plodge?'

'Paddle, wade through watta, water.'

'And if I dither?'

'The incoming tide will not be a gentleman and ignore you, it will sweep you off your feet. Worse still, salt water will seep into your banjo case. Everyone knows salt water is good for killing verrucas and banjos. Am I as good as Mr Lincoln?'

Jeb sort of nodded, 'yes'. He was imagining himself trapped on a sandbank being diminished every second by an incoming tide. He concluded that if he was not to drown, which in his case meant not getting beaten up by the Coxon brothers, he'd best swallow his pride and dress up as a woman.

'I'll do it,' he said.

'What made you change your mind?'

'I don't want sea water damaging my banjo.'

'As a musician I can understand that. No extra charge, I'll be your dresser. I don't suppose I can persuade you to wear the bustle that goes with the costume?'

'Certainly not. The coat and hat will more than suffice to hide my maleness.'

'If you say so.'

With Rowley's help Jeb pulled on a long, black, woman's coat.

'I can do the hat myself, thank you,' said Jeb, pulling the bonnet down hard on his head as if he was a cowboy and the bonnet was a Stetson.

'No, no, Mr Jeb … not like that. Allow me. There, that's better. Pull the veil down and we are ready to sail. Look in the mirror. What do you think?'

Jeb looked in the mirror. What he saw did not please him. God dammit! He was an agent of the United States of America, not a cross dresser. Was he going to have to meet Henry … a stickler for protocol … dressed as a drag queen?

'I will not wear gloves. Give me the muff. Thank you. There,' he said, putting the Colt into the muff-holster, 'anyone attacks me, I'll shoot them dead. Let's go.'

In high dudgeon, Jeb picked up his banjo and slung it over his shoulder; as he did so the gun-weighted muff, hanging loose on a fur ribbon around his neck, swung like a pendulum.

'Just a minute,' said Rowley, shaking his head in disbelief, 'a wife in weeds doesn't carry a banjo strapped across her back.'

'You are saying, Rowley, that my banjo will blow my disguise?'

'As sure as hen's lay eggs. If you don't want two black eyes and a broken nose, leave your banjo here.'

'Where I go, my banjo goes.'

'In the short time I've known you, Jeb I've come to realise you are stubborn.'

'And,' said Jeb, pulling out his watch and, for the umpteenth time, looking at it, 'if I am to meet Mr Adams off the London express, we have no time to argue.'

'Will you trust me to carry your banjo?'

'Do you cherish your fiddle?'

'Aye! I do. But it's not a Stradivarius.'

'My banjo belonged to my father. Its personal associations make it as valuable to me as a Stradivarius.'

'I understand. I keep my grandfather's waistcoat in a chest under the bed. He was a keel man.'

'You will look after my banjo as you look after your grandfather's waistcoat?'

'I will. Give it here–' slinging the banjo in its Mississippi alligator case over his shoulder. 'And, keep your gob shut. Wives in weeds don't have baritone voices like a keel man shouting, "Ahoy!" to a collier. I'll go first. I'm well known around here. I'm your free pass.'

'If the Coxon brothers are waiting for me outside the stage door, I'll blow their brains out.'

'You can't dee … do that, Jeb … the Coxons divent … don't have brains. They have brawn but they divent, don't have brains. Anyway, we're not going out the stage door. We're going out the front door. The Dress Circle door. Have you got a handkerchief?'

'Of course. I do not wipe my nose on my sleeve. Why?'

'It's to wipe away your tears. You're a grieving widow.' Then, lighting a candle in a brass holder from the gas light before turning the latter out, said, putting his ear to the door, 'It sounds quiet outside. They'll aal be at the Turks patting themselves on the back; telling themselves how wonderful they were. It was my donkey that brought the house down. Four encores or was it five? Stay as close to me as if you and me were a pantomime horse. I'm the front part, see? You're the back. A pantomime horse aalways gets a laugh. Last year at the Empire, Sunderland …'

'Rowley!'

'I'm doing it again, aren't I?'

'Yes.'

'Talking too much.'

'Yes. When you and I discuss your terms of employment as my "local knowledge", I will stipulate in your contract that every time you succumb to your inclination to rabbit, you will be fined a sovereign.'

'Rabbit?'

'Talk too much.'

'Follow me, bonny lad and I'll show you things an audience is never meant to see.'

'Just get me to the railway station and I'll show you a purse full of sovereigns.'

'Now, Jeb, is that a promise or is it rhetoric?'

'Rhetoric!'

'A thought as much. Been in a theatre makes some folk gan aal theatrical. Keep your gob shut and divent start shouting "My kingdom for a horse".'

ROWLEY AND JEB LEAVE THE WORLD OF MAKE-BELIEVE

Leaving Rowley's dressing room – the chatter box's 'emporium' – Jeb, a secret agent, and his 'local knowledge', found themselves in an unlit corridor with a cold breeze blowing through it.

Jeb had read that theatres were haunted. He wanted to ask Rowley if the draught was the heavy breathing of the theatre's ghost. He now knew Rowley well enough to know that if he did ask him, he would be lighting a sparkler. This was not the time or the place for an improvised monologue on the supernatural. He stifled his urge to be convivial, not by biting his tongue but by blowing puffs of air at his veil.

The backstage area of the theatre was utilitarian. It was shabby. It was unloved. It was the servant of those appearing on stage. Unlike Cinderella, it would never go to the ball.

'That was Esmeralda's pen,' said Rowley, as, by the light of the candle he was holding, he pointed out to Jeb a wooden pen filled with straw. 'Four encores or, was it five? Watch your head. If it helps you to see where you are going, pull your veil up. But, mind, when we gan public, we're going, don't forget to pull it down again, you know, like the shopkeepers do with their sun blinds. When it's sunny you pull them down to stop your cream cakes getting sunburnt. When it's not sunny and the sun is on holiday, you pull them up to let your customers see your cream cakes are aal smiles.'

'Where are we now?'

'Under the stage. Watch your head … divent … don't bash your bonnet. A widow in weeds with a bonnet on her head that looks as if it has been bashed into her head by one of Armstrong's hydraulic steam hammers won't look right. Widows in weeds aalways look smart, see. Why? Because they are spiders spinning webs to attract another bloke.'

Opening a five foot by three foot door, Rowley advised: 'Watch your heed. Divent bash your bonnet. Look after your props and your props will look after you. That's what Macready told me … this is fact, not fiction. With me own eyes I saw him stow Yorick's skull in a travelling bag as carefully as if he was putting a bairn to bed.'

They came out onto a stone flagged corridor with whitewashed walls. It sloped upwards at a steep angle.

This time, going through a full-sized door, they entered a gas-lit corridor. Its floor was carpeted. It had a dado rail. Its wallpaper showed a repeat pattern of the masks of tragedy and comedy.

'Dress Circle,' said Rowley, blowing out his candle.

As he did so a woman came shuffling backwards through a double swing door. In one hand she was carrying a mop and in the other, a bucket.

'Let me help,' said Rowley.

'Thank you, sir. Eeee! It's Geordie Black. I hear yuh had a gud neet, Rowley. Three encores, Albert telt me.'

'Four or five,' said Rowley. 'Albert never was good at arithmetic.'

'I can smell smoke,' sniffing. 'Should I shout fire? That's what I've been told to dee if a smell smoke.'

'It's my candle,' explained Rowley, showing the char the smouldering candle in its brass holder. 'A favour, Ellen?'

'When men want something they aalways use me first name. What you after, Rowley? A divent come cheap.'

'Take this for me, will you–' handing her the candle in its brass holder.

'A used to dee candles before we had the gas. Give it here.'

'Thank you kindly.'

'Niva mind, "Thank yuh kindly". I want a kiss like what Albert telt me yuh gave Esmeralda.'

Removing his bowler Rowley kissed Ellen on the cheek.

'I've got two,' said Ellen, tapping the un-kissed cheek.

It was on the second cheek-kiss that Rowley smelt gin.

'You been on Mother's Ruin, Ellen?'

'Charring and gin, Rowley, gan together like a coffin and a deed body. Sorry, Missis–' looking at Jeb– 'a shouldn't have said that. If you're wearing weeds yuh must be grieving.'

Behind his veil Jeb looked at the char with his mouth open. Why was she staring at him? Was she seeing through his disguise?

'It's arful been a widow,' continued Ellen, looking Jeb up and down. 'I nar what you're ganin through, pet. I've lost two. One good'n and one bad'n. What's yours die off? Cholera?'

Jeb, unable to reply without blowing his disguise and being ill at ease dressed as a woman, and not knowing what to do, turned up his coat's collar as if to stop a draught.

'You'll be feeling the cad if you're grieving,' said Ellen, patting Jeb's muff with her mop's handle.

Rowley, knowing that inside the muff Jeb was clutching a loaded Colt revolver and fearful that her tapping might make it go off, took Ellen to one side and whispered in her ear: 'Jennifer is my cousin from Jarrow. She's one short of a baker's dozen.'

'A thought there was something funny aboot her.'

'An explosion at the alkali works did something to her brain.'

'Did it kill her husband? Is that why she's grieving?'

'No. No. It killed her goldfish. She's in weeds for her goldfish.'

'Get away. A thought there was something funny about her.'

'Divent spread it about like horse manure that Rowley's cousin's a bit funny in the heed ... reet?'

'Mum's the word, Rowley.'

To seal their bond Rowley tipped her a wink, blew her a kiss and saluted her with his bowler. Flattered to be a confidante of 'Geordie

Black', she dropped him a curtsey. If she told her sister about Jennifer, that would be alreet. Her sister was like herself – good at keeping a secret.

Rowley was well aware that before the next high tide everyone doon the Sandgate would nar Geordie Black had a sister from Jarrow called Jennifer and that she was daft in the head.

Going through another door and into another plush corridor also lit with hissing gas lamps, Jeb asked Rowley: 'Why'd you call me Jennifer?'

When he spoke the veil covering his face puffed in and out like curtains at an open window.

Rowley winced. There was the hint of the start of a sulk in Jeb's tone of voice … a hint of the pet lip.

'You have castrated me, Rowley. You have done to me what slave owners do to their slaves.

Rowley lifted his bowler and scratched his forehead. He was perspiring. Helping a Union secret agent was taking more out of him than a Friday night at the Alhambra, South Shields, where, if they didn't like you, the lascars pelted you with apple gowks. The lascars were seamen. They were used to throwing ropes over mooring buoys. They never missed.

'Howay, bonny lad, a couldn't call you Hercules, could I? You're a grieving widow, not a big hairy bloke strong enough to lift a keel boat. And, another thing, "J' is your first initial. '"J" for Jeb. '"J" for Jennifer … that helps me remember your nom de guerre. And "J" is for Jeremiah … now, there's a bloke who had a lot to worry about.'

'And so have I,' said Jeb, taking the Colt out of its muff-holster and scratching his nose with its barrel. 'This veil is itching me worse than bee stings.'

'If you don't hide that gun and stay incognito, you'll have more to worry about than a few stinging buzzers.'

Going through two more doors and stopping at a third, Rowley, the palm of his hand on the door ready to push it open, said: 'Keep the Colt hidden, your gob shut and your veil doon. On the other side of this door, is … civilisation. After you, Jennifer.'

In the theatre's lounge bar, men wearing long white aprons were tidying up the mess left by the evening's audience.

In Rowley's opinion, Jeb was walking too fast for a wife. To slow him down he took his arm.

'There! There, pet! You'll be better after the funeral.'

'Night, Rowley,' said one of the waiters.

'Night, Davy.'

'Yuh did well toneet, Rowley. Three encores, am hearing.'

'Actually, it was four.'

****

The night was cold, blustery, frosty and foggy. Under a hissing gas lamp in the theatre's portico, Jeb brought Rowley, to a shuddering stop.

'Quit linking me. I'm not your girlfriend.'

'You're walking too fast for a lass.'

'Which way to the station?'

'Follow me … and divent walk like a keel man ganin to the pub, Mince … mince, dainty, like the lasses dee.'

After crossing Grey Street and walking a few yards down its slope – Jeb, not even trying to 'mince' – spotted Waterloo Bob. The busker-beggar was sheltering from the cold in a shop doorway.

Would his paid informer recognise him? The poor fellow looked cold. His Northumbrian small pipes lay in his lap like a dead spider. He was blowing on his fingers to keep them warm.

'Are yuh alreet, Rowley?' said Bob rolling his coffin-chariot a little out of the doorway.

Not everyone in the toon knew Rowley Harrison, stage name 'Geordie Black', but Rowley was a good tipper. Many times, he'd rattled the busker's collecting box. Rowley was also a musician. Many a time Rowley had complimented Bob on his playing of the Northumbrian small pipes.

'Canny,' replied Rowley, dropping a coin into the busker's tin.

'Ta, very much. It's cad toneet.'

'Brass monkey weather.'

'Me playing fingers is as stiff as the deed bodies a seen on the field at Waterloo. I've heard the news.'

'That England is not going to war with America?'

'Nar! Nar! It's your encores am talking about. Three encores, a heard, and aal because your donkey pissed on the stage.'

'It was four encores, possibly five if you count the applause after the curtains closed.'

'Aye, well, yee nar best.' Poking Jeb's banjo in its Mississippi alligator case with his crutch, which Rowley was carrying: 'Nivva knew yuh played the banjo.'

'Do you mind!' said Jeb, 'that's my banjo you are poking.'

The vehemence of Jeb's exclamation made his veil flap like a curtain at an open window.

'Banjos are plucked not poked. You, of all people, Waterloo Bob, should know that.'

'Mr Phelan,' said Bob, looking Jeb up and down. 'A thought there was something funny about yuh … something a couldn't put me finger on. Lasses divent walk like keel men. What yuh deeing dressed as a griever?'

'It's a long story,' said Jeb. 'I was coerced.'

'That sounds nasty.'

'It's his disguise,' explained Rowley. 'The Coxon brothers are after him. He's incognito.'

'Eh? A thought he was in Grey Street.'

'Bob', said Jeb, lifting up his veil, 'have you anything to report? You have not forgotten I am paying you handsome to be my eyes and ears.'

'Divent worry, bonny lad, Bob hasn't forgotten. The word on the street is that the Coxons are looking for a gang of Americans. They weren't beaten up by one American but by a gang of ten. Were you the gang of ten, Mr Phelan?'

'I was.'

'You're a bonny fighter, Mr Phelan. If you'd been fighting on the French side at Waterloo we would have lost and aal the ships in the river would now be flying the tricycle.'

'If I am indeed a "bonny fighter", Bob, it is because my cause is a just one. The Lord is against slavery and so am I.'

'Aye! Am sure you're reet. Trouble is, Mr Phelan, "reet" doesn't aalways win. Take the Sally Bashers. An hour ago, I had a run-in with them. Their brass drowned out me pipes.'

'Compensation for your lost earnings, Bob,' said Jeb, dropping a coin into Bob's bowl.

'Thank-ee, kindly, Mr Phelan. Thank-ee, kindly.'

'Look out,' said Rowley, 'it's the Coxon brothers and they're heading our way.'

'Off yuh gan,' said Bob, 'they'll be wanting to nar if I've seen any Americans.'

'And have you?' said Jeb.

'No, I haven't. Divent fret, bonny lad, your secret's safe with me. Had away. They're coming up faster than the Imperial Guard came at me at Waterloo. I'll play a tune for you. Yuh nar, to say thank-ee kindly for your contribution. A very generous contribution, if I may say so, Mr Phelan.'

'He's called, Jennifer,' said Rowley.

Inside the muff-holster, Jeb gripped the Colt so hard that, if he could have seen his knuckles, he'd have seen they were white. If the Coxons recognised him he'd shoot them. He'd beaten them once and he'd do it again if he had to.

The brothers were interrogating a beggar. Had he seen a black man with an American accent?

'"Mince",' whispered Rowley.

'I'm not an actor,' expostulated Jeb in a hissing whisper.

His 'hiss' making his veil flap, this time, not like a curtain at an open window but like the genoa on a tacking yacht.

'If you don't "mince" you'll be "mince-meat",' said Rowley. 'If the Coxons beat you up they'll put what's left of you into a mince pie and sell you to cannibals.'

The Coxons were armed with cudgels.

Jeb cocked the Colt in its muff-holster.

'They're looking at me,' he whispered to Rowley. 'They're suspicious.'

'They are not looking at you, Jennifer, dear, they are looking at me. I am a local celebrity. Four encores, toneet … or, was it five?'

Jennifer and Rowley … Geordie and Jackie Coxon were on a collision course. The pavement was not wide enough for them to pass without someone giving way.

Rowley was all for 'giving way', but Jeb would have none of it. God damn it! He was a widow wearing 'weeds'. His mother was a Southern 'belle'. In the Southern states men were gallant. A Southern gentleman always gave way to a lady. Rowley had told him to 'mince' and, god damn it, that's what he was doing. He was, also, spoiling for a fight. Part of him wanted to blow the Coxons to smithereens.

There was a saying in the town. If you want to find the Coxons try the Old Grey Horse, and if they are not there, try the magistrate's court.

Rowley was certain they were looking at him. Of course they were. And he knew why. He was a local celebrity. That they might be looking at Jeb because they'd seen through his disguise, was too scary to think about. Heaven forbid that the headstrong American should draw his Colt and shoot them. He, Rowley Harrison, was a song writer, a comedian, a musician, not a bare-knuckle fighter. The butterflies in his tummy warned him he was about to go on stage.

There are different ways of 'giving way'. There is the surly, boorish way where the passers-by, as they pass, rub shoulders the way a keel boat in a choppy sea scuffs a quay. Under the present circumstances that approach was out of the question. It would provoke the Coxons into using their cudgels and into Jeb drawing his Colt. Then there is the 'white flag' approach where one side throws in the towel and rolls on its back like a cat. Rowley could feel Jeb pulling the arm with which he was linking him. Jeb was a keel boat wanting to slip its mooring. As far as Jeb was concerned, giving way was out of the question. Then there is the 'sarcastic' way. The person giving way, as he steps aside, says: 'After you, my lord!' Then there is the 'misunderstanding' way. Then there is the humorous way. There were many ways of stopping a pan of broth boiling ower.

An instinct, honed to a fine point by years of treading the boards, told Rowley it was time to deploy his secret weapon … his bowler hat … modified by a blacksmith … mounted on a track of ball bearings, it rotated independent of the wearer's head. It never failed to win over an audience. When your jokes are falling flat … spin your bowler hat.

As they closed Rowley was shocked by the scars and cuts he saw on the Coxons' faces. It was like looking at the blood-stained cuts you saw in chopping boards in butcher's shops. Dear god, what had Jeb done to them?

To stop them ogling 'Jennifer' … now was the reet time … he played his ace … he spun his bowler. Round and round it went.

When they grinned, he knew he had them, if not in his back pocket, at least in the palm of his hand. It was a good start to taking the pan of broth off the boil.

'Gentlemen,' said Rowley, 'I am presuming you are blocking the passage forward of my good self and my grieving cousin, Jennifer, because you wish to shake the hand of Geordie Black … the man who knows the name of every pebble on Tynemouth beach.'

'Nar!' said Jackie. 'The Coxons give way to neebody.'

'You are "sail" and Jennifer and I are "steam"; is that what you are saying?'

'That's a fancy way of putting it,' said Geordie, 'but that'll dee.'

'Everyone nars,' said Jackie, 'that steam gives way to sail.'

'Jennifer,' said Rowley, squeezing Jeb's arm, which he was holding the way a dog owner holds a straining dog on a leash, 'it would seem that you and I are "steam ships" and the gentlemen are "sail". It would seem, Jennifer, that the laws of the sea apply also to landlubbers. Another example, I am thinking, Jennifer, of the long arm of the law.'

If testosterone had been a perfume, the Coxons would have gagged. Jeb reeked of male aggression.

Watching the exchange, Waterloo Bob rolled his coffin-chariot out of its doorway shelter, the way cannon are rolled out of gun ports. Mr Phelan paid well. He was officer class. He was a fine musician. Would the Coxons spot that Rowley was carrying a banjo in a Mississippi alligator case? It was Bob's opinion that he should go to Jeb's aid the way Blucher had come to Wellington's at Waterloo.

'Geordie! Jackie!' he shouted.

'Jennifer,' said Rowley, 'you have a train to catch. I was wrong. The gentlemen do not wish to shake the hand of Rowley Harrison, stage name Geordie Black. Dear me, cousin, I am not as famous as I thought.'

Once again spinning his bowler, as a diversion, he nudged Jeb around the immovable Coxons.

'Remember, Jennifer, we are "steam" and "steam" gives way to "sail".

'Coxons, are yuh deaf? Ower here,' shouted Bob. 'I've got something to tell yuh.'

'Let's see what Waterloo has to tell us,' said Geordie.

'Mind, whatever he tells us, we divent pay him.'

When they were far enough away from the Coxons, so as not to be heard, Jeb whispered to Rowley that he hoped Waterloo Bob would not betray him.

'Don't fret, Jennifer,' said Rowley. 'Remember the duet yuh telt me yuh played with him. Yee two are crotchets and quaver brothers.'

'Rowley, quit calling me Jennifer. I don't like it.'

'Aye, alreet. But keep your voice down and your veil. And, divent forget to "mince".'

'And quit linking me.'

'I'm helping your disguise. You are my cousin Jennifer and I'm helping you because you are grieving.'

'Well, I don't like it. I'm not into theatricals. Unlink me and I promise to "mince".'

'Now you're talking.'

'What time is it?'

Rowley took from a pocket the hunter-case watch he'd bought second hand off his prospective brother-in-law, Edwin Wakefield.

He swung it on its chain; the momentum enabling him to throw it up into the air, catch it on the back of his hand and flip it over – as if he was flipping a pancake – into the palm of a hand.

'By my reckoning, Jennifer,' said Rowley, having flipped the hunter open with the flick of a finger, 'if you "mince" and the Coxons haven't seen through your disguise we should be at the station in time to meet your friend, Mr Adams, off the London train.'

'He's not my friend. He is a colleague. His father is America's voice in London.'

'He's top drawer, is he?'

'His heart is in the right place.'

'But?'

'He is not musical. He has a red mark on his neck from wearing a starched collar.'

'Where have you arranged to meet? The station is big. It will be busy.'

'At the lectern upon which the station's Bible is chained. Henry is religious. Which way to the Bible?'

'It would have been easier to have met under the clock.'

'Henry has a thing about punctuality. He doesn't trust clocks in railway stations. He claims to have evidence the railway companies make their clocks fit their timetables. That way, their trains are never late.'

'Get away! And here's me thinking only actor-managers fiddled the books.'

'Which way to the public Bible? Henry trusts the Bible.'

'I'm not sure, but I think it's under the clock. Name a public house in the town and I'll tell you where it is.'

'Rowley, never forget, you are my "local knowledge". You are my compass, my guiding star. We are fellow musicians.'

'I'll say, amen to that. Follow me.'

'To Heaven or to Hell?' said Jeb, puffing out his veil.

'Jennifer, bonny lass, you've only been in my company an hour and already you've caught a bad dose of the theatricals. You've gone theatrical faster than the plague spread around Sandgate two hundred years ago. Follow me and divent forget to "mince".'

'Quit calling me Jennifer.'

'Keep your voice down. Folk are staring. Even Cushie Butterfield didn't have a voice that sounded like surf raking pebbles on Tynemouth beach. And she was a big lass.'

IN WHICH HENRY GIVES A FAMILIAR FACE A BOLLOCKING

The station was busy. Lots of people. Lots of porters pushing barrows. Lots of passengers getting off trains. Lots of passengers getting on trains. Numerous pickpockets. Steam engines puffing out black smoke. Folk greeting each other puffing out white smoke. Men in railway uniforms blowing whistles … waving flags. Lots of sightseers; there for no other reason than they'd come to look at the brand-new steam locomotives; machines which had, in the twinkling of an eye, rendered the stagecoach as dead as the creatures' natural philosophers were calling dinosaurs.

'We're late,' said Jeb, looking at the station's large clock. 'Henry's a stickler for punctuality. He'll be polite but he won't be pleased. Where's the Bible?'

'Under the clock. Jennifer, keep your voice down. Folk are looking at you. You keep forgetting you have a man's voice. Try "squeaking".'

'Rowley, I am not a mouse. I am a Union secret agent. What's he doing here?'

'Who?'

'Boris, the pot boy from the Old George. Why is he talking to Henry?'

'You know Boris?'

'I told you, I am lodging at the Old George. Do you know him?'

'Everyone who drinks at the George knows Boris. Regulars call him the "short changer". You have to watch him when he gives you your change, see? I've heard tell he's ambitious. When he's old enough he wants to drive one of the new steam locomotives. He doesn't get on with Nelson. They belong to different worlds. Nelson's "sail" and Boris is "steam".'

'When you and I gave way to the Coxons we were "steam". I don't care to think I have something in common with Boris.'

'Don't worry, Jeb, you haven't. You belong to the New World.'

'And which world do you belong to, Rowley?'

'I belong to the world of make-believe. I am a man of the theatre.'

'And, like my good self, also to the world of music. You play the fiddle. I play the banjo. Shall we, as we approach Boris and Henry, play, in our heads, the respective national anthems of our two countries?'

'I am thinking, Jennifer, you are as much a man of the theatre as you are a secret agent.'

'Quit calling me Jennifer.'

'Keep your baritone down! At least let me link you. Let me help your disguise. Fooling Boris into thinking you're a wife won't be easy. Boris is sharp. Nose like a dog. Eyes like a hawk. Cunning as a rat. Ambitious as Caesar. Mince, Jennifer, mince and keep your veil down. Leave aal the talking to me.'

******

Henry was not a New World Puritan. He was not a witch burner. But, he had standards. Some things were sacred … like, one day America would be the greatest country on Earth.

What he'd seen this young vagabond – with a mop of blond hair – like a haystack in a wind – do, had roused his ire. The urchin needed to be spoken to. He didn't need to be whipped but he needed to be spoken to.

167

As blinkers remove a horse's peripheral vision, 'indignation' had removed Henry's. He was unaware that a dapper-looking fellow of medium height and a tall woman in 'weeds' were trying to attract his attention.

'Look at me when I'm talking to you,' Henry was telling Boris.

Lifting up his head and narrowing his eyes, Boris said: 'Yee an American? Yuh are, aren't yuh?'

'That's none of your business,' said Henry, poking Boris in the chest with a rolled up copy of the Times.

'Ouch!' said Boris, mimicking serious injury. 'Howay, man!'

'Why were you defacing the Bible on the lectern? The "Good Book" is there for the uplifting of weary souls. It is for the edification of travellers as they travel through life using the brand-new railway. Answer me, young man, or I'll call a constable.'

'I'm a train spotter.'

'A what?'

'A train spotter, sor. I comes to the station to watch the trains. I writes doon their names in me book, sir. Me notebook's full, see?' – showing Henry a scrap of paper. 'When the "Bride of Lammermoor" puffed in I didn't want to forget it, so, I wrote its name doon in the Bible.'

'You defaced the public Bible to help you remember the name of a steam locomotive … is that what you are telling me?'

'Me mother writes in the family Bible. She writes the names of aal her family.'

'But not the names of steam locomotives.'

'Will a gan to Hell, sir?'

'I may be an American, young man, but I am not God. I don't know.'

'Henry!' said Jeb - the enthusiasm of his greeting filling his veil with his breath as a following wind fills a spinnaker - 'welcome to Newcastle.'

'A wife with a bloke's voice,' said Boris. 'What's ganin on?'

Henry looked at Jeb the way one can imagine a farmer looking at a sheep which, instead of bleating, has roared like a lion.

That he'd nonplussed Henry made Jeb smile. It wasn't everyday a New York Phelan got to put a Boston Adams on the back foot.

'It would help Jennifer's disguise, sir,' said Rowley, 'if you'd kiss his hand. You know, as if he really was a wife. That way, anyone watching will be more inclined to think he really is a wife.'

'And who are you, sir?'

'Me? I'm "local knowledge", said Rowley, spinning his bowler.

'How'd yuh dee that?' said Boris. 'That's cleva, that is.'

'I am a man of the theatre,' said Rowley, bowing.

'I nar yee,' said Boris.

'And, young man, I know you.'

'You drink at the George.'

'You once short-changed me.'

'Accidents happen, divent they?'

Steadying the Colt inside the muff with his left hand, Jeb brought out his right hand for Henry to shake.

'Kiss it,' whispered Rowley.

Had Jeb gone native? Henry had heard rumours about the English aristocracy, Palmerston … 'Pam' … dyed his hair. Some were fond of boys.

In a foreign country, Americans – and, make no bones about it, to Henry and Jeb England was a foreign country … not as foreign as Arabia but, nevertheless, foreign – stick together and help each other. Never mind that Henry wasn't a musician. Never mind that at dances he had been known to hide in a window nook. He was an American. And in a foreign country Americans stick together.

'God damned pleased to see you, Henry,' said Jeb, pumping Henry's hand.

Stubborn as a stain, the look of shock stayed put on Henry's face.

'Why are you dressed as a woman?'

'It's a long story,' said Jeb.

'Hoy!' said Boris. 'I nar yee. You're the American what's lodging at the George. Best rooms. Gas in the sitting-room. Candles in the bedrooms. You're not a wife. You're a bloke. Wait till I tell Nelson.'

'It would be best, Boris, if you told no one you have seen me dressed as a woman,' said Jeb.

'It costs money to keep a secret. Secrets is like a First Class ticket, aal the way to London … they divent come cheap.'

'We will discuss terms when we are back at the Old George. In the meantime, you may carry Mr Adams' valise.'

'How much?'

'A shilling.'

'It's a deal. Do we shake hands?'

'To help my disguise you may kiss my hand.'

'Hadaway until the tide comes in. Here, give's your bag.'

****

They walked back to the Old George via Pudding Chare. The houses on the two sides of the mediaeval alley leaned towards each other as if their upper storeys had folded their arms and were gossiping.

The alley was a wind tunnel. Gusts blasted through it the way water surges through a pipe. It was unlit. In its darkest corners footpads with cudgels might well be hiding.

Rowley and Boris led the way.

'Gardy-loo!' shouted a voice from somewhere in the blackness above their heads.

'Watch oot!' shouted Boris.

At the alarm Jeb drew the Colt out of its muff-holster. As he did so the contents of a chamber pot splashed at his feet.

'Is my bag wet?' said Henry.

'Not enough to make it shrink or stink, sir,' said Boris.

'That aroma reminds me of Esmeralda,' said, Rowley. 'She pissed on the stage tonight.'

'A woman, pissing on a stage, in public,' exclaimed Henry. 'That would never happen in the New World. Praise the Lord my ancestors crossed the Atlantic.'

'Esmeralda's a donkey,' explained Rowley. 'She was part of my act. Her unpremeditated opening of her bladder got me four encores or, was it five? I am, Mr Adams, in the theatrical line of business. You see, I ...'

'Rowley ... not now.'

'You are telling me to shut up?'

'I am.'

'And he who pays the piper picks the tune?'

'Yes, or, in my case, who plays the banjo picks the tune.'

'Yes, Jennifer.'

'And quit calling me Jenifer.'

JUST WHEN YOU THINK
YOU ARE SAFE ...

Before they got to the 'George', Jeb told Boris: 'Take Mr Adams and myself to the private entrance of our accommodation. We do not wish to pass the front of your public house. Mr Adams and I wish to keep a low profile.'

'It'll cost, mind. Diversions divent come cheap. If yuh want a cabby to take yuh to Hexham via South Shields, you'd expect to pay extra. A nar I would. Follow me and watch oot for rats.'

After taking a left, a right and ganin doon (going down) various chares, lanes and alleyways … ways sometimes no wider than the width of a man's outstretched arms … they came to the door Jeb had left earlier that day to explore the town.

'Bob's your uncle,' said Boris, holding out his hand.

'Boris,' said Jeb, ignoring the hint, 'off you go and tell Nelson I will be wanting room service.'

'Where's me bob for carrying HIS bag?' pointing at Henry.

'Here,' said Henry, dropping a shilling into the cup Boris had made out of his hand. 'Use it, young man, to buy a new notebook. If you do not wish to go to Hell resist the temptation to desecrate the Bible with the names of locomotives. And learn humility, young man. Learn the meaning of "deference". I do believe you'd treat a duke the same way as you'd treat a fishmonger.'

'Yes, sir,' said Boris, doing his best to sound dutiful but not at all pushing hard in that direction.

*****

A centaur is half-man and half-horse. A mermaid is half-fish and half-woman. Boris? Boris was half-boy and half-man. Sometimes he was a juvenile. Sometimes he was an adult. All of which is by way of explaining why, when he left to tell Nelson his American lodger had returned and wanted room service, pronto, he disappeared down a chare … not as Boris the pot boy, but as the steam locomotive the 'Bride of Lammermoor'. Chuff! Chuff! He disappeared into the inky blackness of the chare; his arms rotating at his sides, in impersonation of pistons.

Meanwhile, in the real world …

'Rowley,' said Jeb, 'will you be free tomorrow to be my and Mr Adams', "local knowledge"?'

'If it's local knowledge you are after, sirs,' said Rowley, tapping his bowler, not as a salute but to make it spin, 'I'm your man. I don't wish to boast but I know the name of every pebble on Tynemouth beach. I know …'

'Rowley!'

'Am I doing it again?'

'You were on the verge.'

'Grass or the edge of a cliff? Sorry. Do I sign a contract?'

'We are fellow musicians. We shake hands.'

'The last time I shook hands on a deal was with the manager of the Empire, Sunderland. He never paid me.'

'Rowley, I am not the manager of a provincial theatre. Mr Adams and I are representatives of the United States of America. We have behind us the resources of the New World. You will be paid for your services and paid well. Be here, tomorrow at nine. Good night.'

When Jeb and Henry closed the door and went up the flight of stairs that led to their rented accommodation, Rowley did not walk away. He stayed where he was and began counting to ten.

Before he'd reached 'five' the door reopened.

'My banjo!' said Jeb.

'I wondered when the penny would drop,' said Rowley. 'If you don't mind me saying so, Jennifer, you're in a bit of a state. When a musician forgets the instrument what is the love of his life … the instrument what he knows better than the face he shaves every morning, it means he's not healthy in that organ that keeps his lugs apart.'

'Good night, Rowley.'

'Good neet, Jennifer.'

****

In the lounge of their rented accommodation above the Old George, Henry, all the time shaking his head as if he couldn't believe what he was seeing, watched Jeb shed his disguise.

'That veil itched my nose,' said Jeb. 'What women have to put up with.'

'Wouldn't know,' said Henry, 'never dressed up as a female.' Looking round the room. 'Are there no better lodgings in the town? I don't think Palmerston would lodge here … mind you, I don't spy any cobwebs … that's something. And it is warm. That fire's hot enough to turn water into steam. It shouldn't be in a hearth. It should be under a steam locomotive's boiler.'

Jeb, having thrown off his disguise, was feeling like a chap who has just been told he is no longer going to be shot at dawn. He was feeling upbeat.

'You are not saying, Henry, that if it's not good enough for England's Prime Minister, it's not good enough for you? Are you reminding me, Henry, that you are a Boston Brahmin? That your lineage is as long as that of an English dook. Are you?'

'Jeb, my inheritance weighs me down. My fellow Americans expect too much of me. They expect me to be able to turn water into wine.

174

In England the boot's on the other foot. In England I'm treated like a servant. At least that's how the English upper classes make me feel. When I meet a dook, my jacket feels tight. Its sleeves grow short. I show too much wrist. My trousers show too much ankle. 'Course, I know they don't, but that's how England's aristocracy make me feel. They are so damn superior. To get into one of their clubs I have to be chaperoned.'

'In Newcastle, Rowley Harrison is my chaperone.'

'The show-off, with the spinning bowler?'

'Yes.'

'What does he do for you that you can't do for yourself?'

'He's my interpreter. The dialect the locals speak is, as far as I'm concerned, a foreign language. He is my … he is our "local knowledge".'

'I wonder what "dooks and pearls" see when they look at us two yankees?'

'They see children.'

'I'm out of diapers, Jeb. I am not a child. I don't wet the bed.'

'To the limeys, Henry, we are teenage children. Naughty teenage children. We don't toe the line. We are dangerous. America is beginning to flex her muscles. The Brits don't like that.'

'Jeb, you know what? I'm homesick.'

'Me, too.'

'Newcastle sure ain't no prairie. I ain't smelt so much steam and smoke in all my life. You know what, Jeb, my snot is black. Blow your nose … look into your bandana and you'll see a pit heap. The hairs in my nostrils are working overtime to keep my lungs clean. When I gets home I'll employ a chimney sweep to clean them out.'

'Would that be a job for a slave?'

'Hell, Jeb, my nostrils ain't a stable that needs cleaning.'

'So, cleaning out a stable is a job for a slave, is it?'

'Hell, Jeb, I don't know. I was just saying … I don't know what it's like to be a slave.'

'I do.'

'No, you don't. You're a white man, like me. You've been pampered and spoilt.'

'I'm lucky to be alive. You know my history. As soon as my white ma knew I was in her belly she fled north. If she'd stayed, her plantation-owning father … my grandfather … would have had me aborted, or, after my birth … murdered. The owner of a slave plantation cannot have a black grandchild. It would be contrary to the natural world. It would be like in that story where a man carries his donkey across a river.'

'Or … like a duke cleaning his butler's boots.'

'You may not play the banjo, Henry, but you sure as hell catch on quick.'

'Like the Limeys have been quick to sell guns to the Confederates.'

'To them, it's business.'

'As it is our business to stop them.'

'And we will.'

'The secessionist states must not be allowed to buy the Armstrong Gun. Right is on our side.'

'England's neutrality in our civil war is not sincere. The Limeys will sell their guns to anyone who has money to buy them.'

'They are capitalists.'

'Our capital is the moral high ground. Slavery is wrong. Our constitution says all men are born free. No ifs or buts about it. There ain't a codicil, saying that don't apply to black folk.'

'The British don't have a constitution. The damn fools trust each other to behave like gentlemen. Out dining last week with Pa at a dook's mansion, a lady, looking at me through a lorgnette, as if I was a specimen, called me "Mr America". She asked me if I knew the difference between a footman and a footpad. They do their best to treat me as an equal, but I know they think me inferior. I feel ill at ease among them. They are itching to tell me to go and empty their piss pots. The Brits speak our language but they ain't Americans. How'd you find them, Jeb?'

'They are against slavery,' said Jeb, staring into the fire's flickering flames in an absentminded kind of way. 'Man to man, that's how I find them.'

'And their government?'

'Hypocritical, as are all governments. Mr Lincoln is fighting this war as much for keeping America one nation as he is against slavery.'

'My pa and I are against slavery.'

'Boston does not grow cotton, Henry. You are against slavery Boston-style.'

'Our backgrounds make us look at the world through different prisms. I grant you that. All I'm saying is … it ain't easy being the scion of a famous family.'

'It's a damn sight harder been the scion of a slave family. Don't you go telling me that ain't true, Henry. No fancy arguments will ever convince me a slave inheritance is better than the inheritance a rich, white, free born American gets when he takes his first breath of New World air. His air is full of oxygen … the slave's is full of poison. When you were born, Henry, you inherited wealth and power and influence. I inherited a sacred duty to fight for the abolishment of slavery. You are American royalty, Henry.'

'My family take it for granted that one day I will become President. I won't. You know why? I ain't up to it. You are right, Jeb, whether I like it or not I am a Bostonian. I am instinctively English. England is my grandfather. You and I are his grandsons.'

'England ain't my grandfather,' said Jeb, talking to the fire. 'You are forgetting, Henry, my father was a slave. My pa don't signify the way yours does. As for my black grandpa, I never knew him. He was brought to America in chains; locked in the hold of a slave ship; fed pig swill; bought at an auction for the price of a pitchfork.'

'I'm sorry about that, Jeb.'

'And so you should be, Mr Henry Adams,' said Jeb, looking up from the fire.

'What about your white grandfather?'

'The man Ma said killed my pa?'

'You have never met him?'

'Nope! Wouldn't recognise him if I sat next to him on a park bench in Manhattan. But I know lots about him. Back home Ma was always telling me stuff about him. In the war he is on the other side. He is a slave owner. Ma keeps telling me he is not a bad man. When I ask her how she can say that when she knows he had my pa murdered she takes out a handkerchief and cries. She makes excuses for him. She says he is a victim of the society into which he was born; that, he knows no better. He was born in Virginia. He puts love of state before his morals. He is a cart pulling a horse.'

'America has slavery,' said Henry, looking at the fire, 'the Limeys have "dooks and pearls". Would you like to be a lord, Jeb?'

'Lord Jeb Prior Phelan … don't sound right.'

'What about "Jeb, the Earl of Manhattan"?'

'If the English aristocracy were pigsm which one gets to put his snout in the trough first?'

'What's the pecking order?'

'Yes.'

'I ain't certain but I do know a dook is pretty high up.'

'How'd you get to become a dook?'

'You inherit the title from your pa. Unless you're like the Dook of Wellington. He was made a dook because he won the Battle of Waterloo.'

'I ain't won any battles and my pa was a slave.'

'Your pa wasn't a slave in Africa.'

'Maybe in Africa he was a king. A king's higher than a "dook". I do know that.'

'The service is slow,' said Henry.

'In the snug downstairs there is a notice telling customers to be patient.'

'I don't feel at home in England. I kike its people as individuals but I don't like the place as a whole. I find it claustrophobic.'

ROWLEY TO THE RESCUE

Through the 'Sandgate Semaphore' … through the beggars who were the eyes and ears of the town's underworld … gossip flew up Dean Street and down cobbled chares: forget the collier stuck on a sandbank at Saint Peter's … the Coxons are after a black man with an American accent. The black man's an escaped slave. He plays the trumpet. If yuh nar where he's hiding … tell the Coxons.

Of all of this, Boris, pretending to be the Bride of Lammermoor, was unaware. As far as he was concerned, the cobbled lane was a railway line. He wasn't thinking about footpads. He was checking he had an up-signal telling him it was safe to proceed at full steam ahead.

'We's there?' he shouted, bringing the Bride of Lammermoor to a stop. 'If yuh divent come out I'll shoot. I've got a blunderbuss.'

'No, you haven't,' said Jackie Coxon stepping out of an inky shadow.

'Oot me way, Jackie.'

'And what if I divent?'

'I'll tell Nelson.'

'Am scared.'

'We're both shit'n wor pants,' said Geordie Coxon, materialising, spectre-like, out of the blackness of the same shadow.

'Howay, man! Hoot! Hoot! I'm the "Bride of Lammermoor" ….
Let's pass.'

Boris knew the Coxons' reputation. They were bullies. They'd hit yuh ower the heed for nee other reason than that's what they fancied deeing. What did they want? Fear began pumping sweat out of his pores the way a bilge pump, manned by four big men, pumps water out of a collier with gaps between its planks as wide as the gaps between an old man's missing front teeth.

The Coxons had derailed the 'Bride of Lammermoor'. The tip given him by Henry, left his sweating hand the way a launched ship glides down a greased slipway.

When the coin hit the lane's cobbles it drew attention to itself the way a coughing patient draws attention to himself in a doctor's surgery.

'Shit!' said Boris. 'That's me tip. I've worked hard for that. It's the bob the American gave's for carrying his bag. Where is it? Can't afford to lose a bob. Ouch! Howay, man!'

'Tell us about the American,' said Jackie.

'Aye, the American,' said Geordie.

'The American who gave yuh the bob. What do yuh nar about him? Was he a black man?'

'Howay, man! There's nee need for that,' protested Boris. 'If yuh want to make a parrot talk yuh give it a grape. Yuh divent clip its beak. Ouch! I'll tell Nelson. Ouch!'

'Where is he?' said Geordie. 'We're not keel men waiting for the tide.'

'Do yuh nar where he is?' said Jackie. 'If yuh dee you'd better tell us.'

'Ouch! Howay, man! Give's time to think.'

****

Before returning to his bachelor lodgings in Gateshead, Rowley fancied treating himself to a swift half. First he'd quench his thirst at the Old George, then he'd show his face at the Turk's and meet up with his theatrical pals.

What a night it had been … four encores or was it five? A black American had threatened him with a gun … he was now being employed by two Americans with purses bursting with sovereigns. He was their 'local knowledge'. And tomorrow night he was to be the star attraction at Sir William Armstrong's soiree. The money was rolling in.

To give himself a pat on the back he was about to sing his catch phrase: 'Oh, me name is Geordie Black' when, out of the blackness in front of him he heard voices he recognised. The, Coxons were giving Boris the 'Byker Bounce'.

'Ouch! Me heed! Howay, man!'

'Tell's aal yuh nar about the black American.'

Rowley was not a fighting man. If words were the chosen weapons, he'd challenge anyone to a duel. He was the lord mayor's barge on Ascension Day. The Coxons were men-o-war. He had to warn Jeb that Boris had blabbed. Jeb had a gun. In a fight a gun is better than a cudgel.

The door at which a few minutes ago he'd handed Jeb his banjo did not have a bell-pull; nor did it have a knocker.

'Jeb!' Rowley shouted through the door's letter box. 'Jeb! Oh, me name is Geordie Black, in me time I've been a crack … Jeb! Mr Adams!'

Upstairs, Henry said to Jeb, 'I'm so hungry waiting for room service I'm hearing voices. I can hear singing.'

'From the bar downstairs?' said Jeb. 'What do you expect? This is Newcastle.'

'No. From our private entrance. Listen.'

'Jeb! Mr Adams! Oh, me name is Geordie Black, in me time I've been a crack. Hoy! Help!'

'That's Rowley,' said Jeb. 'What in tarnation does the chatterbox want now?'

Jeb and Henry took the stairs down two at a time … Jeb, brandishing a Colt … Henry, brandishing a poker.

'Abraham Lincoln!' hollered Henry.

Outside, they found Rowley protesting his innocence to a policeman with a Bull's Eye strapped to his belt. The policeman was in the process of handcuffing Rowley.

'What you doing singing songs through a letter box? Casing the joint, were you? Where's your jemmy? I'm a country lad from Warkworth. I've seen drunks telling their woes to horses but … it's alreet, gentlemen, there's nee need for battle cries … everything is under control.'

'Jeb! Mr Adams!' said Rowley. 'Am I glad to see you.'

'You know him?' said the constable.

'He is in my employment,' said Jeb. 'He is my local knowledge.'

'Would you mind, sir, not pointing that gun at me. I am an officer of the law. You're not local, are you?'

'I'm an American.'

'And so am I,' said Henry. 'My father is the Union's legate in London.'

'Leg-it,' smiled the constable, 'does that mean he runs off when he's collared by the long arm of the law? Ha! Ha! I likes a joke.'

'You are, constable,' said Rowley, pulling his coat collar back into shape where the constable had used it as a handle to pull him off the letter box, 'a policeman with a sense of humour.'

'I likes flattery, sir. If I was a cat I'd be purring. I likes flattery the way I likes cream on me porridge.'

'You are no longer ganin to arrest me?'

'For the moment … the tide's out.'

'May I reward your forbearance with a demonstration of theatrical wizardry?'

Rowley spun his bowler.

'How'd yuh dee that?'

'It spins, constable, because I am a man of the theatre. Rowley Harrison, stage name Geordie Black, at your service, constable.'

'Well, yuh bugger! Geordie Black, eh? A seen yuh when yuh were on at the Empire.'

'Did I make you laugh?'

'Oh aye! You did. And cry. You made wor lass bubble. If I have another bairn, it's your fault.'

'My act might be responsible for bringing another life into this … this wicked world?'

'Aye! To stop her bubbling when we got back home she needed … yuh nar?'

'Love?'

'Aye! Aye! Yuh could call it that. Give's your hand, Rowley. It's a pleasure to meet yuh. What the hell's a star like yee, deeing busking through a letter box?'

'I wasn't singing for my supper. Jeb and Mr Adams are my employers. The private entrance to their accommodation has no bell-pull. It has no knocker. I was trying to let them nar … Jeb, the Coxons know you are lodging at the "George". They will be coming to get you.'

'The Coxons,' said the constable, 'where's me whistle? If they are involved in whatever is ganin on, I'll need help.'

'The Coxons are after me, constable,' said Jeb, 'because earlier this evening I scared the hell out of them.'

'You bested the Coxons, sir?'

'Yes, with this–' patting the ivory handle of the Colt in its shoulder holster.

'So,' said the constable, 'you are the bloke what's been blasting the heads off angels in cemeteries, are you?'

'It was two against one, constable. When you need back-up you blow your whistle. When I need back up, I draw my Colt.'

'The Coxons are big lads. Why were they after you?'

'They are working for Confederate agents. They are on Tyneside to buy the Armstrong Gun.'

'Are they now?'

'And we are here to stop them,' said Henry.

'Are you now?'

'You are against slavery, constable?'

'Aye, I am. Divent ask silly questions. Nee man should be a slave unless it's to his missus when she tells him to wash the dishes.'

'Mr Adams and I are against slavery,' said Jeb.

'Aye, I can see why that would be,' said the constable, lighting up Jeb's face with his bull's eye. 'Where are the Coxons now?'

'I think,' said Rowley, 'they'll be in the "George" bullying Nelson into telling them he has an American lodger.'

'Mr Harrison, we'll board the "Old George" the way our brave lads boarded the French at Trafalgar. We'll board through the front door like respectable folk. A constable whose fatha was a beadle from Berwick does not gan skulking into a public house like a draught under a door. Do yuh hear what am saying, Mr Harrison?'

'Aye-aye, constable.'

'Gladys hasn't been out since last week. It's time she had a breath of fresh air.'

'Gladys?'

'Gladys is me truncheon, Mr Harrison. Follow me.'

'What about us?' said Jeb, 'We are armed. Henry has a poker and I have a Colt revolver?'

'This is Newcastle, young man, not the Wild West. Gan back inside until you nar it's safe to come out.'

****

Rowley and the constable set off down the chare leading to the 'Old George's' front entrance, at a snail's pace. They entered its blackness – the constable taking the lead – the way anglers, wading through water, use staffs to warn them of a sudden change in depth … or, in the case of Rowley and the constable, of assassins lurking in the chare's shadows.

'That's blood,' said the constable, shining his bull's eye on a red stain … fresh blood. I fear for Boris. Keep your eyes open for arms and legs.'

'Attached or chopped off?'

'Chopped off.'

'Come, come, constable … that comment belongs to the world of the theatre. It belongs to my world. It is theatrical. The Coxons are bad'ns, we aal know that, but to make Boris spill the beans, surely they wouldn't chop him up into bits and pieces.'

'I'll let you into a secret, Mr Harrison. The Coxons are body snatchers. An arm and a leg won't sell for as much as a body, but I've heard rumours a foot will buy a bowl of broth. Hello! Hello! A body.'

'Divent hit is,' said Boris. 'I've telt yuh aal I nar.'

'Dear me! Dear me!' said the constable, lighting Boris's face with his bull's eye. 'Boris has been to Blaydon Races. Two black eyes and a broken nose. You'll need a steak poultice to make your peepers better, Boris. The Coxons?'

Boris nodded.

'Can you stand?'

'I think so.'

'Follow me.'

'A can't … me legs is hurt'n. The Coxons took me boots. Oh, yuh bugger, the cobbles is cad.'

'Mr Harrison, have you ever played a pantomime horse?'

'Front … Sunderland Empire. An unforgettable experience.'

'Play the part of a horse, now … front and back … the stage is aal yours. Give Boris a piggy-back.'

'Me?'

'There's nee one else here, is there?'

'Gee-up!' said Boris, jumping onto Rowley's back. 'Gee-up! Where's me stirrups?'

As they approached the 'Old George', a chair leg smashed its way through one of the public house's bull's eye windows. It stuck out of the bull's eye the way a musket pokes through the loophole in a redoubt.

Screams … four letter words … came pumping out of the shattered Bull's eye. Bang! Bang! The two gunshots brought silence. Seconds later the screams and shouts began again … as if the two gunshots had not killed the noise but merely wounded it. A third gunshot brought about a lasting silence … the sort you get after a fall of snow.

'That's a disturbance of the peace, if ever a heard one,' said the constable. He blew his whistle three times. 'That's for back-up. In the meantime, I'm boarding … follow me, lads.'

'Oh, dear me,' said Boris, as he slid off Rowley's back, 'the cobbles is cad.'

'Police!' shouted the constable as he charged into the 'Old George's' public bar. 'Well, well, well!'

'Boris!' shouted Nelson. 'Where the hell have you been?'

The way stones can be used as paperweights to stop paper 'flying' the Coxons had been immobilised by a posse of the 'George's' regulars.

Billy (the sceptic) and his girlfriend Edna were sitting on top of Geordie Coxon. John and his wife Brenda were sitting on top of Jackie Coxon.

'Yuh bastard!' said Boris, kicking Geordie Coxon in the ribs.

'Now, now!' said the constable, standing on one of Jackie Coxon's fluttering hands and twisting his boot on it, as if he was putting out a cigarette, 'yuh niva kick a man when he's as helpless as a mouse.'

Jeb and Henry were on the stairs leading to their private accommodation. They were above the fray and not in too much danger of getting a black eye. Jeb was brandishing a smoking Colt revolver; Henry, his face as white as a rice pudding, was brandishing a poker.

'Shoot the bastards!' said Boris. 'Look what they've done to me. They've broken me nose. Me peepers are slits.'

'That would be cold blooded murder,' said the constable. 'There's been fights at the George ever since Adam ate the apple but, as far as I knows, there's never been a cold blooded murder. Geordie, Jackie, have yuh got lugs in ya heeds?'

The two thugs nodded that they had.

'Are yuh ganna use them and listen to an officer of the law?'

The two thugs nodded that they were.

'If I tell these folk to let you up, do you give me your word you'll behave?'

The two thugs nodded that they understood the terms of their parole.

'Any more trouble from you two,' said Nelson, 'and I'll gouge out your eyes the way I uses me hook to take pips out of apples.'

Whether or not the Coxons would have stuck to the conditions of their parole was never put to the test. No sooner were they a-stirring, muttering foul oaths, than the help the constable had summoned when he'd blown his whistle, charged, with drawn truncheons, into the bar. There were three of them … all big men. The Coxons knew when to fly the white flag. Without putting up a feather of resistance they allowed themselves to be handcuffed and escorted out.

'Drinks all round,' said Jeb.

'Who's paying?' said Nelson.

'Abraham Lincoln,' said Henry.

'And steak for Boris's black eyes,' said Jeb.

'Bacon's better than steak for bruises,' said Nelson. 'Yuh nar why? Cos it's cheaper. Howay, bonny lad,' to Boris, 'sit doon afor yuh fall doon.'

'What happened, Nelson?' said the constable who'd caught Rowley singing through the letter box and who had stayed behind to gather evidence.

'What happened?' said Nelson. 'The Coxons came in, that's what happened.'

'They told Nelson,' said Billy, 'they knew he had a black American lodging upstairs and they were going to teach the black man a lesson.'

'A wasn't having that,' said Nelson. 'In the "Old George" as long as a man has money to pay for what he wants, the colour of his skin doesn't come into it. Now, how many free pints have I pulled? How many whiskies have I poured? As Trafalgar wasn't won without sailors losing arms and legs, free drinks have to be paid for.'

'Be generous, Nelson,' said Jeb, 'the good people of Newcastle have saved me and my colleague, Mr Adams, from a beating. For that,' looking round the bar, 'I thank you, one and all.'

'The Colt helped,' said Henry. 'That's what shut them up.'

'When you fired your gun, sir, said Edna, 'a thought the roof was ganna fall in. I was so scared I had to grab Billy. You were so brave, my love. If the drinks are on the house, I'll have a brandy.'

'Oblige the lady, Nelson,' said Jeb.

Pulling the cork out of a bottle of brandy with his teeth and keeping it in his mouth as if it was a dummy, Nelson glugged brandy into a glass.

'Keep pouring, Nelson,' ordered Jeb. 'The lady's in shock. Sitting on top of a Coxon is hazardous work.'

'It was,' said Edna. 'If it hadn't been for my beloved,' taking Billy's hand, 'I might be dead. Yuh were so brave, Billy. A think yuh deserve a medal.'

'A divent feel well,' said Boris.

'That's blood coming out of his nose,' said Brenda. 'Edna, there's blood coming out of his nose.'

'A nosebleed's nowt,' said John. 'Hydraulic cranes dee that.'

'John,' said Brenda, 'Boris is a human being. He is not a piece of machinery. Oh! It's coming out of his mouth as well. I think something's burst inside his heed.'

'Blood's like watta,' said Billy, 'yuh cann't lock it up.'

'He's lolling,' said Edna.

'A once seen a collier sink like that,' said Billy.

'He's ganin to "Fiddler's Green",' said the constable. 'Well, yuh bugger … he's deed.'

'Get Doctor Dagger,' shouted a female customer, 'a double brandy, Nelson, if you please … he brought me twins, screaming their heeds off they were, out of me womb and into this mad world. A divent blame them for screaming. A scream every day for what I have to put up with.'

'Boris does not need a doctor, young lady,' the constable told the woman who thought highly of Doctor Dagger, 'he needs an undertaker.'

'"Young lady", indeed! You flattering me to get something you want?'

'Mrs,' said the constable, 'I nar yee and yee nar me. I am an officer of the law and you are on the game.'

'Cheeky bugger.'

'Drink your drink and flow out of here like the tide.'

'And if I divent?'

'I'll arrest you.'

'Handcuff me to a bed, will yuh? That you should be so lucky.'

'Maud,' said Nelson, gaffing the prostitute with his hook, 'gan and ply your trade at the Grey Horse, there's a good lass. In me rough and ready way I was fond of Boris. He'd have made a good seaman if he hadn't wanted to be an engine driver.'

'My brother's an undertaker,' said a man who looked like a starved horse. 'Here's his card. Mention my name … John Brown and you'll get a discount.'

'The Coxons will swing for this,' said the constable. 'They gave him that bump on his heed. I'm not medical but my guess is that bash they gave him opened taps inside his heed.

'He's starting to smell,' said a woman, putting a rag hanky over her nose.

'Divent tark daft,' said the constable, 'decomposition doesn't come in as fast as the tide. The bad smell we can aal smell is the bone yard.'

'Aye, it's the bone yard,' said Billy.

'Yuh can aalways smell the bone yard when the wind's blowing from the west,' said John.

'And the tide's on the turn.'

'A divent nar aboot that.'

'Poor Boris,' said Nelson, tapping the corpse with his hook. 'Divent worry, bonny lad, I'll give yuh a good send off. I'll have you buried with your train spotter's books. When we commended Flossie-Fenwick's mortal remains to the deep, after Trafalgar, me and his ship mates put his teddy bear in his shroud. Not a dry eye on the ship. Decks awash with tears.'

Boris's corpse emptied the George faster than a downpour of rain chases sunbathers off a beach.

A toper on his way out, nodding at the corpse, said: 'Every cloud has a silver lining. He'll not short-change me again.'

'Now! Now!' said Nelson. 'Apart from me and Queen Victoria, nee body is perfect.'

'Constable?' said Jeb. 'Where have your officers taken the murderers?'

'Innocent until proven guilty, sir. We are in Newcastle, sir, not in your American wild west. Afore a judge puts a black cap on his heed, and tells Geordie and Jackie they are ganna swing, they have to be found guilty.'

'Where is the jail to which the suspects have been taken?'

'Suspects, now, are they? In my book they are murderers and should hang. Let me explain, sir. The law is an ass ...'

'A donkey is a domesticated ass,' butted in Rowley. 'When my donkey pissed on stage she brought the house down ... got me, four or was it five encores?'

'Mr Harrison, you do not interrupt an officer of the law when he's on the verge …'

'Of arresting a criminal?'

'Hit him with your truncheon, constable,' said Henry, 'that is the only way to shut him up.'

'I was on the verge of confiding, sir,' addressing Jeb directly, 'that I have one head but, I wears two hats. Innocent until proven guilty, sir, is my policeman's hat point of view. It is my officer of the law point of view. That the buggers should be hung, drawn and quartered is my bowler hat … my private point of view. It's what I often thinks but never say when I'm wearing my policeman's hat.'

'The jail,' said Jeb, 'where is it?'

'The suspects, sir, the murderers, have been taken to the castle. Aal castles have dungeons. Why spend money on building a prison when the Normans have built one for you? Folk divent like spending money on felons.'

Before they left the bar – Billy, Edna, John and Brenda surrounded Rowley.

'Sir,' butted in John, 'excuse my asking, but are you Geordie Black?'

'I am he,' said Rowley, spinning his bowler. 'Do you come to bury Caesar or praise him?'

'To praise,' said Brenda.

'I raise my eyes to the Lord,' exclaimed Rowley. 'I am a snowdrop with aspirations to become a daffodil … and poor Boris is a daffodil in July.'

'What's he on aboot?' said Billy. 'If that's what reading and writing does to yuh, a think I'll pack in learning.'

'Don't you dare, Billy,' said Edna. 'You've got to G. Am not your wife, yet, but am telling yuh now, you've gone too far to stop. Think of the good job you'll get at Armstrong's if you can dee the reading and writing like what John can.'

'Tonight,' said Rowley, 'I was the recipient of four encores or was it five?'

'It was five,' said Billy. 'I might not be able to read and write but a can count up to five.'

'And up to ten, Billy,' said Edna, 'divent put yourself doon.'

'We know it was five, Mr Harrison because we were in the audience,' said John.

'We were deeing the clapping,' said Edna, 'weren't we, Billy?'

'Mr Harrison …' began John.

'If you are going to pay me a compliment,' interrupted Rowley, 'call me Rowley.'

'Rowley,' said John, 'I wanted to ask you a question.'

'I prefers compliments to questions,' said Rowley, pulling a funny face which made everyone giggle.

'If a compliment will please you, Rowley,' said John, 'I tell you truthfully I and my friends loved your act.'

'You made us laugh,' said Brenda.

'I was in the Gods watching your act, Rowley,' said a tipsy woman, gate crashing the conversation. 'You naughty man, you made me wet mesel. Am still damp like the washing is when yuh hang it oot in fog.'

'I apologise,' said Rowley.

'It's not your fault. Give's a kiss.'

Fame had a downside and was not the bed of roses, those who'd not experienced it imagined it to be.

'Avast!' shouted Nelson. 'Daisy, get your grubby paws of Mr Harrison. Folk are forgetting there's a stiff in the bar. Show some respect.'

'Ugh! Is he deed?' exclaimed Daisy, looking at Boris to whom Nelson had drawn her attention. 'A thought the "Short Changer" was asleep. If he's deed I'm out of here to spread the news doon the Sandgate. When they nar the "Short Changer" is deed, they'll tell the bellman it's Christmas Day and he's to ring his bell, aal day.'

'Have a heart, Daisy.'

'Am aal heart, Nelson. Yee should nar that. And keep your hook to yourself. I'm off to spread the news–' poking Boris with her umbrella to test that Boris really was dead and wasn't pretending like he used to pretend he'd given you the right change when he knew damn fine well that he had not. 'He's deed, alreet. A divent want me gossip to be lies. If yuh tell lies yuh gan to hell. Nee need to throw's out, Nelson. I'm on me way. Do yuh want the door left open?'

'What for? It's cad outside.'

'To keep the stiff cad … that's what for. Wuh divent want Boris ganin smelly, duh wuh? A deed body is nee different to a barrel of herring. Leave the herring in the sun for a week and they'll stink worse than a bone yard. Good neet, Nelson, a nar when am not wanted.'

'She knows a lot about death,' said Edna.

'She should do,' said Nelson, 'when she's not selling herring she's a layer outer. She did me Uncle Tom. Wrapped him up as tight as a mummy as if, instead of ganin to heaven, he was ganin to London in winter on the top seat of the mail coach.'

'What's "death" begin with, Billy?' said Edna, never one to miss a chance at helping Billy learn to read.

'Depends what you've caught,' said Billy. 'It could be the cholera. It could be the booze. A divent nar.'

'I meant, Billy, what letter does the word "death" start with? Yuh nar. "A" is for "apple". "B" is for "ball".'

'Oh, we're back to the alphabet, are we? You're like the tide, you are, Edna. When yuh start coming in, yuh never stop.'

'"Death"?' said Edna.

'"Death",' repeated Billy. '"Death" … starts with a "D". Am I reet?'

'Well done, me bonny lad! You're learning the alphabet quicker than a high tide takes a collier off a sandbank.'

'Am I?' said Billy. 'What about that collier that ran aground on the Black Middens? She was there for months afore waves smashed her to bits.'

'Them was rocks, Billy. You're on a sandbank.'

'Am I?'

'Yes. And me? Am the tide what's ganin to pull yuh off. When yuh nar your alphabet, yuh can write me a love letter. And after practice has made yuh perfect practising on me, yuh can write a letter to Sir William

Armstrong asking him for a job like what John's got. If Sir William is "Master of the Dralickers", you, my love, will be "Master of the ABC".'

'Will a?'

'Yes, you will. I think we'd best leave. A divent like drinking in a graveyard.'

'Before we go,' said John. 'The question a wanted to ask you, Rowley, was … did you know your donkey was going to piss on the stage?'

'It was not premeditated,' said Rowley.

'Was it real piss? A mean it wasn't an oilskin bag full of watta you'd tied under the donkey's belly, was it?'

'It was real … close to … as green and smelly as the watta coming out the Lorte Burn sewer.'

'There you are, Billy … didn't a tell yuh it was the real thing. That information wasn't gossip … it came straight from the horse's mouth.'

'It was a donkey,' said Billy. 'It wasn't a horse.'

'Four encores or was it five?' said Rowley.

'It was five,' said Billy. 'A might not nar me alphabet or the difference between a horse and a donkey, but a can count up to five. A learnt to count up to five when me mother taught me to count the coal bags. When the coal man told me to look after his horse, a never did. Me mother told me if the coal man tells yuh to look after his horse, divent. When you're looking after his horse he'll put doon an empty sack on his counting pile and tell yuh, looking yuh in the eye, bold as brass, "Aal done. Count the bags." Me mother wasn't daft. God rest her soul.'

'I am an engineer,' said John.

'I am a comedian,' said Rowley, 'I sometimes make folk laugh.'

'Speaking as an engineer, Mr Harrison, I think it would be impossible to fit a donkey with a fake bladder.'

'Speaking as a comedian, young man, I sometimes find it impossible to make an audience laugh … nor can I cue a donkey to void its bladder.'

'I telt yuh it was real piss,' said John.

'Alreet! Aal reet!' said Billy. 'Yee were reet and a was wrong.'

'Duh yuh remember wor bet?'

'Nar, a divent.'

'If it WAS real piss and Rowley said it was and he should nar, you have to buy aal the drinks the next time we're out.'

'Hadaway, man! A might not be able to do the reading and writing, but there's nowt wrong with me memory.'

'Yuh nar when the tide's in and when it's out, Billy, don't you?' said Edna.

'Aye, a dee. Am like me mother, am not daft.'

'And you know where Wakefield's the jeweller's is, don't you?'

'Aye, a dee.'

'And you know what they sell?'

'Nar, a divent.'

'They sell engagement rings, Billy.'

'Howay, pet! I'll put a ring on your finger when a can read and write. Forst things forst.'

One by one Rowley's fans bid him 'Gud neet'. They were honoured to have met him. They loved his act. It was the best panto they'd seen.

'Four encores or was it five?' Rowley shouted after them.

'Five!' shouted Billy. 'A might not be able to read and write but a can count.'

When the woman called Edna had mentioned Wakefield's the jewellers Rowley had flinched. It had made him think of the love of his life. Who did Annie love the most? Rowland Harrison, stage name Geordie Black, or playing the trombone? A man needed a drink, now and then, the way an apprentice needed, now and then, to punch a beadle. Why, oh why, had she had to go and join the 'Sally Bashers'?

'It's been a long night, gentlemen,' said the constable, 'and, an eventful one. This is my first murder. I see him,' nodding at Boris's corpse, 'getting me three stripes. A murder's a lucky break for a constable. It offers the prospect of a step up the ladder.'

'Every cloud has a silver lining,' said Henry, brandishing the poker he'd picked up earlier to use as a weapon.

'A word of advice, sir, you be careful what you are doing with that there poker. Put it back … there's a good lad … where it belongs, next to the coal tongs.'

'Sorry,' said Henry. 'I wasn't threatening you.'

'I knows that, sir. If you had been, you'd now be wearing handcuffs.'

'Would I?'

'Yes, you would, sir. Sir has had a narrow escape. Sorry to leave you with the stiff, Nelson. Still, if a high tide can move a collier off a sandbank a landlord can find an undertaker to move a stiff.'

'I'll find a sheet to cover him … it,' said Nelson, 'a jury rig … something to get yuh by afore yuh call into a port with facilities.'

'An undertaker been the "facilities",' said the constable. 'Good neet, gentlemen … careful the bed bugs divent bite. Forgive my levity. As a hot day makes a man thirsty, death makes me humorous.'

While Nelson went off to find a sheet, Jeb said: 'Rowley, my good man … tomorrow I wish you to take my good self and Mr Adams to the jail in which the Coxons are been held. I wish them to tell me all they know about the Confederates employing them.'

'The more we know about them,' said Henry, 'the better equipped we will be to hinder their purchase of the Armstrong gun.'

'You will be, Rowley, our local knowledge, our interpreter … our go-between.'

'That's a lot of jobs to dee. If I was a ship that cargo would put me Plimsoll Line under watta.'

'Be here at ten, Rowley,' said Jeb.

'Have I shown you how I can spin my bowler?'

'Shoot him!' said Henry.

******

Rowley walked home to Gateshead, not across the new High Level Bridge, but across the eighteenth century, many-arched stone bridge. Never mind that this route meant walking down a hill and then up a hill. The weather didn't bother him. He was used to the north-east wind.

Walking helped him think. Often, when walking, an idea for a song popped into his head. What a night. Five encores. Five curtain calls. He knew exactly how many. His asking if it was four or five, was an act. And aal thanks to Esmeralda's bladder. Folk were funny. That chap in the 'George' asking him if it was real piss or a put-up job. He wished it had been a put-up job. If it had been he'd have been able to bring the house down every night. Five encores … every night. He savoured the thought. Wonderful! What would Annie think when he told her he was earning a few bob by showing Yankees round the town? That he was doing his bit to end slavery in America. Would that make her think him respectable?

Annie's brother, with whom she lived in a big posh house in Swalwell, was a councillor. He was on this committee and that committee. He had a house full of clocks and paintings. He bred pigeons. His pigeons had ruffs round their necks like the toffs used to wear in Tudor England.

Rowley's lodgings, in the flat above the Wakefield's, clock makers and jewellers, Gateshead shop, was not gas-lit.

He knew Annie had been when he saw, by candle light, on the kitchen table, a ham sandwich and a bottle of ginger beer. Annie, bless her, did her best to look after him. That was kind. He liked to think she cared for him.

At this time of night she'd be snuggled up in bed with her Bible and trombone. She'd be asleep in a nice warm house. A house with gas in every room. And she'd left him a love letter.

By candle light he read: 'My darling, Rowley, I have left you a ham sandwich and a bottle of ginger beer. I hope the mice haven't eaten it. I mean the ham sandwich not the bottle of ginger beer. I don't think mice like ginger beer. I don't think you do, either. But I do hope you will learn to like ginger beer. If you can learn lines for your act, you can learn to like ginger beer. I know you can.

I have some good news for you. I am going to be promoted to 'Captain'. Do not worry. When my promotion comes through you will not have to call me "Captain". Because we are intimates, you can still call me "Annie".

You will be pleased to know that Captain Starkey is back in the fold. The Army rescued him tonight from the "Devil's Kitchen". He repented under a gas light in Hood Street. Major Starkey is not a shirker. She is determined to save Captain Starkey's soul. How many times must she dive overboard into the stormy sea of sin, to save him?

I look up to Major Starkey. She is my guiding light. More than once she has complimented me on my trombone playing.

She is teaching me how to make sinners repent. I am resolved, Rowley, to make you see the light and give up the booze.

In the name of Jesus Christ Our Lord and Saviour,

Annie Wakefield

PS When I get my promotion do you think I should sign myself: Captain Annie Wakefield?'

Rowley sighed. Annie, dear, dear Annie, had practised signing 'Captain Annie Wakefield' ... 'Cpt Annie Wakefield' five times under her PS.

He washed the ham sandwich down with whisky diluted with ginger beer.

If only his rivals for Annie's hand were flesh and blood. But they weren't. He was up against 'temperance', the 'trombone' and the 'Bible'. Tearing Mathew, Mark, Luke and John out of a Bible and stuffing them down a trombone's bell wasn't the same as telling a bloke: 'Hoy! Divent yee gan giving Annie the eye ... she's mine.'

Once, when he'd wooed her with 'amore' chords on his violin, she'd not gone weak at the knees ... she'd not turned the other cheek. What had she done? She'd played the 'Hallelujah Chorus' on her trombone. 'Hallelujah! Hallelujah!'

How did yuh fight the Bible, a trombone and temperance? He had nee idea. To help him solve the problem he poured himself another whisky ... large.

JEB AND HENRY DISCUSS TACTICS AND EXCHANGE CONFIDENCES

Alone in their rooms in the 'George', Henry reminded Jeb of the reason they were in Newcastle.

'I have with me letters of introduction from London. They are signed by Britain's foreign secretary, Lord John Russell. He and Sir William Armstrong know each other. When Sir William sees Russell's signature, he is duty bound to see us. By all accounts Sir William is an honest fellow. He manufactures guns to protect his country. I have heard he is an inventor first and a businessman, second.'

'As I am a musician first and a secret agent, second.'

'When we meet Sir William, Jeb, you remember which hat you're wearing. In Newcastle you are a secret agent first and a musician, second. My letters of introduction are addressed to Sir William's Hood Street office. Is that far?'

'I don't know. Rowley will know. He is our "local knowledge". Newcastle is not London, Henry … it is a small town.'

'Where does Sir William make his guns?'

'I believe his factory is some two miles upriver from here, not far.'

'When we meet Sir William, I will remind him that in our war, Great Britain is neutral. If he sells weapons to either side, he will be breaking the law. The Confederates need the Armstrong Gun more than we do.'

'Can't see anything wrong with Sir William selling our side the Armstrong Gun. We have right on our side.'

'I agree … but can we stop him selling guns to the South? Business is business, Jeb. I fear Great Britain's neutrality is not sincere.'

'Which is why I intend to use Rowley as a double agent.'

'Can you trust him?'

'Yes.'

'How'd you know?'

'A gut instinct. He plays the violin. I play the banjo.'

'Jeb, that's witch doctor talk.'

'You telling me that because I'm a black man?'

'Hell, no, Jeb … I didn't mean anything.'

'We are from different stables, Henry.'

'I knows where you heading, Jeb. You're going to remind me, not for the first time, that your daddy was a slave.'

'I can't forget that. When I look into the flames of that there fire, I wonder what he looked like. I wonder if he liked music. I'm sure of one thing … he'd have made a good diplomat.'

'How'd you mean?'

'A slave has to learn to hide his feelings. When he's hungry he won't moan. If he moans his master will whip him. Feeling hungry is better than being whipped. Even a well-fed slave will always be hungry. He will be hungry for freedom. He will hunger to be a free man. He will be hungry to walk down a street, whistling as free men do and walk into a coffee shop and buy a coffee with his own money.'

'My pa is a diplomat.'

'Learn from him.'

'I try.'

'Learn from the Brits. They are experts at lying. America scares the pants off them. They keep saying they are neutral in our civil war. They are capitalists. If a capitalist sees a chance to make money, he will take it. The Brits look down their noses at us.'

'Pa told me an earl showed him how to use sugar tongs.'

'Etiquette. The bane of my life, in England. I feel more at home with beggars and buskers. I dress like a gentleman but in my heart of hearts I am a vagabond. A troubadour. A minstrel. I play my banjo to rid America of slavery the way Blondel, travelling Europe, played his lute to find his king. I have played a duet with a Newcastle busker by the name of Waterloo Bob. He is a fine musician. He plays an instrument called the Northumbrian small pipes.'

'My god! You have played a duet with a busker. On the streets?'

'Yes, Henry, on the streets. In the town's smoky air we fought a musical duel.'

'A musical duel?'

'Banjo versus the Northumbrian small pipes.'

'Never heard of them.'

'Nor had I. Their sound is sad … melancholic. Better suited for a dirge than a jig.'

'And you, Jeb, you'd be on your banjo. Jeb, you love your banjo more than I love a cigar.'

'A slave sings to help him forget his chains.'

'You ain't ever been a slave. You're a rich boy from New York.'

'I don't forget my origins.'

'I wish I could forget mine. It ain't a bowl of jelly being an Adams.'

'Avast, me hearties!' shouted Nelson, coming up the stairs from the bar. 'Open up the hatch. Victuals is been served.'

'I've learnt something to neet,' said Nelson, warming his backside in front of the fire, before serving the two bowls of steaming mutton broth he was carrying on a tray fitted with an iron eyelet so it could be carried by a man with one flesh and blood hand and a hook.

'What have you learnt, Nelson,' said Jeb. 'Let me help you with the tray.'

'I can manage, sir,' putting the tray down on the table, 'just give me time to unhitch me grappling iron. There, gentlemen, sirs, your victuals has landed as smart as Colley was piped aboard the Royal Sovereign.'

'"Colley"?' said Henry, licking his lips at the sight of the steaming bowls of mutton broth.

'Lord Collingwood, sir … him as was the first to give the French a broadside at Trafalgar.'

'Would that be" local knowledge"?' said Jeb.

'It is that, sir. And very proud I am of it. I'm boasting, I knows, but I don't care.'

'You were at the Battle of Trafalgar?' said Henry, looking at Nelson the way a visitor to a museum looks at a stuffed bird in a glass case. 'You must be old.'

'When I was on the Sovereign, sir, I was but a bairn. I wasn't wearing nappies but when the fighting started I should have been. I'm an old sea dog. It ain't true an old dog can't learn new tricks. Land dogs can't, but sea dogs can. I learnt something new toneet …bugger, that fire's hot … I learnt toneet, sirs, that a stiff empties a bar faster than a farting lurcher. And, another thing … undertakers is as rare as salmon now are in wor river Tyne. Boris will have to stay where he is for a bit longer. Me and a couple of me regulars have taken him out of the chair and straightened him out on the floor. Coffins is long and narrow. They ain't made to take men what's doubled up and slouched in a chair.'

'The events of the evening,' said Henry, 'exceptional events, have brought storm and strife to your inn.'

'Mr Adams and I apologise for ringing … under the circumstances … perhaps … too often for room service. We are from the New World, Nelson, we are impatient fellows.'

'It wasn't Boris's stiff kept me busy, sir. Nor was it not having Boris … god rest his train spotter's soul … to help me serve. What held me up and kept you gentlemen waiting for service, was me pondering how I could carry two bowls of mutton broth up a lot of stairs on a tray without dropping them. That's what I came up with, sirs,' tapping an eyelet screwed into the tray with his hook. 'What do you think? It wasn't easy screwing it in with one hand.'

'It shows imagination,' said Jeb.

'You are a practical fellow,' said Henry.

'Thank you, sirs. Thank you,' said Nelson, knuckling his forehead with his hook.

'Nelson,' said Jeb, 'before you weigh anchor and sail back to the temporary mortuary Boris's corpse has made of your bar …'

'You want more bread with your soup? Have a not brought you napkins?' –checking the tray. 'I have.'

'What's a "lurcher"?'

'Duh yuh not nar that, sir. It's a collier's greyhound. I wouldn't expect yuh to nar the difference between a jib sheet and a genoa, but a did think you'd nar what a "lurcher" was. Well, well, well. If yuh want oot else, ring the bell. I'll be reet up unless I'm negotiating with the undertaker.'

'In which case we'll have to be patient,' said Henry.

'You are very understanding, sir,' said Nelson, leaving them whistling a hornpipe.

******

'The broth is hot,' said Henry. 'It is like our landlord.'

'Nelson is a philosopher,' said Jeb.

'Is he? He is the sort of fellow who, if he didn't like you, would spit in your broth.'

'In that case, Henry, we'd best keep in his good books.'

'Do you think he likes us?'

'He likes the money I am paying him to rent these rooms. I know that. I will pay him extra.'

'What for?'

'To stop him spitting in our broth.'

'It is my opinion, Jeb, that no amount of money will stop a servant spitting in his master's broth if he is that way inclined. It's like someone making a face behind your back. Unless you catch him at it, you know nothing about it.'

'I am paying the rogue to spy for us, Henry. And for that, I am paying him extra. He is our eyes and ears. He helped us put the Coxons behind bars. He is against slavery. Without his help we might now be sitting here with broken noses.'

'Or worse.'

'In his way, Nelson is an honourable fellow. And he makes excellent mutton broth.'

'He talks a lot.'

'Everyone in this town does. That's what I've found. Geordies are like turkeys ... they can't stop gobbling.'

'Can you understand them?'

'Sometimes, yes. Sometimes, no. I sometimes think I'm hearing a foreign language. Would you like a lesson?'

Without enthusiasm, Henry nodded that he would.

'When two Geordies meet they do not say "hello".'

'Do they not?'

'No, they don't ... they say "are yuh alreet, bonny lad?"'

'Yuh alreet, bonny lad,' repeated Henry in an American accent.

'Learn it,' said Jeb. 'It might save your life.'

A NEW DAY. ROWLEY BECOMES A GO-BETWEEN AND MAKES A SURPRISING DISCOVERY

If the sun rising over Newcastle that cold February morning in eighteen-sixty-three had been able to talk, it might well have said: 'I'm deeing me best.' Penetrating the toon's smoky halo was no easy task. In human terms it was like asking a man with a dicky ticker to carry a bag of coal up Dean Street.

In their private lounge at the Old George, Jeb and Henry sat in front of a fire. They were waiting for Rowley. The full English breakfast Nelson had served them had made them feel sleepy. It looked cold outside.

'Can we trust him?' Henry asked Jeb.

'Rowley is a good sort. I'd bet my banjo he won't let us down. I told you last night … I have a gut instinct about him. We need his local knowledge. He speaks the local dialect. He is our guide and interpreter.'

'He is … theatrical. He's the sort who'd call a few drops of rain a monsoon. He shakes your hand as if he was pumping water out of an artesian well. He is a verbal bull in a china shop.'

'It is axiomatic,' said Jeb, waxing philosophical as he plucked his banjo in an absent minded kind of way, 'that you become like the job you do. Pirates have scars and drink grog. Blacksmiths become big and brawny. Theatre folk become, well, theatrical. I know an opera singer who sings Mozart to his milk man. Comedians can't stop telling jokes. You know what the milk man said to the opera singer?'

'Nope.'

'"You are churning me up" … get it? Or, do I have to explain?'

'I got it. I just don't think it's very funny. Do I look like a diplomat?'

'An apprentice diplomat, Henry.'

'Pray … why not a qualified one?'

'You have not learnt to hide your feelings. Sure, you are making progress, but you have a long way to go. A diplomat must hide his feelings the way a burglar hides his jemmy. Henry, do I look like a spy?'

'The Colt you are carrying in your shoulder holster makes you look like a character out of the Wild West.'

'In public I hide the Colt the way you, my dear Henry, must learn to disguise what you are really thinking. Do you like cucumber?'

'Not as much as I like pastrami on rye.'

'What if Queen Victoria offered you a cucumber sandwich?'

'Her majesty has servants to do that.'

'But what if she did and what if you really hated cucumber? Worse, what if eating cucumber brought you out in spots? Would you smile and take the cucumber sandwich, conscious of the honour her majesty was bestowing on you by serving you herself, or would you say "no thank you, ma'am, eating cucumber brings me out in spots"?'

'Would the spots be life threatening?'

'No but they'd be big and red and you'd be disfigured for at least three months.'

Henry hesitated. He knew the answer he wanted to give was the wrong answer, and if he gave it he'd be in for a pummelling.

'Henry, you are dithering. He who dithers on the horns of a dilemma gets a sore backside.'

'Another axiom?'

'Indubitably! If you were a diplomat you would have told me, without hesitation, that you'd have taken the cucumber sandwich and feigned delight at the great honour her majesty had conferred on you by serving you herself.'

'Would I?'

'Yes, you would. As a sharp shooter must learn to hit a turnip fifty yards off, even in a mist when he can't see it, a diplomat must learn to feign.'

'Anyways,' said Henry, uncrossing his arms and legs as if opening doors and windows to let him get out of the tight spot he found himself in, 'the situation I'm now in, is private. I ain't in a dook's drawing room. You and I are on the same side. We are fellow Americans. With you, Jeb, I don't have to feign anything.'

When they heard a drum-roll knock on the door leading downstairs to the 'George's' bar, Jeb said: 'That has to be Rowley.'

'The fellow's incorrigible,' said Henry. 'How can he turn knocking on a door into a piece of theatre?'

'I've told you, Henry, Rowley is an entertainer. He makes mountains out of molehills. That's his job. That's what he does.'

'Well, I don't like it. It makes me homesick. I'm missing Boston.'

Jeb unbolted the door with the Colt in his hand.

'You're taking no chances,' said Henry.

'The Coxons have friends in the town. If it's not Rowley, who might it be? The Coxons are locked up, but their pals are not.'

'Identify yourself,' Henry shouted through the door.

After hearing coughs: 'Oh, me name is Geordie Black, in me time I've been a crack.'

'If it shuts him up,' said Henry, 'for gawd's sake open the door and let him in.'

'Yuh alreet, bonny lads?' said Rowley, spinning his bowler to show his employers he was a ship with the wind in its sails.

As a man used to dealing with an audience, Rowley sensed at once that his American employers were not 'morning people'. They did not jump out of bed shouting 'whoopee! Let's gan to work'.

'I am asking,' he said in an American drawl, 'if you two guys are still in one piece after all that happened to you last night? I am asking if there is money in your wallets? I am asking if you are old fashioned sail boats or one of the new-fangled steamers. Are you mail coaches or steam locomotives? Newcastle to London in four hours instead of four days. Oh, me name is Geordie Black, in my time I've been a crack.'

'Rowley,' said Jeb, 'shut up.'

'Sorry,' said Rowley, grinning. 'Can you touch your toes? I can. Sorry.'

'And quit saying you are sorry when you sure as hell ain't.'

'Have you ever been hit with a poker?' said Henry.

'On stage I have. Not with an iron poker. That would have hurt. The poker I was hit with was made of balsa wood. Me heed can take balsa but not iron.'

'This poker, Mr Harrison,' said Henry, picking one up from the hearth, 'is the real thing.'

'Henry,' said Jeb, 'Rowley is on our side. He is our local knowledge and interpreter.'

'I am two for the price of one,' said Rowley. 'And another thing you can't hit a man with a poker when he's in mourning. See,' pointing to the black arm band he was wearing.

'Has your cat died?'

'Now, now, Mr Jeb. If you lost your banjo you'd be wearing a black arm band. I know you would.'

'You have lost your violin?'

'Nar! Nar! No. No. It's in remembrance of Boris. Nelson gave it to me. Nelson was fond of Boris.'

'That's reet, Mr Harrison,' said Nelson, entering without knocking, 'I was fond of the lad. To help me remember him I've painted me hook black,' displaying the hook for all to see. 'Divent touch it. The paint's still wet.'

'I've heard of a "Book of Remembrance",' said Henry, 'but never of a "Hook of Remembrance".'

'That's because you're an American, sir,' said Nelson. 'In Newcastle we have wor own way of deeing things. In the pit villages there's many a collier with a black wooden leg. It's the done, thing, yuh see. We are aal victims of fashion. Like the keel men aalways wore silver buckles on their shoes and blue waistcoats and yellow ribbons in their waterproof hats. Aye, they were the days. Happy days, just so long as the Press didn't get yuh.'

'Were you a pressed man, Nelson?'

'Nar! Nar! I was unlucky. I was the cat what got caught licking the cream. A frigate, HMS Arcadia she was called, sailed into the Tyne for victuals. When she was moored at the quay I sneaked aboard to see what a could get me hands on. I divent nar exactly what happened. Aal a nar is, a woke up at sea. Nine years old … a powder monkey at Trafalgar. Aye, aal a long time ago. More coffee, gentlemen?'

'A coffee for Mr Harrison, Nelson. Yes, Rowley?'

Rowley nodded that he would like a coffee.

'And a stottie filled with bacon, Mr Harrison,' suggested Nelson.

'What's a "stottie"?' said Henry.

'It's a flat loaf as big as a Doge's turban,' said Rowley. 'When they are filled with bacon they are delicious.'

'A splendid idea,' said Jeb. 'Put it on the bill, Nelson. When Rowley is munching he can't be talking.'

'But, gentlemen, I will be listening,' said Rowley. 'I am your local knowledge. Nelson, take horse to your coffee pot … take horse to your bread bin. If you have no bacon in the pantry … take horse to a butchers. Let it be proclaimed by the town crier: "Geordie Black wants coffee and a bacon stottie."'

'Jeb,' said Henry, 'shoot him.'

'I'll get Cushie to serve the victuals,' said Nelson, looking at Rowley and shaking his head. 'Cushie's me jury rig to replace Boris. Until me hook's dry, I'm out of action. 'am smearing the way a bairn dribbles. Me hook's a paint brush. 'am painting question marks with it aal ower the place.'

******

As a dummy dipped in honey only sometimes shuts up a howling bairn, a stottie, with bacon hanging out of its dough the way excited travellers hang their heads out of railway carriages, failed to shut up Rowley.

'You gentlemen married?' said Rowley.

Jeb and Henry shook their heads. They watched him munch and chatter the way a westerner, new to Thailand, watches a python eat a dog.

'I'm in the process. I keep asking Annie to marry me, but she keeps saying "no". You see … she's respectable. She lives in a grand house opposite Saltwell Park … that's in Gateshead, across the river. Her brother makes clocks. He has two shops. One in Newcastle, one in Gateshead. I live above the Gateshead shop. He's me … my landlord. I pay him rent. He doesn't think much of me. You see, he's stationary … I'm peripatetic. He's a councillor … I'm a music hall entertainer. To keep me heed above watta … to keep my head above water … I have to take any job that's ganin … that's going. Annie knows I'm fond of a glass of ale … or, two … or, three. You see, gentlemen, I have rivals … not, flesh and blood rivals. If they were flesh and blood rivals, I'd knock their blocks off and tell them … "Annie's mine!" Nar! Nar! My rivals are the Salvation Army and the trombone. The Salvationists hate booze as much as the devil loves a sinner. Annie's after Edwin … that's her brother's name … to open a ginger beer tavern. Outside in big letters it will say "Beer Shop". When the silly buggers gan in … go in … they'll not be supping Kent hops … they'll be supping Asian ginger.'

'Have you tried wooing Annie with your fiddle?' said Jeb.

'I have … I played her a happy song… and duh you know what? It made her cry. How can a happy song make you cry?'

'Women are a mystery,' said Henry.

'So,' said Jeb, 'your music can make this lass, Annie, cry but it can't make her say "Yes" to your proposal of marriage.'

'Yes.'

'Have you tried wooing her with a sad song? If a happy song makes her cry, perchance a sad song will make her laugh.'

'If I sang a sad song to an audience and they laughed, I'd be worried. It's a terrible thing when your audience gan … go … absent without leave. Annie's always ganin AWOL. If she's not learning to play the trombone, she's marching the streets, saving souls.'

'Learn to like drinking ginger beer,' said Henry. 'I like ginger beer.'

'As a student of human nature, Mr Adams … that comes as no surprise to me. The trouble is, Geordie lasses are chaste … mind you … I have heard rumours … Ha! Ha! What's the world coming to when the lass yuh love is more interested in playing the trombone … I hate trombones … and saving souls? When I say to her "Give's a kiss, pet", she'll ask to smell me breath. Then it's "you've been drinking, haven't you?" I protest: "Annie, aal I've had is a swift half doon at the "Hydraulic Crane"." That's when she first told me, "I'm learning to play the trombone". I was shocked. Strings and brass never were the best of pals. Can I use your mirror? I wish to check me cravat is straight. Nature gave me rubber lips. I can pull funny faces. I can make mermaids smile, but not Annie. I love Annie. I divent … I don't know why.'

'You are "smitten", Rowley,' said Jeb. 'Against the cholera and the "smittens" there ain't no cure.'

'You ever been "smitten", Jeb?'

'I'm in love with my banjo. Can you be "smitten" with a banjo?'

'Annie loves her trombone more than she loves me.'

'Do you not love your violin?'

'Course, I do … but I also love Annie.'

'If your rival is a trombone, I don't think you need to worry. Use the trombone as a Trojan horse. Buy Brasso. Volunteer to clean it. If she lets you near something she loves, it means she likes you.'

'My jokes divent … don't make her giggle.'

'Rowley, I will put my cards on the table and, fingers crossed you are big enough to take criticism, some of your jokes are not funny.'

'Once I tried a Shakespeare speech on her.'

'"Romeo and Juliet"?'

'"Richard the third" … "Now is the winter of our discontent made glorious summer by this … son of York".'

'Did it go down well?'

'She threw a potted geranium at me. If I hadn't ducked I'd have had to go on stage that night with a shiner and tell the audience "Yuh should see the other bloke". The "smittens" has me in chains and shackles. I'm a slave to Annie.'

'In that assertion, Rowley, you go too far. To my ears the word "slave" has unpleasant connotations.'

'In Virginia, Mr Harrison, your levity would get you lynched.'

'Slavery cannot be joked about,' said Jeb.

'I apologise,' said Rowley.

'I accept your apology. You are a free born Englishman. You have no experience of real slavery … of shackles and whippings. Rowley … Mr Chatterbox … does Annie know you are helping the Union to rid America of slavery?'

'I have not yet had time to confide in her. We are both very busy … she in saving souls and me in making folk giggle … not to mention her practising to play the trombone.'

'She is against slavery?'

'Yes.'

'If she knew you were helping Mr Adams and I on such a noble cause, I put it to you … would she not think you heroic?'

'I like your drift … but I divent … don't want to be a dead hero. I don't want to be a ghost to the neighbours doon below … down below.'

'Down below?' said Henry. 'Are you talking about Hades?'

'Nar! Nar! No! No! You see, Mr Adams, on Tyneside lots of folk live in flats. There's an upstairs flat and a doonstairs flat. If yuh live upstairs, the neighbours doon … down below are aalways knocking on your front door telling yuh to take your boots off and walk on tip toe because the bairn's trying to get to sleep.'

'When are we going to skidaddle?' said Henry, shaking his head in disbelief at Rowley's loquacity.

'What's that mean?' said Rowley.

'It means, Mr Harrison, when you are finished telling us about your love life … when are you going to help Mr Phelan and I do the work our President has sent us on Tyneside to do?'

'You are our local knowledge,' said Jeb. 'You know where Hood Street is?'

Rowley nodded.

'Is it far?' asked Henry.

Rowley shook his head.

'I also wish to talk to the Coxons,' said Jeb. 'You know the castle jail?'

Rowley nodded.

'Is it far?' asked Henry. 'Will we need horses?'

Rowley shook his head.

'A cab?'

Rowley shook his head.

Rowley's miming was not due to the fact that he'd learnt to padlock his volubility … it was due to the fact that while he was being questioned he was struggling to remove a piece of bacon fat, trapped, like a rat in a trap, between two molars.

'Got yuh!' he exclaimed, flicking the fat into the fire. 'Where to first, gentlemen? Hood Street or the castle jail? The Coxons will be chained to walls dripping with green slime like the hair of the Tyne God. The "Tyne God's" a Roman statue. It was dredged up when they were making the river deeper. I wanted to put the Tyne God in Abdullah and the Forty Thieves. I was overruled. Some folk have nee imagination. What do you think, gentlemen?'

'I think Hood Street first,' said Henry.

'I meant the "Tyne God",' said Rowley.

'Rowley,' said Jeb, 'I wish you to imagine you are an open door and I am the wind.'

'You are going to blow me shut?' said Rowley.

'I am,' said Jeb.

'Bang!' said Rowley. 'Now I'm shut up the way the wind bangs shut a netty door and stops the defecator watching stars when he does his dump. If you're constipated, watching stars is a wonderful laxative. As good as two spoonfuls of castor oil. Bang! Now, I'm silent as the grave.'

'Shoot him,' said Henry.

'I want to know more about the Coxons' relationship with the Confederates. After visiting the jail, we will post-haste to Hood Street where we will present Sir William with our letters of introduction. Henry, you agree?'

'Mike's mutton pies,' said Rowley.

'You intrude, Mr Harrison,' said Henry.

'Explain,' said Jeb.

'If you two think you can go into the Coxons' cell like a tea clipper under full sail and tell them to sing like the canary I had when I was a bairn and afore Adam had eaten the apple, I'm telling you now, in what you might call a stage whisper, to think again. After what you've done to them, Jeb, the Coxons will hate you worse than the neighbour down below hates the clog dancer in the upstairs flat. To get their hands on you they'll pull their chains off their cell walls. They'll be at you the way a seal gans … goes, after a cod.'

'As usual, Mr Harrison,' said Henry, 'you exaggerate. Your hyperbole is irritating. You need to be reminded of the seriousness of the matter in hand. Mr Phelan and I are here on Tyneside to make damn sure the United States of America stays united. We are here on Tyneside to rid America of slavery.'

'Your point, Rowley, is?' said Jeb.

'The Coxons will be hungry. It's bread and water in jail. Let them sniff one of Mike's mutton pies and they'll blab faster than a spring tide covers the sandbank at Newburn.'

'Where do we get these pies?' said Henry.

'At the Bridge public house … Mike … I nar him … is the pub's landlord.'

'I know him,' said Jeb. 'I was introduced to him by Waterloo Bob.'

'You've been in the toon nee longer than three tides and already yuh know as many locals as me who's lived here aal his life and knows the name of every mussel on Tynemouth beach.'

'As usual, Rowley, to make your point you exaggerate. I have told you … the duet I played with Waterloo made him and I, crotchet and quaver brothers. He introduced me to Mike. Mike recommended I lodge here at the Old George. Waterloo Bob, Nelson and Mike are my eyes and ears in the town. You see, Rowley, as a musician … you will know this … music opens doors into men's souls. And men's souls are safe deposit boxes. They are where men store their secrets. Looking into men's souls lets a spy know who he can trust.'

'How are you paying them? In two bob bits or sovereigns?'

'Sovereigns.'

'You can trust them. When are we weighing anchor?'

'Now,' said Henry. 'The sooner we bribe the Coxons with mutton pies …'

'Hot mutton pies,' said Rowley.

'The sooner we bribe the Coxons with hot mutton pies and get them to tell us all they know about their Confederate employers, the sooner Jeb and I will get to Hood Street to present our letters of introduction to Sir William.'

'What if he's not there?' said Jeb.

'We will make an appointment to see him. London has informed him we will be calling.'

'London?' said Rowley.

'Britain's foreign secretary, Mr Harrison. You are providing local knowledge to people who drink tea with those who rule the British Empire.'

'Get away! That's showing off, that is. Did I ever tell yuh, I've shaken hands with Dan Leno and flicked a flea of Anna Pavlova's tutu?'

'Shoot him,' said Henry.

******

At the Bridge public house, Mike, leaning across the bar counter and putting his hand on Rowley's shoulder, said: 'Rowley, Mr Harrison, is it true?'

'That I had five encores last neet?' said Rowley.

'That your donkey pissed on the stage. That's what I'm hearing.'

'Gossip never lies except when it tells yuh a priest never kissed a nun.'

'So, it's true.'

'Aye. The stage was flooded. The stage carpenter had to build an ark. Before they abandoned their instrument the musicians in the pit played "Abide with me". A trombone player drowned. I hate trombones.'

'Annie?'

'Aye.'

'The musicians entered the ark in twos?'

'Aye, they did. Strings first. Brass second. Percussion last.'

'There's always a pecking order. At Waterloo the officers were the strings and I was the percussion. Nowt changes. It's the rich what gets the pleasure … the poor what gets the blame. What can I get you?'

'Mutton pies,' said Jeb.

'Hello, Mr Phelan,' said Mike.

'You have a good memory for names, landlord.'

'As Rowley has to remember his lines when he gans on stage a landlord has to remember the names of his customers. You were introduced to me by Waterloo Bob, Mr Phelan. That's like been introduced by royalty. And you tip, sir, like a gentleman with a big heart. I couldn't forget your name and the face that gans with it if I tried. It's mutton pies you're wanting, is it?'

'Two mutton pies, landlord,' said Henry. 'They are to take out. We want them in a bag.'

'Another American,' said Mike. 'Are there any Americans left in New York?'

'My colleague, Mr Adams,' said Jeb.

'Pleased to meet you, sir,' said Mike, extending a hand as big as a bear's claw.

Henry took the proffered hand with the enthusiasm of a chap who, terrified of snakes, is told to overcome his phobia by stroking a python.

'Call that a handshake,' boomed Mike. 'Aal me regulars have noms-de-gardy-loo … helps me remember wee hasn't paid … I'll call yee … "Floppy Paws".'

At the put-down, Henry looked sick.

'"Floppy Paws",' repeated Rowley. 'I'll use that in my act. Four encores or was it five?'

'The gossip in the chares says it was five,' said Mike.

'"Floppy Paws",' said Jeb.

Henry squirmed. Damn them! They were laughing at him. A few months ago his pa had flushed at a function given by the Duke of Devonshire. The cause of the blush? A flunkey had whispered into his pa's ear that Pa was using his dessert spoon to eat his soup. Damn them! Damn America's civil war.

'You were saying, Mike?' said Jeb.

'You gentlemen take a seat in the snug ower there. I'll bring the pies ower when they're ready. Will yuh be drinking?'

'Whisky,' said Jeb.

'Double whisky,' said Rowley.

'"Floppy Paws"?'

'A Fentiman's ginger beer, landlord, with froth on the top … as strong as it comes out the greyhen.'

'Oh, the gentleman has a sense of humour. I like that.'

'I can give as good as I get.'

'Divent push your luck, bonnie lad.'

'That's reet, bonny lad,' said Jeb, 'divent push ya luck.'

What would Mike think of his attempt at speaking Geordie?

'You're a quick learner, Mr Phelan,' said Mike. 'But duh yuh nar what "Peggy's Waistcoat" is?'

'"Gateshead",' said Jeb.

'Is there nowt yuh divent nar?'

'How to abolish slavery without shedding blood.'

'Aye, that would be as hard to dee as gannin doon Scotswood Road on a Saturday night without getting your face bashed in.'

'Just a Saturday night?'

'I was trying to be kind, I have a heart of gold, see. I'll get the mutton pies.'

'We want them in a bag,' said Henry. 'They are to take out.'

'I hadn't forgotten, sir. Mike might be old and have lost his baritone voice at Waterloo and be closer to Jerusalem than New York but I still have a good memory. I never forget to keep a customer I divent like waiting. I calls it "landlord's manners". As the wind said to the snowflake, sir, "do you get me drift?".'

'No,' said Henry, bristling. 'I'll have you know, landlord, I am a Boston Brahmin.'

'And I'm a landlord what doesn't sing lullabies. I'll get the pies. I might be a while. You see, afore I makes them, I have to find the shepherd who's looking after the mutton that's ganin into them. Aal not be longer than three shaves.'

'What was he on about?'

'Ask Rowley,' said Jeb, smiling, 'he's our local knowledge.'

'He was putting you in your place,' said Rowley. 'Like the way folks who don't like my jokes, when I'm on stage, throw orange peel at me. I'll bet you didn't know that when I'm not on stage, I'm a hanger.'

'A hanger?' said Henry.

'A public executioner?' said Jeb.

'Nar! Nar! No! No! I'm a painter and decorator. I hang wallpaper. Do you think that's funny?'

'Not particularly,' said Henry.

'It made me smile,' said Jeb.

'Afore I use my jokes in my act I try them out … yuh nar … you know … toe in the watta.'

'I object,' said Henry, 'you are using me the way a tailor uses a dummy. In this town my status sinks into quicksand. A landlord calls me "Floppy Paws". A comedian uses me, in lieu of an audience, to see if his jokes work. Folk around here think I am a deckhand. I am not. I am an officer.'

'Henry,' said Jeb, 'calm doon, bonny lad.'

'And you … Jeb Prior Phelan have gone native. I am not your "bonny lad". I am Henry Adams, the son of Charles Francis Adams, America's legate to the United Kingdom.'

'Was your mother called Eve?' said Rowley.

'I beg your pardon?'

'Yuh nar … you know … Adam and Eve?'

'I don't think that's funny.'

'Nar … nar … no … no … you are reet … you are right. It's not. Forget I said it. I'll not keep that in a bottle the way I used to keep spiders when a was a bairn.'

'Excuse me, sirs,' said a young girl with her hands behind her back as if she was hiding something.

'Hello, Jenny,' said Rowley, blowing the lass a kiss, 'catch that and you'll turn into a princess.'

'Please, sirs,' said Jenny, 'Mike says I've to ask yuh if yuh want nail files in the pies or do yuh want aal meat?'

'What are you talking about, girl?' said Henry. 'Mutton pies are not pedicures.'

'It's Mike's sense of humour,' explained Rowley. 'He knows the pies are for the Coxons. He's asking if we want to help them escape.'

'Is he indeed! Well, we don't. We give the Coxons the pies only after they have told us all they know about the Confederates. The pies is for information, not to help them escape. No ifs and buts about it … that's the deal. Am I not right, Jeb?'

'We can't aid and abet murderers,' said Jeb, shaking his head at Mike's silly joke. 'What we can do is fatten them up for the gallows. If they are found guilty of murdering Boris, they will hang.'

'Jenny,' said Mike, popping his head over the snug's wainscot the way a nosy parker looks over a wall, 'give the gentlemen the pies.'

From behind her back Jenny produced two brown paper bags. Fat from the pies had stained the bags the way a receding tide leaves the sand it has recently covered a darker brown from that above the tide line.

'Here you are, sirs,' said Jenny, 'mutton pies full of meat and nee files, toothpicks or knives in them to help murderers escape. I like a public hanging. Did I dee well, Mike? Was me acting, gud?'

'What do you think, Mr Harrison?' said Mike. 'You are a man of the theatre.'

'I think Jenny should gan to London and audition for the stage. That's my advice,' said Rowley.

'Aye!' said Mike. 'That's for the crystal ball. Nelson's lost Boris. I can't afford to lose Jenny. Back in the kitchen, lass. Table number five want two broth. Give them the stale bread. I divent like them. Now then, gentlemen, I've been ruminating. You'll see if you looks in the bags Jenny has given you, not two but four mutton pies. Divent worry, I'm not ganna charge yuh for them. I'm not even ganna charge yuh for the two you ordered. Like aal landlords I have a heart of gold. It's my contribution towards ending slavery. The reason I've given yuh four is because I nar the jail and I nar the turkeys.'

'Turkeys?' said Henry.

'Turnkeys,' said Rowley.

'The turkeys loves my mutton pies the way turkeys with feathers loves Hindhaugh's grain. The mutton pies, gentlemen, are … wait for it, Mr Adams …are graveyard keys.'

'Skeleton keys,' said Rowley.

'Mr Harrison, will yuh not butt in and spoil me fun. A joke what doesn't make its hearers dee a bit of thinking is like a mutton pie with nee lamb in it. Do yuh get what am saying, Mr Adams, bonny lad? When you've eaten one of Mike's mutton pies you baa like a sheep and fart like yuh dee when you've been at the herring. What I'm saying is, by way of gannin to Heaton from Newcastle via Gateshead is that two of the pies is to bribe the "turkeys" to let yuh in. My mutton pies open doors. When yuh tell them they are Mike's mutton pies and Mike sent them, they'll let you in, nee bother. My name opens doors.'

'That's a well-known fact,' said Rowley. 'In Abdullah and the Forty Thieves, Abdullah did not say "Open sesame" to open the cave, he said, "Open Mike".'

'You taking the piss?' said Mike.

'That's what "Esmeralda" did last neet. Four encores or was it five?'

'Shoot him!' said Henry.

'And another thing,' continued Mike, shaking off Rowley's interruption the way a wet dog shakes off water, 'divent give the Coxons the pies until they've told you aal you want to know. That's my advice. Let a customer eat a mutton pie afore he's paid for it and you'll never get your money.'

'I thought you had a heart of gold,' said Henry.

'That's bullshit, bonny lad,' said Mike. 'Some gentlemen divent nar a lurcher's arse from its gob. When yuh hand ower the pies divent forget to mention my name. Hoist ya sails and off yuh gan.'

'Pies for spies,' said Rowley, standing to leave. 'Magic pies! Pies what opens doors. Let us make flowers bloom in a desert.'

'Shoot him, Jeb. Shoot him!' said Henry.

******

The public house and the castle jail were neighbours.

The cobbles they walked over to get there were slippery with ice.

'It's like walking ower the backs of them tortoises that swim in the sea,' said Rowley.

'Turtles,' said Jeb.

'Aye, that's them.'

'Are we safe?' said Henry, looking at the hawkers and stall holders. 'The people look vicious. They are shabbily dressed.'

'Safer than you would be, Mr Adams,' said Rowley, 'if you were back home fighting in a battle in your civil war.'

'Is it always this busy?' said Jeb.

'It's visiting time at the jail. Look at that good wife ower there. See the weight she's carrying in her shawl? She's doing what we are doing. She's visiting. She'll have something in her shawl for the "turkeys" to let her in and give her extra minutes with the poor bugger she's visiting. If she's not a visitor with a bribe in her shawl, I'll stop telling jokes. If the "turkeys" are not too greedy there might be something left for the prisoner. It's alreet for the Bible to say 'man does not live by bread alone' but when you're in jail, after a week of bread and water, an apple or a gooseberry will be better than the spread the toffs gave themselves when they opened the Grainger Market.'

'And one of Mike's mutton pies will, to the Coxons, be a cornucopia,' said Henry.

'You've put the pies on a pedestal there, Mr Adams … a very high pedestal. I am not a familiar of the Coxons. Like everyone else in the town, I know of them. I speak their language. I nar … I know how they duck and weave. Will you trust me, gentlemen, to dee the negotiating?'

'Will we be with you?'

'I'd rather you weren't.'

'Why not?'

'Think about it, Mr Adams. Think about it.'

'Explain,' said Jeb.

'If the Coxons were to see you two gentlemen in the flesh they'd see a Colt revolver and a man brandishing a poker. They'd see humiliation … have I not telt yuh? To get their hands on your necks they'd pull the wall brackets holding their chains off the prison's walls. Rage would choke them afore they could tell you what you want to know … even if they wanted to tell you. Do you take my point, gentlemen?'

Jeb and Henry were quick to see that Rowley was talking common sense. They belonged to the New World. They were practical fellows. They agreed to let Rowley do the negotiating.

'We'll meet you back at the Bridge,' said Jeb. 'I have a soft spot for Mike.'

'Do you?' said Henry. 'To me he is a carbuncle.'

'I'll play the Coxons, gentlemen, the way I play an audience. I'll squeeze the pips out of them. When they start singing … not a real song, if you know what I mean …'

'Jeb and I know what you mean, Mr Harrison,' said Henry.

'When they start singing, by which I mean, telling me all they know about their employers … the Confederate agents … I'll hoist sail for the Bridge and tell you aall I nar faster than it takes a collier to take a cargo of Tyne coal to London.'

'One of the new steam colliers, I hope, Mr Harrison,' said Henry. 'Steamers do not need wind, though I fancy if you were a sailing ship your sails would never be short of wind.'

'Mr Adams, sir, there's a saying in the toon … niva upset a go-between.'

****

Jeb and Henry watched Rowley set off on his information-gathering mission the way punters watch the start of a horse race … full of confidence they've backed the winner.

They watched him jangle the bell pull at the side of a nail-studded door, set into the keep's soot-blackened stones, like a crab hiding under a rock. They heard him sing through its grill 'Oh, me name is Geordie Black.'

A big man holding a circle of white-hot metal, in tongs, opened the door.

'Torturer or the town's blacksmith?' said Henry.

'Blacksmith,' said Jeb. 'As a Salem witch needs a black cat, a jail needs a blacksmith. Who else can make shackles? Plenty of work for blacksmiths in the slave states.'

On their amble back to the 'Bridge' they passed the top of 'Castle Garth Stairs'.

'Listen!' said Jeb. 'Ignore the hawkers and listen.'

'What for?' said Henry.

'Music.'

'The only music I'm hearing, Jeb, is a steamer hooting on the river and that steam locomotive going over the bridge.'

'That's the music of industry, Henry. That's the music we make back home in Cleveland. That's the music, will win us this goddamned civil war. The South can't make that music. The music I'm hearing … just hearing …listen … belongs to, King Arthur and the Knights of the Round Table.'

'Jeb, don't you go letting your love of music make you forget the reason you and I are here on Tyneside. We ain't here to pick primroses.'

'Follow me,' said Jeb, heading off down the stairs. 'I will introduce you to a Union spy.'

Jeb found Waterloo Bob sheltering from the cold in the passageway he'd found him yesterday.

'Crotchets and quavers to you, Bob.'

'Minims and semi-breves to you, Mr Phelan. We's your posh pal? By the cut of his jib he's not a Byker lad. And tell him to stop look'n at me as if I was a deed halibut washed up on Byker sands?'

'Henry, may I introduce you to Waterloo Bob, a survivor of the Battle of Waterloo and a fine musician.'

'And a spy,' said Bob, 'divent forget that. Spying pays better than busking.'

Henry acknowledged Bob, with a movement of his head that had more in common with a twitch than a nod. He wasn't au fait with this bond between musicians. It struck him as being unhealthy.

'Any news, Bob?' said Jeb dropping a sovereign into Bob's bowl.

'That's very generous, sir. Very generous. If that doesn't make Bob form a square and get ready to tell charging French cavalry to gan back to their stables and eat oats instead of English red coats, then nowt will. The game is afoot, sir. Mr Jeb, sir, the game is afoot. The Coxons were asking me last neet to keep me peepers open for Americans. Of course, a said a would. I didn't tell them … let on like … that they'd just walked past you dressed as a wife linking Geordie Black. I've heard tell he's a good act to gan and see but … I've got nee legs. Even with me crutches a can't manage the music halls.'

'The Coxons are in police custody,' said Jeb.

'A nar they are, sir. Underworld gossip travels fast in this town. I hear tell they've done for Boris. Neebody liked Boris. Still, there was nee need to gan and murder him. Divent fret, Jeb, with or without your sovereigns, I'm on your side. I'm as much against slavery as a was against the French at Waterloo. Where's your banjo?'

'Under lock and key at my lodgings.'

'We musicians love our instruments.'

'We do.'

'I can live without wearing underpants but not without me pipes.'

'Quite,' said Henry, sniffing.

'Have yuh got a cold, sor?'

'I might have and I might not.'

'Aye and am a Waterloo veteran with nee legs. Have yuh tried pulling on pants when you've got nee legs?'

'But you have eyes and ears, Bob,' said Jeb.

'Aye, a have, sir.'

'And you will continue to use them to help us abolish slavery?'

'How many times do I have to tell, yuh? I'm on your side. It's good money being a spy.'

'A very good morning to you, Bob. Before I return to America you and I must play another duet. The Northumbrian small pipes and the banjo. What a combination.'

On their way back up 'Castle Garth Stairs' Jeb and Henry, heard: 'When Johnny Comes Marching Home'.

'A Rebel song and a Union song,' said Jeb.

'If you say so, Jeb,' said Henry, 'you know I ain't musical.'

'Our side sing it. The Reb's sing it. When this bloody civil war is over and our side is victorious and slavery is abolished, let's hope our great nation can find more common ground than a song.'

'I'll say amen to that,' said Henry.

'Amen!' said Jeb.

'Amen!' said Henry. 'That busker, Waterloo Bob, am I right in thinking his wheels were screwed to a coffin?'

'Quite right.'

'I'll wager, Henry, not many Union agents are paying a spy with no legs and whose chariot is a coffin on wheels. Think aboot it, bonny lad. I do believe I am getting the hang of the local dialect. I am starting to feel quite at home saying "are yuh alreet, bonny lad".'

'Are yuh alreet, bonny lad?' said Henry. 'Are yuh alreet, bonny lad?'

'In my short time on Tyneside I have woven a spider's web of spies. I have Nelson at the "George", Mike at the "Bridge" and Waterloo Bob who, in spite of having no legs, is peripatetic.'

'Can you trust them?'

'They are against slavery. I pay them well. Waterloo Bob, Nelson and Mike are my eyes and ears in the town.'

'And I have in my pocket a letter of introduction to Sir William Armstrong from Britain's foreign secretary.'

'In this foreign land, Henry,' said Jeb, 'we are being looked after by the high and low.'

'By its "dooks and pheasants",' said Henry.

'By those who eat Mike's mutton pies and by those who eat cucumber sandwiches.'

'With cocked fingers,' said Henry.

****

At the 'Bridge' Mike sucked up to Jeb and Henry like a piglet at a sow's teat. The Americans were gentlemen. He was a publican on a camel crossing Sinai. When he looked at them he saw an oasis. He saw sherbet and dancing girls.

'Did me mutton pies open the jail's doors?' Mike asked.

'We left all that business to Mr Harrison,' said Henry.

'Aye,' said Mike, 'a suppose that's for the best. Rowley nars his way around the jail. Last year it was he spent a night in there. Drunk and disorderly. Under the influence he punched an officer of the law. Lucky to get off with a fine. One more punch and he'd have been sent on a transport to Australia. The kangaroos divent nar what they are missing. I suppose if yuh divent nar what you are missing you can't be missing it. Aye, it's the rich what gets the pleasure and the poor what gets the blame. What'll yuh be having, gentlemen?'

'A pint of brandy, a jug of warm water and three glasses, Mike,' said Jeb.

'The third glass is for Mr Harrison,' said Henry. 'He will be joining us, later. In the meantime, landlord, Mr Phelan and I wish for a booth away from eavesdroppers. When Mr Harrison joins us, we wish to talk in private. And slices of lemon in our hot water, if you please. Neat brandy gives me heartburn.'

'That doesn't come as a surprise to me, sir,' said Mike.

'You are a medic as well as a landlord?'

'I nars folks, sir. Looking at you, sir, I sees heartburn. Now then, gentlemen, if you'll be so good as to follow me the way ducklings follow their mother, I'll show you to a booth away from eavesdroppers. I'll put you in what I call the "leper booth". It's tucked away yuh see, the way a leper colony is. Neebody would ever build a leper colony doon on the Sandgate … it's too busy, see? But they might build one on the Town Moor. Funny things gan on, on the Town Moor. I've heard talk there's ganna be a "temperance" meeting there.'

****

An hour later Rowley joined them in the 'leper' booth, munching a mutton pie.

'Would that glass be for me?' he said, spying the unused glass. 'If it is, fill it up. Talking to murderers is thirsty work. Keep pouring, Mr Adams; keep pouring. As a fish needs water, a go-between needs brandy. There,' said Rowley after taking a swig of the drink Henry had poured him, 'that's better, as the cow said after she'd been milked.'

'Rowley, cut to the quick,' said Jeb.

'Well,' said Rowley, 'Mike makes a canny mutton pie. It gans well … it goes well with brandy.'

'Shoot him,' said Henry.

'The Coxons, Rowley … the Coxons.'

'They weren't what I'd call "chatterboxes". They think they are going to hang for killing Boris. Aye, their minds were more on angels and harps than on keel boats and booze. I never thought they were religious. But they are now. They want to see a priest the way I get this urge to gan and kiss Annie. I telt … told them: "Tell me aal you know about the Americans and I'll get you a priest". That's what I telt … told them. When they looked at each other to see if I meant what I said I told them, "to keep you going while you still have bodies to feed I'll throw into the deal a couple of Mike's mutton pies".'

'What did they tell you?' said Henry.

'Not a lot. All they could talk about was not wanting to hang. Couldn't stop them talking about how they'd never wanted to send Boris to kingdom come. To take their minds off their doom I spun my bowler. Never fails to amuse. It did this time, though. When they didn't look gobsmacked I was mortified. This morning, gentlemen, I learnt a painful lesson … as the lion tamer said when the lion told him to balance a jug of water on his head. This morning, gentlemen, I learnt the sad truth that my spinning bowler has limitations. It can take a sewer worker's mind off turds, but it can't take a murderer's mind off the gallows.'

'Shoot him,' said Henry.

'Mr Adams, sir,' said Rowley, 'you have shot me so many times my body is a colander.'

'If you are a "colander", Rowley,' said Jeb, 'let it drain information. The Coxons … what did they tell you about the Confederates?'

'The Confederate spies … there are two of them. They are staying at the Station Hotel. One of them is a French-American. I'd say he was the front of house man. The stage manager. Did I ever tell you about the stage manager at Sunderland?'

'No,' said Jeb. 'Nor do I wish to know about him. The Coxons, Rowley … the Coxons.'

'Shoot him,' said Henry.

'Aalreet! Aalreet! Give's time to take me jock strap of the washing line. As I was saying there are two of them. A French-American and an older bloke. They are not short of money. They smoke cigars. One of the Coxons' sisters, Ursula by name, is a maid at the hotel. Like me this morning she was in the jail paying her brothers a visit. She knows more about the Confederates than her brothers.'

'Did you speak to her?' said Jeb.

'Of course I did. When she knew I was Geordie Black she wanted to give me a kiss. I told her you can give me a kiss, pet, if you tell me aal yuh nar … know, about the Americans. She said "that's a funny bargain". I told her "life is full of mysteries, pet". I asked her if she'd heard the story that the Tyne was once full of salmon.'

'Shoot him,' said Henry.

'The Americans were employing the Coxons, gentlemen, in the same role as your good selves is employing … moi … that's French for, "me".'

'Rowley,' said Jeb, a twinkle in his eye, 'do you know what a double agent is?'

'Aye, I do. He's a stage manager. He tells one story to the theatre's owners and another story to the performers. And the difference between the two stories is the sovereigns which gan … go clink! Clink! Into his back pocket.'

'Are you against slavery?'

'I am.'

'And you know the Station Hotel?'

'I do. Divent forget … don't forget … I am local knowledge.'

'You will be well paid, Rowley. Abraham Lincoln is a generous paymaster.'

'To do what? Am I to play more than one part in the same play? I have done that before. At the Empire … that's Sunderland not Newcastle … when the conjuror's assistant went doon … down with the cholera I stood in for him. On the same night when the wolf in Little Red Riding Hood went doon … down with typhoid I stood in for him, yuh nar … you know … in that part of the play when the wolf is dressed as the little bairn's grandmother. So, I was playing a wolf dressed as an old dame when ten minutes before I'd been a conjuror's assistant. I liked playing the conjuror's assistant. I had to wear tights. I have good legs. I like to show them off.'

'Shoot him,' said Henry.

'I had bells on my shoes and a pig's bladder on a stick. When the conjuror gave me the nod I'd to hit him ower the heed … hit him over the head … with the bladder. All part of the act. That's how a comic learns timing. Then … you won't believe this, after the interval I was back on stage … in front of the gas … as my good self. Well, not me but my character, Geordie Black. "In his time a man plays many parts." That's Shakespeare. Have you read him? What do you want me to dee … do?'

'I want you to go to the Station Hotel and tell the Confederates that …'

'Me name is Geordie Black,' sang Rowley.

'Shoot him,' said Henry.

'I'm doing it again, aren't I?'

'Yes, you are. If I had my banjo with me I'd play it. If Orpheus's music could charm the underworld then surely my banjo can shut up a Tyneside comedian …'

'Singer, songwriter and double agent.'

'Then surely my playing the banjo should be able to shut up a Tyneside comedian, singer, songwriter, comedian and double agent. What do you think, Henry?'

'Shoot him,' said Henry.

'Rowley,' said Jeb, 'I want you to go to the Station Hotel and tell the Confederates … the Coxons … their "local knowledge" are in jail. Hint to them that you are willing to take their place.'

'Like in the theatre,' said Rowley, 'when the big star gets the pneumonia it's the understudy's big chance. Like when the sun isn't shining you can see the moon.'

'You will be Abraham Lincoln's mole in a nest of Confederate spies.'

'I've never played a mole. Will I have to wear a mole mask?'

'Shoot him,' said Henry.

'Before I do that,' said Jeb, 'I want, you, Rowley to take us to Sir William Armstrong's Newcastle office.'

'It is in Hood Street,' said Henry. 'Britain's foreign secretary, Lord Russell, told my pa that's where it is and my pa told me.'

'Chinese whispers,' said Rowley, shaking his head, 'that's how the Manx cat came to have nee … no tail. You see when the Almighty was giving out his instructions on how to make a cat, on the Isle of Man, he tried out a system he'd never used before. He used middlemen. The middlemen were a bit like theatre managers. He used them to pass on his instructions to the lads and lasses making the cats. It is my opinion the cat was lucky to be just missing a tail. Chinese whispers …very dangerous.'

'The cat might have had five legs,' said Jeb, laughing at Rowley's nonsense.

'For goodness' sake, Jeb, do not encourage him,' said Henry, 'shoot him.'

'While Henry and I introduce ourselves at Hood Street,' said Jeb, laughing, 'I want you, Rowley, my fellow musician … Rowley plays the violin, Henry … to find out all you can about the Confederate agents. You agree?' pressing a sovereign into Rowley's palm.

'I agree,' said Rowley, looking at the sovereign and wondering if he should treat Annie to a bunch of flowers or be practical and buy her a book on how to improve her embouchure, not for kissing, but for playing the trombone.

'I suggest we all rendezvous back at the "George" as and when events make it possible for us to do so,' said Jeb.

'How do we get to Hood Street?' said Henry. 'Do we walk or take a cab?'

'Shanks's Pony,' said Rowley.

'What kind of vehicle is that? The Far East has rickshaws. Tyneside has … Shanks's Ponies. Is it pulled by more than one horse? If it rains, does it have a hood?'

'Mr Adams, sir,' said Rowley, shaking his head (the ignorance of foreigners never ceased to amaze him) 'we will be walking to Hood Street.'

'Why didn't you say so?'

'I did.'

******

Outside Sir William Armstrong's Hood Street office Rowley told Jeb and Henry: 'I'm off to the Royal, now.'

'I thought we were paying you to visit the Confederates at the Station Hotel,' said Henry.

'Quite right, Mr Adams. Afore I see them I wants to dress for the part I'll be playing. It's nee good … no good me going to see the Confederates dressed in my Sunday best. When I see them I will be dressed as a waterman. The Theatre Royal's property department has just the outfit I'm after. I have a pal in "props". He is called Mr Pitt. You'll never guess what his nickname is.'

'"Pit Props",' said Jeb.

'How'd you know that?' said Henry. 'Have you met him? Is he someone else you have spying for our cause?'

'Jeb nars … knows the nickname, Mr Adams, because he is sharp. He is a musician. He nars how many crotchets make a quaver.'

'I don't follow,' said Henry.

'You can lead a horse to water … niva, mind,' said Rowley, shaking his head. 'Jeb, sir, I will meet you and Mr Adams at the "George" as soon as I am able. In the meantime, adieu!' (Bowing) 'I must to horse to meet on the stage of real life at the "Station Hotel" … dastardly

Confederates who wish to break up the United States into little pieces and who support the keeping of slaves. Adieu! Adieu!'

******

Jeb and Henry watched Rowley do a hornpipe dance in the direction of the Theatre Royal, with mixed feelings. They watched him … somewhat lost for words … disappear into Grey Street the way sailors who, having abandoned ship and are in a lifeboat, watch their maritime home disappear beneath the waves.

'Don't say anything,' said Henry. 'I am thinking the same as you. I know I am.'

'That our fate … perhaps the outcome of our civil war, lies in the hands of a Tyneside singer, songwriter and comedian?'

'And "spy", don't forget that.'

'He is quite a character. I like him. We are fellow musicians.'

'Well, I ain't a musician. I'm a diplomat.'

'An apprentice diplomat, Henry.'

'OK, an "apprentice diplomat". But I'm telling you now, Jeb, when we go into this here office of Sir William Armstrong, I will swagger in. I'm an American. My boss is Abraham Lincoln.'

'We will flow into this here office, Henry, the way the Mississippi flows into the Gulf of Mexico.'

******

The flow of the mighty Mississippi was reduced to a trickle when Richard told the two Americans: 'Sir William is out on the moors, sirs. He is testing a new gun.'

'He is hands-on?' said Henry.

'Sir William is not afraid of getting his hands dirty, sir.'

'Good for him,' said Jeb. 'He'd fit in, in the New World.'

'We have letters of introduction from the British Foreign Secretary,' said Henry. 'It is important that I and my colleague, Mr Phelan, see him. We are representatives of Abraham Lincoln. Our letters of introduction are our bona fides. Do you wish to see them?'

'That will not be necessary, sir. Sir William was expecting you to call sometime soon.'

'Was he indeed!'

'London advised Sir William to expect visitors from the New World. If you called when he was out Sir William told me to tell you that if you are free tonight he would like to offer you dinner.'

'Where at?' said Henry. 'At his club?'

'Newcastle is not London, sir. Up north we do not have an abundance of exclusive gentlemen's clubs. Sir William has invited you to dine with his good self and Lady Armstrong at their private residence.'

'Where do they live?'

'Jesmond Dene.'

'Is it far?'

'A twenty-minute walk, sir. Sir William's private card, sir. The address is printed on it.'

'Local Knowledge will know where it is,' said Jeb. 'What time does Sir William wish us to call on him?'

'Sir William, sir, said any time after six.'

'How should we dress?' said Henry.

'Sir William, sir, said to tell you the occasion would be informal.'

'What does that mean?'

In his short time in England Henry had fallen foul, too many times, of England's etiquette rules.

'All I know, sir, is that Sir William said "informal". May I show you how to make an Armstrong Gun out of paper?'

****

Jeb and Henry flowed out of Sir William's Hood Street office not as they had flowed in, as the mighty Mississippi, but as babbling tributaries of the Tyne. In their hands they carried origami Armstrong Guns. Under Richard's tuition they had made the paper guns themselves. They were proud of their handiwork.

'I think mine is better than yours,' said Henry.

'Richard helped you more than he helped me,' said Jeb.

ROWLEY RETURNS WITH INFORMATION JEB FINDS DIFFICULT TO BELIEVE

Back at the 'George', in their private sitting room, in front of a blazing coal fire, Jeb and Henry looked at their origami Armstrong Guns, with as much awe, as if the twenty-first century had back pedalled into Victorian England and they were looking at a computer.

'I've marked mine with an H,' said Henry. 'That way I will know which one is mine.'

Jeb smiled. Henry was so possessive. He was an American version of an English 'dook'. 'Dooks' had to HAVE. If you were an Adams you had to own and possess.

To pass the time while they waited for Rowley to return, Jeb strummed his banjo; Henry cut his fingernails with a clasp knife.

The origami Armstrong guns reminded them of why they were on Tyneside.

'Can we trust him?' said Henry, splaying his hands, one after the other, to look at his fingernails. 'What if the chatterbox has told the Confederates about us? What if he's double crossing us the way he is double crossing them?'

'He won't do that,' said Jeb who having tired of strumming his banjo was loading his Colt revolver with his eyes closed.

'How'd you know he won't?'

'He plays the violin. He and I are fellow musicians. We are crotchet and quaver brothers. You know what, Henry? I have loaded my Colt with my eyes closed. Rowley is against slavery.'

'I don't like being kept waiting. It's like wanting to go to the toilet when you know, you can't.'

****

A short while later they heard, through a keyhole: 'Oh, me name is Geordie Black, in me time I've been a crack … let's in, will yuh? It's me, the prodigal son. Howay man, let's in.'

'What a welcome,' said Rowley, eyeing the poker and the Colt, Henry and Jeb were respectively holding. 'And silly me thought Sunderland Empire on a Friday night was dangerous. I am of the opinion, gentlemen, that while the spying game pays better than comedy, it is more dangerous. No one ever died from having eggs thrown at them. Guns and pokers are different. The Byker bite. The Hebburn heartburn. The Jarrow jaundice. The Gosforth gosh! The Toon truncheon. The Newburn nod. They are aal less dangerous to flesh and blood than pokers and truncheons.'

'Rowley!' said Jeb.

'Shoot him,' said Henry.

'Sit down, Rowley, and spill the beans.'

'Would that be an American expression?' said Rowley.

'It sure is,' said Jeb. 'It belongs to the New World. It means tell us all you have learnt about the Confederates.'

'Do you like my disguise?'

'Pit-Props has done you proud … now, cut to the quick.'

'When I went to see the Confederates I wasn't Geordie Black the famous Tyneside comedian and songwriter; no, sirs, I was playing a part. When I met them I was on stage. I put on the local accent as thick as me mother … god rest her soul … she's in Jesmond cemetery … put strawberry jam on the muffins she used to make or the way in the old days keel men put butter on their bread or …'

'Shoot him,' said Henry.

'Rowley, stick to the point. Cut to the quick.'

'I told them the Coxons were in jail. Drunk and disorderly. Maybe even murder. I was there in place of them like when you canna get cabbage at the Green Market and you have to have sprouts instead. There were two of them.'

'What did they say when you told them about the Coxons?'

'Took it on the chin the way a duke takes the death of a footman. One of them is a French-American. He talks English with a French accent. I once shared the bill at the Hippodrome … Alnwick … not London with a French dog trainer … poodles … who spoke the Queen's English like that. It takes aal sorts. We have spiders and hedgehogs and …'

'Shoot him,' said Henry.

'Alreet! Alright! The other bloke, I'll call him the American-American … if yuh nar … know what I mean. The American-American was old. He looked tired. The French American did most of the talking. He wanted to know if I was local. Did I know my way around the town? I told him I was as local as the weather. He wanted to know if I knew the river. I told him I knew a keel boat from a cobweb. To knock them off balance … by way of a diversion … to stop them asking me questions I didn't want them asking I told them … no extra charge … that a knew a "guzzunder" from a milk jug.'

'A "guzzunder"?' said Henry.

'Yuh nar … you know … a piss pot. When yuh wake up in the middle of the neet … night and want a piss … need to pass water, gentlemen, and divent … don't want to get wet ganin aal the way doon the yard to the netty … the privy … you use a chamber pot. We call them "guzzunders" because they gan … go under the bed. Neebody … nobody likes emptying them. It's a job yuh delegate. I once saw an advert in the Chronicle: "Wanted. Guzzunder emptier. Peg for nose provided. Cost of replacing a lost peg will be deducted from wages". I'd have to be hard up afore a worked for a master who'd charge me for losing me nose peg.'

'Mr Harrison,' said Henry, opening and shutting his clasp knife, 'you are a long winded fellow. The Confederate agents …'

'The American-American wanted to know if it was true there were men of colour in South Shields. I asked him if there were, was he was going to enslave them. He told me not to be cheeky … that he asked the questions. His tone was sharp. "Any negroes?" he wanted to know. I told him about the Somali community living in South Shields.'

'So, you are working for them?' said Jeb.

'I am, gentlemen, their "local knowledge".'

'Are they paying you?' said Henry.

'I cut a deal.'

'I'll bet you did.'

'When you are used to dealing with stage managers, Mr Adams, cutting a deal with two Confederate agents was like sailing doon the river to Tynemouth when the tide is going out and the wind is blowing from the west … nee bother!'

'"Knee bother",' said Henry, giving Rowley the full knitted eyebrows' puzzled look, 'your knees are giving you pain? Mr Harrison, you jump from subject to subject like a mosquito in a mangrove swamp.'

'Nar! Nar! No! No! You misunderstand, Mr Adams. "Nee bother" is a local expression. It means, "Not a problem". It has nowt … nothing to do with human anatomy.'

'Your use of nautical metaphor, Mr Harrison, and Tyneside argot has not hidden … at least from me, it has not … your avarice. With two paymasters you will anon be driving round Newcastle in a phaeton with coachmen in livery.'

'I like the sound of that. Money! It can buy booze and baccy but it can't buy top of the bill at Sunderland Empire.'

'Money,' said Jeb, 'if the Northern States had enough gold, I'd use it to buy every Armstrong Gun Sir William and his engineers are capable of making … anything to stop the Confederates getting their hands on them. Rowley, my fellow musician, while you are being paid by the North and by the South, I am assuming, come what may … no matter how much money the South offer to pay you … you will stay loyal to myself and Mr Adams.'

'In other words, Mr Harrison,' said Henry, 'you will not double cross us?'

'Divent worry … don't worry, bonny lads … I'm against slavery. I know right from wrong. I dislike slavery as much as I dislike stage managers.'

'You may "dislike it", Rowley,' said Jeb, 'I hate … detest slavery. When I think of my fellow men being chained and whipped with no redress, my blood boils. It makes me feel more like an animal than a human being. I refuse to be diminished. My solace is my banjo.'

'I know what you mean,' said Rowley. 'When I get more orange peel than claps I play my fiddle. Aye! The fiddle is a great soother of stormy emotions.'

'Mr Harrison,' said Henry, 'comparing an entertainer's failure to be entertaining to … slavery is, in my opinion, inappropriate. It is, Mr Harrison, an altogether inappropriate comparison.'

'Mr Harrison,' said Jeb, 'has no experience of slavery. We must excuse him the way the British aristocracy excuse Americans who slurp coffee out of saucers.'

'Don't you go belittling your country, Jeb. We belong to the New World. We have our own way of doing things. We do things our way … the American way. Mr Harrison, the Confederates, they do not suspect you are a double agent?'

'If they were an audience I'd say they were in my back pocket … Byker Grande, first house … Thursday night. Mind you. They were "tres" … that's French for "very" … nervous … hair trigger nervous, if you ask me. They were as nervous as I get afore I go on stage. There's a sword swallower I know has to have a piss pot waiting for him in the wings. Swallowing swords in front of an audience opens his bladder, see? You know, I'm thinking … is that why Esmeralda pissed on stage?'

'Who is "Esmeralda"?' said Henry.

'Don't ask,' said Jeb. 'Rowley, not for the first time I must ask you to stick to the point.'

'If you don't,' said Henry, 'I will shoot you.'

'Alreet! Alright! I hired the Confederates a cab and took them to Sir William Armstrong's works at Elswick. Aal the way there they kept asking me about the river … how deep was it? How much cargo could a keel boat carry? They kept me waiting on a bench in the work's yard. My disguise, see? Watermen divent … don't gan … go into offices. Offices is for toffs. While I was waiting I asked one bloke … he was passing by like … he'd a tab behind one ear and a pencil behind the other. Lugs, yuh nar … know … have more than one use. In that respect, gentlemen, lugs, are like screwdrivers. Screwdrivers are meant for screwing but they can also be used like crowbars. Lugs can be used as baskets for tabs and pencils as well as for listening.'

'Shoot him!' said Henry.

'Now! Now! Divent … do not spoil me ramble. I asked the bloke what he did. He told me he was a draughtsman. I asked him … cheeky like … if that meant … pointing at a barrow … if he drew it round the yard. He was ganna … going to smack me one for my cheek when to mollify him … like buying the missus flowers when you come in late from the pub … I sang him a chorus of … (taking a deep breath and singing) "Oh, me name is Geordie Black, in me time I've been a crack" … well, yuh should have seen his face. It was a picture. You'll never guess what he asked me.'

'Why,' said Henry, expressing his frustration with this chatterbox by raising his eyebrows, 'was the famous Tyneside song writer and comedian Rowley Harrison dressed as a common waterman?'

'Now, you are talking. I'm beginning to like you, Mr Adams. We'll never be on first name terms, but if you knocked on my front door I'd open it. Before I proceed to a matter of more import, I must take you up on your phrase "common watermen". Watermen, Mr Adams, are not "common"; that is, if by that adjective you were implying they are vulgar fellows. They are not. They are knowledgeable fellows. They know the name of every grain of sand in the river. They are, however, "common" in the sense that there are lots of them. Which do you mean, Mr Adams? My grandfather was a waterman. Watermen stick together. The honour of my family is at stake. Insult my family and I will challenge you to a duel with wooden swords at twenty paces. We will face each other, back-to-back. Red paint in pots will simulate blood.'

Henry put his head in his hands. He knew when he was beaten.

'Henry meant,' said Jeb, 'that watermen were "common" in the sense that there are lots of them on the river. Didn't you, Henry?'

'I will interpret Mr Adam's groan as an affirmative,' said Rowley. 'It made my day that my catch song stopped me getting smacked. Fame has its upside as well as its doonside.'

'It would make my day,' said Henry, raising his head out of his hands, 'if I was more of a man and had the courage to shoot you.'

'Now, now, Mr Adams, don't you go belittling yourself. I have information about the Confederates … at least one of them … that, if my suspicions are reet … are right will make the hairs on a bald man's head rise up the way when you brush your hair with a comb you can use the brush to pick up little bits of paper. The French-American says he can't understand anything any local says. The cheeky bugger said he doesn't think Geordies speak English. The American-American … the old guy … has a habit of scratching his crotch. I am an observer of mannerisms. I watch folk the way my Uncle Tom watches hot iron. He nars … he knows, when it's ready to pour by its colour. I think he has worms.'

'Your Uncle Tom?' said Henry.

'Nar! Nar! No! No! The American-American.'

'Worms! More like eczema or fleas.'

'I quite agree, Mr Adams.'

'If you agree with me, why did you say this Confederate has worms?'

'I was by way of been an agent provocateur, Mr Adams. I was provoking you into suggesting a suitable alternative.'

'And, did I?'

'Yes.'

'You manipulated me?'

'Yes.'

'I don't like that.'

'I expect that's what the fleas and eczema said when they were scratched. Jeb, Mr Phelan, sir, I wish to ask you a question. Is America a big country?'

'America is a vast country, Rowley. It grows bigger every year.'

'England is an antimacassar, America is a blanket,' said Henry.

'Get away,' said Rowley.

'Why do you ask?' said Jeb.

'If it is big, it has lots of everything?'

'It sure has,' said Henry. 'We have an abundance of everything … you name it … we got it to the power ten.'

'What about names? People's names?'

'Christian names or surnames?' said Jeb.

'Both.'

'Lots of Irish in New York … lots of Scots … lots of Germans … lots of Italians. America is a melting pot.'

'I told you, Mr Harrison,' said Henry, 'we got lots of everything in America. We got more coal than Newcastle.'

'So,' said Rowley, 'let us imagine this abundance of variety to be a field of daffodils.'

'Why?'

'Humour him, Henry,' said Jeb. 'Rowley's meanderings remind me of Mr Lincoln's stories. He may be leading thirsty men to water.'

'I'd rather die of thirst,' said Henry, folding his arms.

'Now, now,' said Rowley, pulling a funny face.

'OK,' said Henry, 'I'm splitting my sides … what about the daffodils?'

'Thousands of daffodils grow in this field. In this abundance, two daffodils have a red spot on their leaves. They have a red spot on their leaves because they are related. If a blind man goes into that field and pulls up two daffodil bulbs, what would be the odds, gentlemen that the blind man would pull up the two daffodils with a red spot on their leaves?'

'Where you heading, Rowley?' said Jeb.

'He's theatrical,' said Henry. 'He's the sort of guy who hails a cab the way Caesar wooed Cleopatra.'

'Answer my question, gentlemen.'

'A betting man would give you a thousand to one,' said Jeb. 'He'd be lucky to pull up one, never mind, two.'

'What if he did pull up two?'

'It was his lucky day,' said Henry, who, despite himself, was wondering where Rowley's ramble was heading.

'Chance,' said Jeb. 'It could happen.'

'What if the two daffodil plants, instead of having a common red spot on one of their leaves, had the same Christian name and a shared surname?'

'Rowley, cut to the quick,' said Jeb. 'I sure hope your story has a good punchline.'

'Shoot him,' said Henry.

'You and the American-American, Jeb, have much in common.'

'He is a black man?' said Jeb.

'Nar! Nar! No! No! I'm not sure how to put this to you, Jeb. I'm thinking it might have consequences. Speaking personal, I've aalways found coincidences have consequences. Yuh nar? You know? When I was after asking Annie if she'd walk out with me, I kept bumping into her. "Rowley," she said, "this can't be a coincidence … our bumping into each other, like this." And she was reet … right. We'd kept bumping into each other because I'd been trailing her. My desire to walk out with her made me her shadow. When I saw her go into a fish shop … there I was waiting for her when she came out … bending down to tie my boot laces. "Hello, pet!" I'd say. "Fancy meeting you here." Then I'd try and be clever … yuh nar … you know … to try and impress her like the way Mr Peacock fans his tail to impress Miss Peacock. "Have you been buying a new bonnet?" I knew she loved me when she clouted me with

the haddock she'd bought … but not too hard … more playful … like a
once saw a vixen under Byker Bridge pick up a sausage from a puddle.
Foxes are scavengers. Did yuh nar that?'

'Rowley,' said Jeb, 'your knowledge of Newcastle's chares, back
streets and alleyways is invaluable to myself and Mr Adams … your
knowledge of your town's local wildlife, is not.'

'Shoot him!' said Henry.

'Rowley, what in your roundabout way are you trying to tell me?
Pray, spill the beans before, out of sheer desperation, I obey Henry's
exhortation and do shoot you.'

'As I telt … as I told Alfredo the knife thrower … Sunderland Empire
last year when he accidently killed his female assistant … lovely figure
… "You'll get over it. Pull yourself together." He blamed his hay fever.
Said it was an accident. Everyone knew he'd murdered her. She was
having an affair. The love of her life was the weight lifter … bottom of
the bill … Jock Strap. His wife was called Liz Truss. I'm not an expert
in these matters but if you're wearing a jock strap can you wear a truss?
If you can is it not like wearing a belt and braces to keep your pants up?'

'Shoot him!' said Henry. 'And this time I mean it.'

'Rowley,' said Jeb, drawing his Colt.

'Alreet! Alreet! What I'm saying is … it wasn't an accident when
the knife thrower's knife pierced his wife's heart instead of the wheel
to which she was tied so she could spin round like my bowler hat. His
throwing was … wait for it … wait for it … I'm ganna … I'm going to
use a long word … it was premeditated.'

'I'm sorely tempted,' said Jeb, cocking the Colt.

'Jeb, sir,' said Rowley, 'do you believe in coincidences?'

'No, I do not.'

'You are like Annie. From what I have told you, do you believe
Alfredo the knife thrower murdered his missus? Remember a
professional knife thrower never misses.'

'I ain't missed with my Colt … ever. Yes, Alfredo murdered his wife.'

'America is a big country, yes?'

'America, Mr Harrison … how many times must I tell you? Is a bedspread … England is a lady's pocket handkerchief.'

'Our Empire, Mr Adams … the British Empire … makes us a floor carpet.'

Mr Henry Adams was like aal the stage managers Rowley had known. To keep them in their place and let them know who was boss you had to have the last word.

'That's as maybe,' said Henry, down but not out, 'but as sure as mosquitos bite, England ain't going to get her hands on the United States of America and the Confederates ain't going to get their hands on the Armstrong Gun.'

'Rowley,' said Jeb, 'why were you asking if I believed in coincidences?'

'Cut to the quick, Mr Harrison! Cut to the quick!' said Henry. 'Your levity and fondness to digress will be your undoing.'

Rowley prided himself on his ability to read an audience … now was the time to 'spill the beans'.

'One of the Confederate agents has the same name as you, Jeb.'

'He is called "Jeb",' said Jeb, as if to say, 'so what?'.

'Yes, he is.'

'Plenty of "Jebs" in America,' said Henry.

'On your banjo case, Jeb,' said Rowley, 'you have your full name: Jeb Prior Phelan. Am I reet? Am I right?'

'We know you are literate, Mr Harrison,' said Henry, 'too literate, if you ask me.'

'On the valise of the older Confederate I read: "Property of Jeb Montague Prior".'

It took a few seconds for Jeb to react. When he did, he looked like a man who has had a bucket of cold water thrown over him. He stood up. He sat down. He explored the room the way a trapped wasp looks for a way out of a greenhouse. He picked up the fireside poker. He poked the fire.

'Plenty of "Jeb Priors" in America,' said Henry, sotto voce.

'But,' said Jeb, 'not so many "Jeb Montague Priors". My grandfather's mother was a "Montague". How old is this American who has my name?' said Jeb.

'Old enough be your grandfather. What's more, Jeb, he looks like you.'

'A white man, looks like me … a black man?'

'Aye, he does. He is whiter than the beach at Tynemouth … so is his hair … but he looks like you, Jeb. When I was talking to him I thought I was talking to you. This "Jeb" ain't my "Jeb" who plays the banjo I had to keep telling myself. This ain't "Yankee Jeb", this is "Confederate Jeb". You have his eyes, Jeb … and his nose. You are profiles of the American eagle.'

At that moment if Jeb had ordered a brandy and been served whisky, he would not have noticed. Nelson could have short-changed him … he would not have noticed. Was he jumping to conclusions? Did he need more proof? His thoughts were racing ahead so fast that in a race they'd have overtaken cheetahs.

'Jeb,' exclaimed Henry, 'don't you go thinking this "Jeb Montague Prior" is your grandfather. Lots of "Jeb Montague Priors" in America.'

'Apart from the colour of your skin, Jeb,' butted in Rowley, 'he could be your twin.'

'I want to meet him,' said Jeb.

'Jeb,' said Henry, 'he's a Confederate agent. He is our enemy.'

'If he is my grandfather maybe I can talk sense into him about this god damn awful civil war. Maybe I can persuade him slavery is wrong.'

'Jeb, you are not thinking straight. If he is your grandfather he is a plantation owner. He is a slave owner. The only thing that will change his mind is when we win this war. Mr Harrison, you do not know my fellow American's history … I do. You do not understand the ferocity with which Americans are fighting each other. Back home a father fighting for the North can have a son fighting for the South. Back home, Jeb, the two Confederate agents Mr Harrison met, would be sticking their bayonets into us.'

'I was named after my grandfather. My mother told me that. She was always telling me … never forget you are a Prior. In your veins there flows "Prior" blood. "Phelan" is your step-father's surname. You ain't a "Phelan", my son, you are a "Prior". Rowley, you say this old man with white hair, looks like me?'

'The spit,' said Rowley.

'Jeb,' said Henry, 'I know what you are thinking. I can read you like a book. Don't you go making two and two make five. Before you dive into a river you need to know how deep the water is … right?'

'Right,' said Jeb.

'But that ain't going to stop you diving in, is it?'

'Right again, Henry.'

'Mr Harrison?' said Henry.

'Mr Adams?' said Rowley.

'The fact that one of the Confederate agents you have met has the same name as my colleague is …'

'And looks like me,' said Jeb.

'The spit,' said Rowley.

'Ok! Ok! He looks like you, Jeb. He has your name. But, damn it, he is a Confederate agent. He is our enemy. Your possible blood link with this man, Jeb, is a diversion. Mr Harrison, what can you tell us about the Confederate's plans? You are our go-between. You are our "Local Knowledge". How far down the road are they to buying the Armstrong Gun?'

'I want to meet this man, face to face,' said Jeb. 'I want to look him in the eye and ask him … is it true, you had my father murdered for falling in love with my mother, your daughter? I must meet him. I will meet him.'

'Jeb, "Jeb Montague Prior" is a Confederate agent. He is our enemy.'

'He is my grandfather. I know he is. Do not argue with me, Henry. Do not stand in my way. I will meet him … and what is more, I know how to do it. Rowley will be my modus operandi.'

'That's another hat for me to where, is it?' said Rowley. 'I'm "local knowledge" … I'm a "double agent" … I'm a "go-between" … now I'm "modus operandi". The "swan of Avon" was reet … right … in his time a bloke plays many parts.'

'Play this part, Rowley, and you will be doing your bit to help abolish slavery. Your fiancée, Annie … the Salvationist …'

'The trombone player …'

'She who has your heart …'

'She who hates booze …'

'She will be against slavery?'

'She likes me been her slave.'

'Beware, Mr Harrison,' said Henry, 'that your levity is not your undoing.'

'I played the Empire, Sunderland with a magician who could levitate. When he murdered the knife thrower, the law tried to hang him. Every time he "dropped" he "levitated". In the end he got transported. "Levitation Loll" he was called … wonderful man.'

'Shoot him!' said Henry.

'Rowley, I am thinking, if you told Annie you were helping abolish slavery it would make her see you as a shining light. Your fondness for a glass of ale would be indulged.'

'I doubt it. It takes a lot to knock "temperance" off its pedestal … not to mention the "trombone". "Temperance" and the "trombone" have Annie, in a straitjacket. They are her jailors. I'm the unfortunate trying to pass her bread and water through the bars of her jail. A thankless task. But, because she has stolen my heart, I keep trying.'

'Supporting the fight against slavery will make you her knight in shining armour. I know it will. You will be the Union's double agent … well remunerated …'

'Now, you're talking.'

'You will be the Union's "go-between". The babbling brook both sides trust.'

'It is true I nar … know, both parties.'

'Parties? Enemies, you mean.'

'As I nar … know, Mr Adams, that the salmon and the seal are not the best of pals, I nar Americans are killing each other in a civil war.'

'And in our civil war, Mr Harrison, let me remind you … the Union is the "seal", and the Secessionists States are the "salmon".'

'Rowley,' said Jeb, 'when Henry and I visited Sir William's Hood Street office we were informed that Sir William was out testing a gun on some moor or other. London had informed him that we might be calling. Henry and I are to meet him tonight at his home in Jesmond.'

'Is that far, Mr Harrison?' said Henry.

'A twenty-minute walk, Mr Adams.'

'Sir William is holding a soiree, this evening.'

'I nar … I know,' said Rowley, 'I am providing the entertainment.'

'You will be there?' said Jeb.

'Aye, I will. Me and my fiddle.'

'In that case I will take my banjo.'

'Jeb!' exclaimed Henry, 'remember your status. When you visit Sir William you are not an itinerant musician, you are a representative of Abraham Lincoln.'

'Music, Henry, opens hearts more easily than argument, rhetoric and verbal persuasion. Rowley,' producing Sir William's invitation card from a waistcoat pocket, 'I wish you to deliver this invitation to the two Confederate agents, one of whom I am pretty certain is my grandfather. Here,' taking up a pen, 'I have altered the invitation time to an hour later than the time shown on the card. I do not want Henry and I bumping into these agents, on Sir William's doorstep. If Sir William was out testing a gun, I am assuming the Confederates did not meet him at Elswick. By all accounts, Sir William is a hospitable fellow. For two such important customers, an invitation would be an appropriate way of thanking them for their business.'

'I'm not happy with involving Sir William. He and I gan … go back a long way. Me grandfatha taught him to fish on the Coquet. In case yuh divent nar … don't know … that's a river. I've done soirees for Sir

William, before. Lovely man. Pays well; calls me "Mr Harrison" … appreciate the "Mr" … not, "Harrison".'

'The cause, the ending of slavery in America, justifies our skulduggery. That is my argument. If Henry and I meet these Confederates … one of whom, I am certain, is my grandfather … on neutral territory, in civil surroundings, we will be less likely to kill each other. But, just in case, I will have my Colt with me.'

HOW ROWLEY HARRISON, STAGE NAME GEORDIE BLACK, SINGER, SONG WRITER AND COMEDIAN, IN BECOMING A POSTMAN, DID HIS BIT IN HELPING TO ABOLISH SLAVERY IN AMERICA

A veneer of hard wood glued to a newel post of soft white wood makes the casual passer-by assume the newel post is a pedigree newel post and not a mongrel.

Rowley was a 'mongrel' newel post. His theatricality was his veneer. It made unassuming folk think he could not peel a potato.

The 'un-assumers' were wrong. Not only was Rowley good at peeling potatoes, he was good at planting them, harvesting them and cooking them … mash or roast. In other words, Rowley was a practical fellow, which was why he'd no intention of delivering the forged invitation to the Confederates personally. He wished to keep as much distance between himself and the slave owners as possible. He had not warmed to them. He felt guilty about involving Sir William.

****

Rowley entered the brand new 'Station Hotel', still in the disguise of a waterman, by a side entrance marked: STAFF AND VEGETABLES.

If anyone asked him what he was doing, he would say he was a cauliflower looking for a chef. Watermen did not use the front entrance of the Station Hotel.

For him, it was a new experience not wanting to be seen and heard. He consoled himself by telling himself a new experience was good for his creativity. If he could find Ursula, the Coxons' sister – she who, at the castle jail, had given him so much information about the Confederate agents – he'd give her a generous tip. He would get her to deliver the invitation.

He found the backstage of the hotel to be much the same as the backstage of aal the theatres he'd worked in … lots of corridors and short flights of stairs … aal unloved … aal in need of tender, loving care.

In a kitchen smelling of boiled cabbage, a big man with a beard, dressed all in white and who was chopping the wings off a pheasant with a cleaver, said: 'What yee want?'

'Ursula?'

'Niva hord of hor.'

Going up a short flight of stairs he spotted a char with a bucket and a mop, lighting a pipe.

'Divent report me,' she said, 'as a horse needs oats, I need baccy. You're not management, are yuh?'

'I'm looking for Ursula.'

'Which one? Char or chambermaid?'

'Ursula Coxon.'

'Chambermaid.'

'Can you take me to her?' handing over a shilling.

'Ta very much, me darling. Follow me.'

****

Behind a trolley piled high with sheets and blankets, Rowley asked Ursula if she knew the room in which the Americans were staying.

'What's that to you?'

'I wish to ask you, if you will deliver them an invitation.'

'Porter's job, that. Me? I'm "bed linen". Me middle name is "Clean Sheets".'

'Do you know who I am?'

'Aye, a do. Rowley Harrison … Geordie Black.'

'But I'm disguised as a waterman.'

'Didn't fool me. I recognised yuh from when a seen yuh at the prison. When yuh pumped out of me, aal a knew about the Americans. And now you're deeing it again. Pumping.'

'I do not have flatulence.'

'Would that be when your arse has hiccups?'

'A Sandgate euphemism?'

'Eh?'

'Never mind. Ursula, aal I'm asking you to do is to pop this invitation under the door of the room in which the Americans are staying.'

'Why can't you do it?'

'I don't know the hotel. You do. You have local knowledge I do not possess. Here's a shilling for your trouble.'

'For two shillings and a kiss I'll put it in their room like an aspidistra they can't miss. I have a pass key. I'll have the kiss first. Changing beds aalways makes me think about sex.'

****

Back in his lodgings over the Wakefield's clockmaker and jeweller's shop in Gateshead, Rowley discarded his waterman's disguise. If Ursula had seen through it, had the Americans? He thought not. Ursula was local. It flattered him that she'd recognised him.

To prepare for the soiree he read his 'patter' book; the notebook he kept of gags and pithy sayings. The performance for Sir William and his guests needed to be planned. He hoped it would look spontaneous but it would be planned. His maxim was: plan but leave loopholes for improvisation … for repartee … for one-liners.

He wanted to see Annie. To keep himself in her good books he would boast to her that he was helping to drive slavery out of America. He'd warmed to Jeb's argument that he should tell his beloved that, like her, he was a soldier … a soldier camping on the moral high ground. Now, they were both crusaders. She for 'temperance'; himself for the abolition of slavery.

******

Asking in the shop downstairs if his prospective brother-in-law, Edwin Wakefield (fingers crossed, some day he would be) was there and being told he was at home feeding his pigeons, Rowley set off down Coatsworth Road to the Wakefield family home; a three storey terrace house with bow windows, overlooking Saltwell Park the way Buckingham Palace overlooks Green Park.

Florence, the maid, opened the door to him. Her real name was 'Agatha' but Edwin, who'd a passion for Italian renaissance art, insisted she be called 'Florence'.

'Hello, Mr Harrison,' said Florence, dropping a 'Gateshead curtsey', that is to say, the hint of a bended knee. 'If you want to see Annie, she's out at trombone practice. Master is feeding his pigeons. That's why I'm keeping tight hold of "Ginger",' giving the large ginger tom cat she was cradling in her arms, a squeeze. 'It's to keep him off the pigeons. I don't like cats. Here, you take him. Whenever you come to see Annie, he aalways sits on your knee.'

'Is that Rowley, I hear?' said Edwin, coming into the lobby to join them.

'I came to see Annie.'

'Trombone practice. Keep tight hold of Ginger, Rowley. I don't want him eating Phoebe,' pointing to the pigeon perched on top of his head.

'Chocolate?' proffering Rowley the box of chocolates he was holding.

'Thank you,' said Rowley, taking one.

'Careful you don't get a ginger one. I like ginger cats but I cannot stand ginger chocolate.'

'If Annie's not in, I'll not stay. I am performing at a soiree this evening.'

'And I'm attending one.'

'Mine is at Sir William Armstrong's Jesmond Dene house.'

'In that case, Rowley, I will see you there. As a thank you for all the clocks my business has supplied his works, Sir William has invited me into his home for entertainment. He and I have a passion for Italian art. I hear your donkey urinated on stage.'

'Brought the house down. Four encores or was it five?'

'Let us see if your performance at Sir William's, tonight, can do the same. Florence, retrieve Ginger. Put him on his lead. Short rein. What centre did your chocolate have?'

'Ginger.'

'Good, that's one less for me to worry about. If Sir William has chocolates at his soiree, I do hope I avoid ginger ones. On my own I am in the habit of spitting out ginger chocolate. A private whim. In public one has to hide one's dislikes. Do you know who will be at the soiree?'

'Americans.'

'Americans! They are pirates. They have boarded one of our mail ships in international waters. Why are they here? Why are they not at home fighting in their civil war?'

'They are fighting their civil war, here … on Tyneside. Agents … Confederate agents … are here on Tyneside to buy the Armstrong Gun. Agents from the North are here to stop them.'

'Both sides are on Tyneside?'

'I believe so.'

'How do you know all this?'

'They are my employers.'

'They … both sides?'

'The North are paying me to double cross the South. It pays better than the music hall. Please tell Annie, when you see her … I am working for the abolition of slavery in America. That will impress her, surely? If that doesn't make her love me more than she loves her trombone, then, nothing will. Tell her, it is my private opinion, that a brass band playing "The Battle Hymn of the Republic" outside Sir William's house this evening will be proof of the pudding that Geordies are against slavery. Edwin?'

'What?'

'Phoebe has shit on your head.'

'That's good.'

'You mean a bird shitting on your head means you are going to be lucky?'

'I have a bald patch. A Lobley Hill barber told me he'd read in an almanac that bird shit cures baldness.'

'You believe him?'

'Not sure … you see, the barber was as bald as a coot. It did cross my mind that if bird shit was a cure for baldness why had it not worked its magic on his pate? Never mind … have another chocolate. Try to pick one with a ginger centre. I dislike ginger.'

'Meow!'

'Not you, "Ginger" … not you.'

'As much as you hate "ginger", Edwin, I hate trombones.'

'Annie loves her trombone. She cuddles into at night the way a bairn cuddles its teddy bear.'

'Annie loves her trombone more than she loves me.'

'Woo her with your fiddle.'

'Brass is louder than strings.'

'And Americans, I have heard, are louder than an orchestra. Do put on a good show tonight, Rowley.'

'I had four … or was it five encores last neet.'

'It was five.'

'How'd you know that?'

'The barber from Lobley Hill told me.'

'News travels fast.'

'It does when you have a carrier pigeon. Phoebe brought the good news from the toon to Gateshead. The Romans had carrier pigeons … did you know that?'

'No … nar, a didn't.'

SIR WILLIAM ARMSTRONG'S HOUSE: JESMOND DENE

Sir William never stopped working. When he was eating his meat and two veg, he was in the habit of making mashed potato dams to hold back lakes of gravy. He made conduits out of slices of beef. In bed at night, he dreamed of hydraulic cranes, breech loading guns and a bridge that would swing open and shut like a door.

On the night of the soiree he confided to Meggie: 'Emma is all smiles. That is because Richard is with us. I have invited him to stay for the soiree. I invited him to make Emma smile.'

'No, you didn't. You invited him because you wanted to talk to him about your swing bridge.'

'You know me too well, Meggie. I hope Mr Wakefield and the Americans are on time. I have heard rumours that Americans are not punctual.'

'I do believe, William, you are hoping they will be late so that you can have more time chatting with Richard about your swing bridge.'

'What is wrong with the old bridge?' said Doris, who was sitting with her hosts, sipping a medicinal brandy.

'Its arches are too low. Even at high tide a keel boat has to lower its sail to pass under it. To enable the ships I am planning to build at Elswick to pass down river, I am planning to build an iron bridge that will open and shut like a door.'

'What if the wind blows it open when it is shut?' said Doris. 'When my footman in London left my front door open, wind barged in like a riot. It opened and shut every door in the house. Bang! Bang! Bang! Richard and Emma have taught me how to make an origami Armstrong Gun.'

'Come with me to Elswick and I will show you how to make the real thing.'

'Factories, William, are noisy and dirty. They are not my cup of tea. They are like pickled onions. They do not agree with me. Mr Disraeli is fond of pickled onions. He persuaded me to have one at one of his soirees. He is such a flatterer. I felt obliged to try one. It gave me frightful heartburn. Goodness knows how my disposition might react if it was to hear a real Armstrong Gun go bang! Dear Emma had used a love note from Richard to show me how to make an origami Armstrong Gun. I told the pair of them "never underestimate the power of a widow's lorgnette'. Another brandy. Talking of love makes me think of my dear departed. I do not wish my grief to attenuate my enjoyment of the soiree. I told Richard, "You are a passionate young man." When he hung his head, I told him straight: "Do not look so hang dog. That was a compliment. A man who loves a dog is humdrum. A man who loves a woman is sublime."'

****

Phillips, the butler – a man who could do twenty press-ups with one hand tied behind his back – opened the door to the first guest to arrive for the soiree.

'Good evening, Mr Wakefield, sor. Sir William is in the sitting room with the ladies.'

'No, he's not,' said William, 'he is playing hide and seek behind his butler's coat tails. Come along in, Edwin. How's the clock and watch business?'

'Ticking along quite nicely, Sir William. Thank you. The order you gave me for a dozen clocks at your Elswick works has made my business most profitable.'

'Heavy engineering and precision clocks.'

'Dwarves and giants, Sir William.'

'Newcastle is a boom town, Edwin.'

'Thanks to your engineering works at Elswick, it is.'

'And thanks to coal. Coal is the town's black gold.'

'I have brought you a present–' handing Sir William a pigeon in a cage.

'Shall I take it to the kitchen, sor?' said Phillips.

'Whatever for?' said Sir William.

'I am assuming, sor, it's for a pie.'

'It is a carrier pigeon,' said Edwin.

'What's it carry, sor, begging your pardon for asking?'

'It will carry,' said Sir William, 'news from Alston Moor to my Elswick works of the results of tests I am carrying out on the improvements I am making to the Armstrong Gun.'

'A postman with wings, well, I neva. Where shall I put it, sor?'

'In my study. Put it in Polly's cage. Polly, if you remember, Edwin, was Meggie's pet parrot. She fell off his perch last week.'

'It comes to us aal, sor,' said Phillips. 'If we divent end up in a pie we end up in a coffin.'

The door-bell jangled.

'I'm on the horns of a terrible dilemma, sor,' said Phillips, as echoes of the jangled door-bell travelled through the lobby. 'I need instructions, sor. Am I a butler carrying a carrier pigeon to its new quarters or, am I a butler, on duty in this here lobby, to answer doors?'

'You look after the pigeon, Phillips. I will look after the door.'

'Phillips,' said Edwin, 'the pigeon is called "Pamela". All my pigeons have names starting with the letter P.'

'Have you one called "Phillips" sor? Yuh nar, sor, like after me.'

'I did have a "Phillip".'

'Did? Did it die in a pie?'

'It might have done. I don't know. It disappeared under mysterious circumstances. The official in charge of the race it was in was a butcher.

Need I say more? Are you bald?'

'Begging your pardon, sir, your horse has left its stable without its carriage.'

'Are you going bald?'

'No, sir.'

'Pigeon shit cures baldness.'

'Verrucas?'

'Good heavens, no … it's not a panacea.'

****

Opening his front door, Sir William found himself looking at three people who reminded him of a dream he'd once had of an out-of-control hydraulic crane. The engineer in charge of the crane had not been able to switch it off. No matter what valves he had closed or opened; what levers he'd pulled, the crane had just gone on lifting, more, and more barrels of gunpowder until it had blown itself up.

In the tableau now confronting him, Henry Adams was the distraught engineer.

Henry was tut-tutting and shaking his head in disbelief at the fact that his fellow American, Jeb Prior Phelan … his fellow diplomat and secret agent … was getting ready to strum a banjo and that Rowley Harrison … their 'local knowledge' … their employee … had a violin stuck under his chin like a pharaoh's postiche.

'A one … a one, two, three,' said Rowley.

In the kitchen, the stirring music of 'John Brown's Body' stopped Richard kissing Emma. In the lobby it stopped Edwin explaining to a sceptical Phillips, that pigeon shit cured baldness. It tugged Meggie and Doris off their cosy fireside seats. To find out what was going on they dashed into the lobby, as excited as children going to a birthday party.

In the lobby, Doris, said: 'Has the soiree started? In London, soirees do not have impromptu beginnings. They begin with sherry and start, only when all the guests are seated. In London soirees, entertainers and the entertained do not mingle. Can you imagine Disraeli playing a didgeridoo? I saw one at the Great Exhibition. William, assert yourself.'

'I will lead the applause,' said Sir William.

'Bravo!' shouted Edwin Wakefield.

'Long live Abraham Lincoln,' shouted Richard.

Lady Armstrong and Emma clapped, Doris scowled. Such informality made her feel uncomfortable. Last night she'd a nightmare. She'd been standing naked on top of Grey's Monument. Worse still, no one had seemed interested in her nudity.

'If you were carol singers,' said Sir William, 'I'd be more than happy to put money in your collecting box.'

'You can thank us, Sir William,' said Jeb, 'by not selling the Armstrong Gun to the Secessionist states.'

'Allow me to introduce myself, Sir William,' said Henry. 'I am Henry Adams, son of America's legate to the United Kingdom. Your man, Richard, who I see behind you, informed my colleague and I …'

'Jeb Prior Phelan, Sir William,' said Jeb, playing a selection of chords on his banjo.

'Your man Richard informed us you had instructed him to invite our good selves to this evening's soiree. I believe London has informed you to expect us. Our letters of introduction are signed by the highest in the land.'

'Welcome! Welcome!' said Sir William. 'Do come in. And you too, Mr Harrison. You are no stranger to my home. You have entertained us before, though … never with Americans.'

'That's Rowley Harrison,' Lady Armstrong whispered to Doris.

'The man we saw on stage last night? The man whose donkey … whose donkey, wet the stage?'

'Yes. Now, will you clap?'

And so it was that Doris ended up clapping louder than anyone.

******

Prior to the arrival of his guests, Sir William had instructed Phillips, with the help of Richard and Emma, to rearrange the furniture and seating in the lounge in such a way as to turn the lounge into a theatre. Comfy chairs had been dragged out of alcoves and lined up in rows in front of a grand piano.

In an annex, Mavis – transported from Hood Street for the occasion – served hot sausage rolls and steaming broth in mugs.

Phillips, who'd partaken of the mulled wine, not on the sly (heaven forbid) but to make sure it was not too hot and tasted not too spicy, filled the glasses of Sir William's guests as if he was conducting a symphony orchestra playing an adagio. The butler's flowing gestures reminded Rowley of the gestures of a Spanish sword swallower he'd once appeared with at the Adelphi, Alnwick.

In a corner, waiting to be called if they were needed, Richard and Emma held hands.

'Please feel free to dunk,' said Sir William.

'"Dunk"?' said Henry.

'Before eating your sausage roll, you "dunk" or, if you like, "dip" it into the broth. My mood tonight is euphoric. Let self-indulgence ride roughshod over etiquette. What do you say, Mr Harrison?'

'I'd say, Sir William, if it's good enough for folk doon on the Sandgate, it's good enough for Jesmond.'

'And I'd say, Sir William,' said Jeb, 'if the Armstrong Gun is good enough to be sold to the South … to the slave states … it is good enough to be sold to the North … where slavery is an abomination.'

'In your civil war, gentlemen,' said Sir William, 'England is neutral.'

'With respect, Sir William,' said Henry, 'Mr Phelan and I have it on good authority that Confederate agents are on Tyneside to buy the Armstrong Gun.'

'That is news to me, gentlemen. When Mr Rendel, my sales manager, returns from Paris, I will ask him point blank if he is selling guns to the slave states.'

'And if he is?' said Jeb.

'Gentlemen, with respect, may I remind you … this is a social occasion. It is not a political meeting. Pax Romana. For an hour, minimum, let us draw a red line of demarcation between business and pleasure. We will discuss the delicate question of England's neutrality in your civil war, later, in a civilised manner over cigars and brandy. What do you say, Doris?'

Taking a deep breath, like a pearl diver does before duck diving down three fathoms and eying Jeb and Henry through her lorgnette, Doris said: 'You sold guns to the Russians in the Crimean War. My husband was killed in that war.'

'The charge of the Light Brigade?' said Henry.

'It might have been and, then again, it might not have been. I wasn't there. You are culpable.'

'Not personally, ma'am.'

'Call me Doris but never Dot. I will not be abbreviated.'

Henry forced a smile. Doris was a four decker with open gun ports.

'Doris,' said Lady Armstrong, 'do stop bullying our American guests. You will rust their spurs. An expression, gentlemen, used by the men of the families who lived on the border between Scotland and England in Tudor times. It was their way of telling someone if they did not shut up they would kill them. My husband's family come from such stock.'

'My family, Mr Adams, Mr Phelan, were not dukes and lords. They were cattle thieves and burners of villages.'

'That makes you very American, Sir William,' said Jeb.

'I think, Sir William,' said Henry, 'you have more of the New World in you than you have of the Old World.'

'Thank you, gentlemen. I will take that as a compliment.'

'Mr Harrison is tuning up,' said Meggie.

'A musician tuning up is like a dinner gong,' said Doris. 'If one doesn't get to the dinner table on time there may be nothing left to eat. When I get the chance I will compliment Mr Harrison on his donkey wetting the stage.' To Jeb and Henry: 'I did not mean to give offence, gentlemen. Am I forgiven?'

Jeb and Henry bowed. Jeb smiled. Henry kept a straight face.

'I am a patriot, gentlemen. I love my country as much as I loved my dear departed. He who died in the Crimean War. I am but recently out of weeds. If you have experienced grief, you will know it is a chameleon. It comes and goes in all kinds of shapes and disguises; two of which are irritability and intolerance. Mr Phelan, I would be honoured if you would escort me into the lounge.'

'Call me Jeb,' said Jeb.

'Jeb, you may link me. When one has a choice of escorts I always say, choose a musician. Do be careful your banjo does me no damage. I am a Ming vase on a pedestal, not a croquet ball to be whacked through a hoop.'

'It is an honour to escort the widow of a hero of the charge of the Light Brigade. Perhaps later you will permit me to play my instrument.'

'You wish to strum for me?'

'I do, Doris. We have much in common.'

'Do we?'

'As you grieve for your husband, I grieve for my fellow Americans who are slaves. My passion is to set them free. My passion and my banjo playing are out of place in polite society.'

'Not out of place in my house,' said Sir William.

'Your hand, Mr Adams,' said Meggie. 'I do believe I can hear Mr Harrison gargling.'

Henry wanted to tell Lady Armstrong to call him 'Henry'. He just couldn't bring himself to do it. He was an 'Adams'; the son of America's legate to this snooty island. He had status. He wasn't a turnip in a field.

****

Rowley eyed the audience the way a collier after eight hours underground blinks at the sun.

Sir William and his guests were in the comfy seats at the front of the ad hoc stage. Richard and Emma and other servants hovered in the background.

A captive audience. A guaranteed remittance. No fear of being hit in the eye with an orange. He enjoyed the intimacy of soirees. He put to the back of his mind the deal he'd done with Jeb and Mr Adams. If the Confederates did come, would there be a fight? Surely not. Jesmond was not the Sandgate.

In particular he eyed Edwin Wakefield, his prospective brother-in-law. Fancy bringing a carrier pigeon to a soiree. Edwin was not as respectable as he made himself out to be.

'Ladies and gentlemen,' said Rowley, 'I was on Tynemouth beach the other day. My fiancée, Annie, and I had taken the train there, aal the way from Newcastle. I was keen to show her my prowess at rowing. So, we hired a rowing boat. The lad doing the renting out said that as I was from Newcastle he'd not charge me full price. I would have none of it. I was showing off, see,' giving Edwin Wakefield the eye. 'I wanted Annie to know she was out with a bloke with money. I got the boat at half price because I charged him for this song. My songs are like travelling First Class on the railway, they divent … begging the company's pardon … they don't come cheap.'

Picking up his violin and playing an introduction, Rowley sang, in a fine baritone, a song about a man who could get no sleep because his child was cutting its teeth. It was humorous and as it had a happy ending it made everyone clap and smile.

'Do you know a sad song, Rowley?' said Jeb. 'A song that will help me remember my people are slaves.'

'I nar … I beg your pardon, Sir William … ladies … I am forgetting the company I am in. I know a sad song about a keel man who lost his wife. Would that, yuh nar … you know … fit the bill … be appropriate?'

'I will know if it's a good, sad song,' said Doris, 'if it makes me cry. You see, Mr Harrison …'

'Call me Rowley.'

'That, Mr Harrison, would make you and my good self, familiars. You are encouraging me to be naughty. We are a long way from London but in my short life … I am not as old as I look … I have found that scandal sticks. I once had the temerity to call Lord Palmerston "Pam". Such a ladies' man. And do you know what? He gave me a kiss … cheek not lips. And winked at me. He thought I was egging him on. As if I would. William … Meggie, how many small brandies have I had?'

'Enough, my dear Doris,' said Sir William, 'to make you a most delightful companion.'

'I am not tipsy?'

'You are merry.'

'When I am "merry", I gossip. Am I naughty? Being "naughty" eases my grief.'

'The way paper soaked in vinegar eases tight fitting shoes,' said Rowley.

'Mr Harrison … Rowley, if your comparison was an arrow fired from a longbow it would have hit the target … but sadly, not the bull. William, my darling, if you don't mind I'll have another brandy. What the hell? That's what my beloved used to say. I am three hundred miles from London. I have heard rumours about our Queen and a Scotsman called Brown. Mr Harrison … Rowley, I do declare you are a flirt. You have a twinkle in your eye.'

'I have a spinning bowler hat as well.'

'If you were a meal … Rowley, your sad song would be my main course and your spinning bowler hat, my dessert. If it is a good, sad song it will make me cry. You see, Rowley, though I am not wearing weeds, I am still, in my heart, a widow in mourning. My husband … my dear Charles was taken from me by war … the Crimean War.'

'Ah!' exclaimed Rowley. 'The charge of the Light Brigade.'

'Charles's passion was for horses.'

To show she'd been ambushed by powerful emotions, she wept into an antimacassar.

'There! There!' said Meggie, removing the soaked antimacassar from Doris's trembling hands the way a doctor removes a blood-soaked bandage from a wound.

'Where's Romeo-Richard? Origami would help. No, I do not need smelling salts.'

Rowley, not knowing the word 'origami' but knowing it sounded like 'Harry Gimme' – a Turkish strong man he'd worked with at Sunderland Empire – looked around for a servant twirling a dumbbell. Harry's catchphrase had been 'Gimme' when he'd wanted an iron bar to bend into the shape of a horseshoe.

'Mr Harrison … Rowley,' continued Doris, 'I want to hear a sad song. Rowley, make me bubble. A good cry makes me feel better.'

Rowley was a professional. He prided himself on having a song, a joke for every occasion. Tell me a joke, Rowley, about a cauliflower … not a problem.

'This song,' said Rowley, 'is aal about a keel man who has lost his wife … his missus … his good woman … the love of his life … his bonny lass.'

Rowley picked up his fiddle. He closed his eyes. He composed himself. He concentrated. The 'wife' from London was 'way ower the top'. She would need more than an antimacassar for the tears he was going to make her shed.

He took his time. Divent rush. Build up the suspense. On his fiddle he played … by way of tuning his ear … the opening bars of the sad song he was going to sing.

'Shall I go on?' he asked Doris as her sobs drowned out his playing.

'No … yes. Please continue. I am not a spoilsport. I refuse to let my grief spoil the evening. I am an English woman. I have a backbone. I have ridden to hounds with Mr Trollope. I know Lord Palmerston … Mr Disraeli … not intimately but I do know them. Pray continue, Mr Harrison.'

'Are you sure?' said Rowley.

'Mr Harrison, do not nag … sing your song. What do you say, Mr Wakefield?'

'I agree with you, ma'am.'

'You are not married, Mr Wakefield?'

'Never found a filly who fancied me.'

'I am a widow.'

'I am a bachelor.'

'Confirmed or are you waiting for your tide to come in?'

'I am not Charles the second, ma'am.'

'And I am not Nell Gwyn. What a naughty man you are, Mr Wakefield, to suggest such a thing. You have a twinkle in your eye. I do believe you are a heart breaker. I apologise … hiccup … grief and brandy make me loquacious and flirtatious. William, Meggie, I do hope you have not invited Mr Wakefield to the soiree on the chance that he and I might become an item.'

'I invited Edwin to the soiree,' said Sir William, 'to thank him for the clocks he has provided for my engineering works at Elswick.'

'Bachelors know nothing of grief.'

'I'll have you know, ma'am,' said Edwin, 'that when Penelope died, I shed buckets of tears.'

'Penelope? A sister? Girlfriend?'

'A racing pigeon, ma'am. I breed them.'

'Doris,' said Lady Armstrong, 'Mr Harrison is coughing.'

'He has a cold?'

'He is hinting he wishes to sing his sad song.'

'Get on with it, Rowley. Where's my antimacassar?'

A few weeks ago he'd sang this song at the Music Hall in Collingwood Street. Not a dry eye in the house. There'd been so much watta on the floor folk had joked the Tyne had burst its quays; that the toon was Venice and its streets were canals.

He took a deep breath. His target was the 'gobby wife' from London. Looking straight at her, he sang:

'I have no one to look after and kiss

The missus is a terrible miss

It's like losing inside your head

An arm and a leg

It's the first time in fifty years

I've slept diagonal in the double bed.
Space I don't need. Space I divent want.
Please God fill it up again with wor lass
A bed without her is an empty glass … an empty glass.'
The wife … the lady from London was blubbing like a babbling brook. The song had gotten to her the way fog makes yuh cough.

Folk's emotions were sheets on a hospital bed. To stop the patient falling out they were tucked in tight. His job was to help the patient kick herself free. But playing with folk's emotions was like smoking a pipe in a gunpowder factory. You had to be careful. You had to judge your audience the way the iron man at Hawks's knew when to pour the iron just by looking at its colour.

To keep folk's emotions aal tingly you had to use the whip and the feather. After the sour cherry of a sad song you gave them the sweet plum of humour. You took them into your heart and told them a story.

'Aye!' said Rowley. 'The keel man missed his wife. When it was dark he'd sit by his fireside and talk to her. He'd tell her, 'I wish you were here, my dear. But you are not. Give me a ghostly sign, my dear; that you are here. Light the gas in the middle of the night … dear me, if you did I'd get such a fright.'

Without being asked, Jeb played mournful chords on his banjo.

'The keel man liked it best,' continued Rowley, indicating to Jeb by a slight raising of his eyebrows, that more mournful chords would be welcome … background music was aalways a help … 'when he fell asleep and in his dreams thought his missus was still alive' (plangent chords from Jeb) 'When he woke up the keel man aalways said: "When I wake up, it's like ganin … going for a plodge in the sea at Cullercoats. The water is cold and crabs bite your toes." That's the keel man's song.'

Doris was in a dreadful state. She was sniffing, smiling and bubbling all at the same time. She was one of those days in May, when, in the space of an hour, it rains, hails, snows and the sun shines.

Everyone was clapping when Phillips entered.

'What is it?' said Sir William.

'Your American guests are here, sir.'

'Mr Phelan and Mr Adams are my American guests.'

'I know, sir.'

'Mr Phelan … Mr Adams, do you know if there are any of your compatriots in Newcastle?'

'I suspect, Sir William,' said Henry, 'they are the agents the Secessionist states have sent over to England to buy the Armstrong Gun.'

'They are your enemies?'

'They are.'

'For personal reasons, Sir William,' said Jeb, 'I wish to meet these slave owners. I promise you their blood will not stain your carpet. To show you my good faith I give you my Colt. If they are armed and wish to blow out my brains I will not stop them.'

'Mr Phelan,' said Doris, 'Mr Harrison's sad song made me weep. The sight of that firearm is close to making me faint. Do all Americans carry guns the way English men carry snuff boxes?'

'America is a new country, ma'am,' said Jeb. 'It is a wild country. It is full of coyotes, bears and rattlesnakes.'

'And Confederate rebels,' said Henry.

'An American has the right to bear arms. With your permission, Sir William, I'd like to meet my fellow countrymen. Where are they?'

'Phillips?' said Sir William.

'The gentlemen are in the lobby, sir.'

'Confederate agents are not gentlemen,' said Henry.

'They are slave owners,' said Jeb. 'I hate them.'

'Yet, you wish to meet them,' said Sir William.

'For personal reasons, Sir William.'

'They gave me your card, sir,' said, Phillips.

'How the devil did they get that? The time for guests to arrive has been altered … why?'

'Begging your pardon, Sir William,' said Rowley, 'I gave it to them … I was under instruction.'

'Who was instructing you?'

'I'm not allowed to say, sir.'

'I gave him the order,' said Jeb.

'Why?'

'I wished to meet my fellow countrymen on neutral territory.'

'You have taken advantage of my hospitality.'

'For that, Sir William, I apologise. My excuse … a civil war makes good manners obsolete.'

'Sir William,' said Henry, 'Jeb wishes to confront the Confederate agents for personal reasons … on neutral territory.'

'Mr Harrison,' said Sir William, turning to Rowley and handing him the Colt Jeb had handed him for safe keeping during the proposed parley, 'drop it in a bucket of water.'

'By which, sir, you mean, for me to put it somewhere safe … am I reet?'

Sir William nodded that that was exactly what he'd meant.

'Behind the aspidistra looks a good place to me,' said Rowley. 'When you see a conjuror on stage with an aspidistra you can be sure it's hiding a rabbit.'

'Sir William, I apologise for bringing the American Civil War into your lounge,' said Jeb. 'It is an unforgivable breach of bad manners.'

'Jeb,' said Henry, 'allow Sir William to show us the back door and let us skedaddle back to the Old George.'

'No. I want to meet these agents. I want to meet them on grounds of my own choosing. I wish to ambush them not with guns but with truth. It is a great liberty, I know, Sir William, but would you be able to provide me with a room for such a meeting to take place? When two slave owners see a black man, they will not be drawn to applause, they will want to clap me in irons. I will use my banjo as Orpheus used his harp. I will strum it not to bring Eurydice back from the dead, but to resurrect in the soul of Jeb Montague Prior memories of a time when he had a baby daughter. A daughter he loved before she committed the crime of falling in love with a slave. Sir William, I have reason to believe one of the Confederate agents is my grandfather. I wish to confront him.

I wish to confront the man my mother says had my father murdered. I ask you, Sir William, do you have a room where I may meet, face to face with these agents, one of whom is more than likely my grandfather?'

'Phillips, take Mr Phelan to the parlour. Take him there via the kitchen; that way, Mr Phelan, you will not have to go through the lobby. When Phillips has reported back that you are ensconced and ready to look them in the eye, I will usher them into the parlour.'

'Thank you for your understanding in this matter, Sir William. It is much appreciated. I give you my word that my meeting with these agents will not lead to bloodshed. When your butler shows the Confederates into the room I will be playing my banjo. If one of the Confederate agents is my grandfather, he will recognise the tune I will be playing. It's a song my mother taught me. It's the song she said her father played and sang to her when she was a child.'

'Is it a sad song?' said Doris.

'It is a song slaves sing to help them forget.'

'To forget what?' said Doris.

'To forget, madam,' said Jeb, 'the pain and anguish of their slavery.'

'Sorry,' said Doris, 'you must remember, young man, I am a freeborn Englishwoman. I know nothing about slavery. You must also remember, young man, that I am on your side. William, if you allow your sales manager to sell guns to the slave states you will not be doing God's will. You will be doing the devil's work. I feel faint.'

'Smelling salts,' said Maggie, 'where are they?'

'I don't want smelling salts. I need Mr Phelan's Colt. I want to give it to the Confederate agents, right between the eyes. I have shot grouse. If you can shoot grouse you can shoot Confederate agents.'

'Doris, calm down,' urged Meggie. 'If you get over excited you will faint. Have another brandy.'

'I do not need a restorative. I want everyone in the world to be as free as I am … regardless of the colour of their skin.'

'Doris,' said Jeb, 'if I may address you familiarly by your Christian name, I appreciate the fervour with which you support the abolition of slavery, but I do not want your over excitement for that cause to damage your health. If you were to shoot these agents, you might be hung for murder.'

'Mitigating circumstances,' said, Doris. 'Folk in England who have kissed Lord Palmerston do not hang. My position in society puts me above the law.'

'Origami,' said Meggie.

'What about it?'

'Paper folding will calm you down.'

'I'd rather have a brandy.'

'What about a brandy and paper folding?'

'Like wearing braces and a belt? My late husband always wore braces and a belt … such an anxious man. I loved him. I loved him as much as I hate Confederate agents … slavers … rule Britannia. Jeb … Mr Phelan, you go and do what you have to do. When you are about it never forget if you need help you just have to holler. When we hear your "holler" your reserves will charge to your rescue. That's how Wellington won at Waterloo … I met him when I was a child … all I remember about him is his hooked nose. He hid his "reserves" from Napoleon the way smugglers hide brandy from the excise. To horse, Jeb! To horse! Off you go.'

'Phillips, take Mr Phelan to the parlour via the kitchen.'

'And me,' said Henry. 'There are two of them. Two against one is not fair. Jeb, I insist I go with you. When they look an Adams in the eye they will know with whom they are dealing.'

'No,' said Jeb, 'you, Henry, will be my reserve witness, If I am killed it will be on your shoulders to tell my mother … your father killed his grandson.'

'This way, sir,' said Phillips. 'When we are gannin through the kitchen be careful yuh divent get flour on your frock coat.'

As Phillips and Jeb left, Sir William said: 'I will welcome these agents into my home the way I welcomed clients when I was a solicitor … with a certain hint that I am a representative of the majesty of the law. I will explain there has been a mix up; that their invitation to dine at my table is a counterfeit. That, events out of my control have led to this confusion.'

'Rowley … Mr Harrison,' said Doris, 'retrieve the Colt from behind the aspidistra. I don't trust Americans. Stand guard behind the parlour door. If you hear shouting burst in and shoot the slavers between the eyes. Taking away a man's freedom makes me bloodthirsty.'

'I've never fired a gun in my life,' said Rowley.

'You are an actor … all you have to do is act as if you know what you are doing. Point the gun at them and say Bang!'

'Doris,' said Meggie, 'do not incite Mr Harrison to violence. If he was to kill the Confederate agents, he would hang.'

'Do you not know Lord Palmerston?' said Doris.

Rowley shook his head. Having orange peel tossed at yuh on a Friday night at the Grande Byker was nowt compared to being told to point a loaded gun at Confederate agents.

'A compromise,' said Sir William, retrieving the Colt from behind the aspidistra. 'I will take out its cartridges, see? The Colt is now unloaded. It may be used as a club but not as a firearm. Mr Harrison–' handing Rowley the Colt– 'by all means stand guard outside the parlour. If you hear raised voices by all means rush in and point the gun at the Confederates. I will be by your side.'

'I'm coming with you, William,' said Meggie.

'And so am I,' said Doris. 'Do you know Origami, Mr Harrison?'

'I knew his mother,' said Rowley.

'A witty answer, Mr Harrison, does not hide ignorance. Your humour, however, makes you acceptable company.'

'Can you speak Geordie?'

'Certainly not! Why should I want to?'

'Let me teach you.'

'Gan on then!' Looking pleased with herself. 'You see, Mr Harrison, I have an ear for languages. I speak French.'

******

On his way to the lobby to meet the Confederate agents, Sir William marvelled at the thought of Doris … posh Doris … she who had dined with royalty … learning the Tyneside dialect. What stories she'd have to tell of the wild north when she returned to London.

What sort of people would these Confederate agents turn out to be? Would they be aggressive? The Americans he'd met in London had all thought very highly of themselves. Should he warn them that in his parlour a Union spy was waiting to meet them? His heart and soul were against slavery. Yet, the businessman in him saw nothing wrong with selling them weapons of war. If he didn't, someone else would.

'Good evening, gentlemen,' said Sir William. 'I do apologise for keeping you waiting. I fear there has been a mix-up. I am Sir William and you are?'

'Jeb Montague Prior,' said the older American.

'Francois Lafayette,' said the younger man, bowing. 'I don't understand what you mean, Sir William, about a mix-up. You were kind enough to invite us to your soiree and we are here.'

'The history of your invitation is,' said Sir William, 'how shall I put it? Ambiguous.'

'As is England's so-called neutrality in the American civil war,' said Lafayette. 'Sir William, let me remind you that Mr Prior and I have a contract with your sales agent to buy the Armstrong Gun. As I speak, Mr Rendell is in Paris cashing in our bonds. You have our money. All you have to do, Sir William, is turn a blind eye when a keel boat, tonight, loaded with guns leaves your Elswick works and is met at Tynemouth by a Confederate warship. All under cover of darkness. You will be richer and the cause of the Secessionist states will be stronger. Cotton is king, Sir William. Don't you go forgetting that.'

To show he meant business Lafayette let Sir William see the butts of two Colt revolvers. They were crossed, in his waistband, the way Black Beard the pirate would have carried them.

While Sir William – awed by this display of fire power – was wondering what to do, there came through the closed parlour door the faint but unmistakable sound of someone playing a banjo.

'I know that tune,' said Jeb Montague Prior. 'Who is behind that door, Sir William? I demand to know. I know that tune.'

'The door is not locked,' said Sir William. 'Open it and find out. Please, gentlemen … no shooting. Newcastle is not the American frontier. I suppose, sir,' to Lafayette, 'it would be pointless to ask you to hand me your weapons for safe keeping?'

'It would.'

'Who the hell is playing that god damned tune? It's plucking at my heart strings. It's taking me back to happier times. It's making me forget I am at war. It makes me feel I am more of a parent than a warrior. I'm going in. I want to know who the hell is breaking my heart playing that tune.'

When the two Confederate agents entered the parlour, Sir William heard Lafayette say: 'Mon dieu! A black man. Why ain't you in chains? You a runaway?'

Back in the lounge Sir William told Richard: 'It would seem, Richard, my Americans are not your Americans.'

'No, sir.'

'As the steam locomotive has made it possible to travel from Newcastle to London in four hours, the steam ship has enabled Americans to cross the Atlantic in days rather than in weeks. Do you know what a monsoon is, Richard?'

'Yes, sir, a down pouring of heavy rain.'

'It is indeed, Richard. What I am wondering is … is it possible to have a monsoon of Americans?'

'It's looking that way, sir.'

'Indeed it is, Richard. Ladies, Edwin, my American guests have given me their word that they will be on their best behaviour. I am fearful that passion for their cause will make them eschew their oath. It is quite possible they will not behave like gentlemen. Richard, I want you to go to Pilgrim Street police station. Explain the situation and ask for reinforcements. Phillips …'

'Sor?'

'Get Richard a horse.'

'I'll get Jimmy to put him on Dobbbin, sor.'

'Dobbin … the cart horse? We need Richard to reach the police station today, not tomorrow.'

'A nar what yuh means, sir, but there's method in me madness. The polis station is next to a brewery. Dobbin used to be a dray horse. That brewery is his aad haem. If he thinks he's ganin haem for molasses, he'll gallop there like the favourite a backed at Hexham did last week.'

'You'd put money on him?'

'I would, sir.'

'Well done, Phillips. Off you go.'

'Thankee kindly, sir. If yuh want me to bash these Americans' heeds in, sir, divent be frightened to ask. It'll be a change from showing off me strength by pulling out nails with me teeth.'

'You can pull out nails with your teeth?' said Doris.

'Yes, ma'am.'

'If Phillips was my butler,' said Doris, 'I'd let him loose on those Americans. I would.'

'Doris,' said Meggie, 'circumstances are making you bloodthirsty. William, what should we do?'

'I suggest we sit outside the parlour and wait. If we hear shouting, gun shots …'

'Gun shots?' said Doris.

'One of the Americans has two Colts.'

'A two Colt American! Mr Harrison … Rowley … reload the Colt.'

'I refuse to allow that,' said Sir William. 'None of us are familiar with handguns … a Colt is a powerful weapon. A ricochet from one of its bullets might kill us. Phillips …'

'Sor?'

'When you have Richard mounted on Dobbin, I want you to stand guard at the front gate. When Richard returns with the police, bring them to join us outside the parlour. What we do after that depends on how these Americans behave … Doris, what are you doing with that poker?'

'I'm arming myself.'

'Put it down.'

'I'll not be disarmed.'

'What about swapping the poker for a large brandy and warm water?'

'You know my weaknesses … you know my weaknesses.'

'Why don't we all have a brandy before we take up our siege outside the parlour? In the absence of Phillips, I'll do the honours.'

'Mr Harrison … Rowley,' said Doris, 'while William pours us fortifiers … make us laugh … amuse us.'

'I was courting this lass called Pal,' said Rowley. 'I was showing off to her like Phillips was when he said he could pull out nails with his teeth. I told her I was a draughtsman at Stevenson's factory. She says: "Rowley, what do you draw?" A passer-by with big lugs … ears, ma'am … said: "He draws the bogey round the yard".'

When Doris did not laugh, Rowley was puzzled.

'Is that it?' said Doris. 'I have a draughtsman at home. In winter it is his job to place bolsters under doors. I hate draughts. Thank you, William,' accepting a brandy.

CONFRONTATION

On the night they'd been ambushed the Coxons had reported back to the Confederate agents. They'd told Jeb Montague Prior and Francois Lafayette that the American who'd taken pot shots at them was a man of colour.

These owners of bellum mansions had been forewarned. They should have been prepared. But, they weren't. The reality of seeing a man of colour dressed as a gentleman made them bristle.

The black man with the banjo was tall, young and well dressed. Lafayette, who was a bit of a dandy, was certain he recognised the style of the New York tailor who'd cut the black man's coat and trousers. Before the civil war it had been his tailors. He was sure of it. Was it possible that he and the banjo player had the same tailor?

It was an aberration for them to be dealing with a man of colour on equal terms. It made them feel hot under the collar. Looking at this black man dressed as a gentleman flared their prejudices the way one of the new Lucifer matches flared when you dragged it over emery paper.

Jeb Montague Prior looked at the man of colour and found himself, much to his surprise, thinking he was looking at his daughter. He was looking at a sunrise he couldn't believe he was seeing. Could it be? No … it couldn't. Yet … yet there was something … he couldn't put his finger on it … about the well-dressed man of colour that reminded him of his daughter. How could a coloured man look like your white daughter?

Jeb was well aware that if the two men had had bull whips, they'd have flayed him alive. He just knew that was what they wanted to do.

To break the impasse, he again strummed the song his mother had sung to him when he was a child … the song his mother's father … his grandfather, had sung to his mother when she was a child.

He was now more certain than ever that the old man staring at him was, indeed, his maternal grandfather. The white-haired Confederate agent looked like his mother. Furthermore, the tune he was playing was making this old man look as if a bucket of ice cold water was been poured over him. It was making the old man tremble. It was draining the blood from his face. Or, something was.

The tune was getting to Jeb Montague Prior the way drizzle, after an hour, penetrates a waterproof ulster. It was getting to him the way a mouse, over a long period of time – but this time in under a minute – is able to gnaw down an oak tree. It was getting to him the way sunshine melts a block of ice. He did not wish to thaw … no, sir, he did not. The white man was superior to the black man. That was a … fact. He belonged to the New World … the can-do world. He believed that when Pennsylvania Avenue was finished it would make England's Mall look like the back lane of a west end slum. A curse on the 'Peculiar Institution'. A curse on Abraham Lincoln. A curse on this civil war.

He loved that tune. It made him forget the civil war. It was a lullaby. A sad, sleepy, lullaby; with it he'd sung his daughter to sleep … many, many times. It was the song his daughter's wet nurse had sung to his daughter after his wife had died in childbirth … his daughter … his dear daughter … the daughter he loved but who did not love him … the daughter who had fled north to escape his wrath when she had fallen in love with Abraham, one of his black slaves. Southern belle society did not approve of interbreeding between slaves and their masters. What an understatement that was. A glorious understatement … like calling an erupting volcano a log fire. To save face he'd not disputed the rumour that his daughter had been raped. Without her knowing it he'd facilitated her flight to New York. By back door methods … contacts he had in Boston and New York … he knew he had a mixed-race grandson. He knew his daughter had married a wealthy, Irish, New

York businessman. He knew his grandson's name was Jeb Prior Phelan. His daughter had not forgotten her roots. She had named her love child after her father. When he had first heard this, he had wept.

He knew … he knew his daughter had not been raped … her crime was falling in love with a black slave. Why, oh why could she not have fallen in love with a free, white man?

The tune was resurrecting emotions he had, for years, kept locked away. He knew they were there. He knew he had not destroyed them. But as long as they were under lock and key months could pass without him thinking about them. How could a simple tune … a lullaby, played on a banjo … be the cause of releasing demons? The lullaby was a jailor with a skeleton key capable of unlocking every padlocked dungeon in his subconscious mind. He didn't feel well. Why was he sweating?

The Union agent playing the banjo … the black man playing the banjo … he found this hard to admit … unbelievably hard to even think about admitting … the black man playing the banjo looked like his daughter. The possibility that circumstances … circumstances he could never have foreseen … had brought him face to face with his grandson began to assert themselves the way a spider, ever so slowly, begins the long process of spinning a web.

The lullaby was overwhelming him the way the Mississippi in flood overflows its levees. He didn't feel too good. He believed in slavery … didn't he? The 'Peculiar Institution' kept the price of cotton low. Cotton was 'king'.

He loved his bellum mansion … his gardens full of magnolias. His slaves were wonderful gardeners. How well they looked after his flower beds. Not a weed in sight. His black grandson's black grandfather had been a wonderful gardener until … until, their respective children had fallen in love.

For the umpteenth time … asked many times over many years … Jeb Montague Prior asked himself: why, oh why did my daughter have to fall in love with a slave?

Old Abraham, the father of Byron, the slave who had seduced his daughter … seduced, was that fair? Had his daughter not told him they were in love? Old Abraham had been an excellent servant … an excellent gardener … an excellent polisher of boots. Old Abraham had doted on him. Old Abraham had made sure the frills on 'master's' shirts were the same on both sides of their buttons.

Was it a sin to make another man a slave? He found that question difficult to answer. What he did know was that keeping slaves had given him a wonderfully comfortable way of life. He was loath to lose his creature comforts.

If slavery wasn't wrong, why did slave owners call slavery the 'peculiar institution'? The 'peculiar institution' … a camouflage phrase … a euphemism. A phrase designed to make slavery sound only a little out of the ordinary, like someone seeing a daffodil flowering in England, in August, might say: 'that's peculiar'.

Jeb played the lullaby … a lullaby sung by slaves to their children … a sad, sad, lullaby … without thinking. He was on today what we'd call 'automatic pilot'. If he'd stopped to think he'd have played the wrong notes. In a voice, creaking with emotion, he sang the words to the lullaby his mother had taught him. The old man with white hair looked so like his mother … the resemblance was uncanny. The old man with white hair … he had to be his grandfather. Was he looking at the man who had had his black father murdered?

He knew a lot about his white grandfather; both the good and the bad. His mother had told him her father was the victim of a system. She had told him her father found slavery uncomfortable. But not so uncomfortable, thought Jeb, to support the Union.

The lullaby was overwhelming the emotions of both of them.

As he strummed, Jeb watched the look on his grandfather's face begin, ever so slowly, to turn from one of confrontation to one of bewilderment.

For just about the first time in his life Jeb Montague Prior found himself looking at a black man … a slave … not as an artefact but as a fellow human being. An emotion he did not recognise ... 'reconciliation' ... was taking one of those little hammers confectioners use to break toffee... tap ... tap ... tap, to his prejudices. A lullaby was telling him that all his life he'd been a damn fool.

Jeb stopped playing.

'Good evening, Grandfather.'

The salutation put the sort of startled look on Jeb Montague Prior's face that might be expected to be seen on the face of a man whose horse, instead of neighing, had spoken to him in English.

The more he looked at this black man the more he saw the face of his daughter. He had her eyes. He could not ... would not go to war with his daughter.

'Damn, you! Damn, you!' he exclaimed.

'You recognise the tune, sir?' said Jeb.

'Yes. It was a favourite of my daughter. How'd you come to know it?'

'I think you know how I know it, sir. My mother called the song "Daddy's Lullaby". You sang it to her when she was a child. When I was a child, my mother, your daughter, sang it to me. Will you join me in a duet?'

'Go to hell!'

The old man didn't look well. Jeb wished he'd been a white grandson. If he'd been a white grandson, they'd now be shaking hands and drinking brandy.

Was the white-haired old man ... his maternal grandfather, going to ask for forgiveness? Jeb doubted it ... but one never knew. The old man looked ill.

His mother had told him a lot about this man. If it hadn't been for the 'peculiar institution' he'd have been a good man.

Jeb junior knew a lot more about Jeb senior than the latter knew about him ... or, so Jeb junior thought.

When he looked at the old man ... the man who had made his black father disappear ... more than likely had had him murdered, why was he not looking at a devil? Why didn't his grandfather look evil? Why didn't he have horns? Why did he look like a kind old man? Why did he look so vulnerable? So, run-of-the-mill?

Inside his head Jeb Montague Prior … slave owner, bellum mansion owner … was fighting a war between a nurtured prejudice and an instinctive love of kith and kin.

He did not feel well. He had chest pains. A stabbing pain was shooting down his left arm. That tune … that lullaby, reminded him of happier times. Against his wishes, the lullaby had taken him back to the time of his first marriage; to the time when he was about to become a father for the first time. If only his beloved wife had not died in childbirth. He'd prayed for her not to die. But she had. And prayers could not bring back the dead.

He loved his bellum way of life. Picking cotton was hard work. Who'd do it if he didn't have slaves?

As a slave owner it was impossible for him to admit he had a black grandson. He had done his best to hide his daughter's love affair with a slave. In the slave states no slave owner could admit to his bellum neighbour he'd a black grandson. To have done so would have been social suicide. Worse … he'd have been ostracised; worse still, his social equals would have taken the law into their own hands … he knew that's what they'd have done. They might have horse whipped him.

He didn't think he was a bad man. He treated his slaves pretty well; he'd never forgotten that Abraham – Jeb's black grandfather – had saved his life. If Abraham, at risk to his own life, hadn't pushed him out of the way of runaway horses pulling a carriage, he'd have been trampled to death. He hadn't given Abraham his freedom, but he had done his best to look after him.

He knew his Bible. He wasn't a bad man … 'do to others what you would have them do to you'.

He would have hated for a black man to have made him, a white man, a slave. He could not imagine what it was like not to be free.

Was it a sin to be the owner of slaves? Would he go to Hell when he died? He didn't know.

The young black Yankee, staring at him the way a botanist stares at a rare flower … could he really be his grandson? Was a civil war responsible for bringing them together in a smoky northern town thousands of miles from the New World?

His mouth was dry. He was sweating. If this young man was his grandson, would he be able … be able to bring himself to tell … to confide in him? Damn it! He wasn't going to apologise for loving the bellum way of life. If he didn't have slaves, who would polish his boots? He wasn't a bad man. He wasn't a murderer.

Back home in Virginia everyone knew Jeb Montague Prior had a runaway daughter. When she had disappeared, so too had Byron. Slaves who'd done bad things often disappeared. There was a code. Slave owners stuck together.

His second wife bullied him. When his daughter had fled north she'd said: 'Good riddance!'

'That tune you are playing. I know it. It is called "Mary's Lullaby".'

'That is correct, sir,' said Jeb. 'My mother told me all about Mary.'

'Did she indeed? What did she tell you?'

'She told me, sir, that when her mother … your wife, sir … died in giving birth to my mother, Mary was her wet nurse … as far as my mother was concerned, Mary was her mother. The breasts that suckled my mother, suckled my father. The black man with whom my mother fell in love was Mary's son. Byron, my black father, and my mother … your daughter, sir … were brought up together. They were the same age. They played together. You encouraged their childish companionship. I know you remarried … Grandfather. I know my mother disliked her step-mother.'

'What's my second wife's name?'

'Rose, sir. You see, sir, I know all about you. How much proof do you need to make you accept me for what I am … your grandson? Mother never got on with her step-mother, did she?'

Jeb Montague Prior nodded. He nodded real slow. He wanted to sit down. Pride kept him standing.

'I know your first name is Jeb, sir. So is mine. I am named after you, Grandfather. Your colleague is pointing a Colt at me. Would you countenance the killing of your own flesh and blood?'

'You are a Yankee and a negro. You are the cholera and the plague,' said Lafayette.

'Jeb Montague Prior … Grandfather, do I not look like your daughter?'

'Yes. Damn it! You do!'

'If I was a white grandson and not a grandson of mixed race, I would inherit your plantation?'

'Yes … you would.'

'A man of mixed-race keeping slaves would be a novelty … would it not?'

'That will never happen.'

'Did you have my father murdered? Did you have him whipped? Did you hang him? Was he bludgeoned to death?'

'He raped my daughter.'

'No he didn't … and you know he didn't.'

'How'd you know that?'

'Mother told me. She told me she begged you to be forgiving. Ma loved my pa. My pa loved my mother. They were brought up together … as children they played together. You let them. You encouraged their fraternity. Pa was Mother's servant. Mary was my pa's mother. Abraham was my pa's daddy. Abraham was my black grandfather. You, sir, are my white grandfather. You see, sir, I know all the names of those involved.'

'Shut your mouth, boy,' said Lafayette.

'Don't call me "boy".'

Lafayette's eyes narrowed. Handing Jeb senior a Colt he said: 'Will you blow him away or will I? In our war with the North a grandson is of no more consequence than a fly. You are Yankee trash, boy. Back home in the States we'd be firing muskets at each other.'

To his grandfather, Jeb said: 'You ain't a killer, sir. You and I are kith and kin. Folk don't kill their kin. Why can't you love me the way my ma loved my pa?'

'Love!' expostulated Lafayette. 'Your pa was a slave, boy. Back where I come from, I pay slaves molasses to pick cotton, not to fall in love with white women. It ain't possible … it just, ain't possible for a white woman to fall in love with a Negro. I knows about such things. Everyone in Virginia knows your pa raped your mother. And that, boy, is a fact.'

'Do not call me "boy".'

'Don't you get touchy with me, boy! Are you armed? The Coxons said you were. Put up your arms. Back home I'd have you whipped and put in irons.'

'And what if I refuse? Will you shoot me in cold blood?'

'If your grandfather won't–' cocking his Colt and pointing it at Jeb's head– 'I will. You ain't my grandson. I have no qualms about killing a Union agent.'

'I scared the Coxons,' said Jeb, folding his arms to show he was not going to raise his arms in surrender, 'do I scare you? Scare you so much you'd kill me in cold blood? Are you not forgetting you are guests of Sir William Armstrong?'

'He didn't invite us … we know that now. You did.'

'Look at me, Grandfather,' said Jeb. 'Would you kill in cold blood your own kin? Your own grandson? Do I mean nothing to you? Am I a cotton mouth … a viper to be got rid of to make the plantation safe? What kind of man are you? Do you need spectacles to see I am a human being? What does prejudice make you see? A Mississippi swamp rat? A dangerous alligator? A piece of vermin? Do I scare you, Grandfather? Does an unarmed man scare you? You scared of an unarmed man with his arms folded? Why'd you call slavery the "Peculiar Institution"? That's like calling a viper, a rosebud. Why not call it what it is … slavery. You know what, Grandfather, I'm thinking that, deep, deep, down … somewhere inside that trumpet blowing … ever so proud … Southern bravado, you are, sir, ashamed of yourself. You know slavery is wrong. Worse … you know it to be sinful to keep slaves. That's why you give it a fancy name. The "Peculiar Institution" indeed! How'd you make enough money to build a mansion, Mr Jeb Montague Prior? I owe it all, sir, to the "Peculiar Institution". To join the institution, sir, you have to believe black folk are inferior and don't need liberty. Does it hurt, Mr Jeb Montague Prior, when I call you grandfather? Does my familiarity make you wince? Does it make you want to shoot me? Does it make you feel as I feel when you call me boy? Whether you like it or not, I am your flesh and blood. Prior blood flows through my veins. Look at me. When you look at me you are looking in a mirror. You see yourself. You see your ancestors. You see your daughter. You see your late wife. Shoot me.'

'Don't provoke me, boy.'

'I am not your boy! You, sir, are my maternal grandfather. Abraham and Mary were my black paternal grandparents. Abraham polished your boots. He was your personal slave.'

Jeb ached to hear the old man say: 'I love you'.

'Ma told me, Abraham was vain about his looks. He didn't want to be whipped. He didn't want a scarred back. You see, Grandfather, sir, I know all about the bellum way of life. Ma told me it was lovely for white folk but hell for black folk.'

Jeb paused. The Colt, the old man … his grandfather … was pointing at him, was wavering all over the place.

The flesh and blood man in front of him was a stranger. Yet he knew so much about him.

More confusing still, this flesh and blood man, didn't look like a villain … the village bad guy … the spiteful peasant who poisoned the village well. He didn't look like a man who owned slaves.

'Ma told me, sir, that things changed when you remarried. For better or worse, sir, you took a new wife. Your new wife, my step-grandmother, sir, was a new broom. Ma told me you let her have all her own way. She had Abraham demoted from butler to cotton picker. She had my ma's wet nurse, my black grandmother, scrubbing floors. I don't like thinking of her having to do that.'

A tear rolled down Jeb Montague Prior's left cheek.

'If you know so much, tell me, what was your black father called?'

'I've told you, sir … his name, sir, was Byron.'

'Yes, that was his name. In my way I was fond of him. Byron … dear Byron. He laughed at my jokes. I told him and your mother fairy stories. In one of them the Mississippi was a brown god … a brown god. What colour was the porch ceiling where Mary sang that lullaby you just played?'

'Blue, sir. To keep evil spirits away.'

'That's right … blue. Looking at you, young man, I am reminded of the faces of those I once loved. I see my daughter. I see my wife … my dead wife.'

'You are, sir, admitting, I am your grandson?'

'You presume too much, boy. You are a black man.'

'Half a black man, Grandfather … and do not call me "boy". I am not one of your black slaves. I am your grandson.'

'So you say.'

'Look at me! Look at me! Look me in the eye. Tell me again what I remind you of. If you were not prejudiced against black people, you would see your grandson, sir. I knows you would.'

'You stir deep emotions in me, young man.'

'Call me Grandson …'

'I can't do that …'

'Your estranged daughter loves you. My mother, sir, loves you.'

'Does she indeed!'

'Yes, she does. To get me to sleep when I was young she told me stories about you … about the bellum way of life … about my black grandparents.'

'What was your black grandfather's name?'

'I've told you, sir … Abraham, sir. He was your butler. He was six-foot three inches tall. He had a limp … a limp caused by being shackled too tight in the slave ship that had brought him, all unwilling, all the way from Africa to America. He was from the Yoruba tribe. Am I right, sir? Is my knowledge not proof I am your grandson?'

'You know more about Abraham than I do … yes, he was tall … yes, he had a limp. He was limping when I bought him … got him cheap because of the limp. Never knew he was from the Yoruba tribe … or the cause of his limp. His job was to wait at table … my table. His job was to make my home run smooth. His job was to be the blinkered donkey that worked the gin.'

'The donkey was called "Western".'

'How'd you know that?'

'I told you, sir. I am your grandson. My mother told me.'

'What was special about "Western"?'

'Before he was put to working the gin, he was Mother's pet.

'My daughter's pet, you mean.'

'Your daughter … my mother … we speak, sir, of the same person. We love, sir, the same person.'

'My daughter …'

'My mother …'

'If you say so. My daughter committed an unforgivable sin. Circumstances beyond my control forced me to allow her to be removed from my life. She means nothing to me.'

'If you no longer love her, sir … if she means nothing to you … why, in your renunciation of her, do you tremble? Why does the blood drain from your face?'

'Damn you, Jeb Prior Phelan … damn you for being born.'

'Love brought me into this world, Grandfather … is that wrong?'

'It is impossible for a free white woman to love a slave. Slaves should fall in love with other slaves …they should never fall in love with a free white woman. Slaves clean my boots. Slaves saddle my horse. I use slaves the way I use knives and forks. Slaves are utensils. Slaves are sails on a sailing ship. They are not the wind. I … I am the wind.'

'It is your fault, sir, my mother … your daughter, fell in love with my father … a black slave.'

'Who told you such nonsense?'

'My mother.'

'My daughter told you that?'

'Yes.'

'So, it is my fault my daughter went behind the wood shed and did things she wasn't supposed to do before she was wed … ridiculous.'

'When they were children you were happy for them to play together.'

'They were the same age. Your father was her personal slave. He pulled her round the estate in a baby chariot. He was meant to be her property, not her lover.'

'Ma has told me, sir, that when you remarried, you changed. Did grief, sir, at losing your wife … my white grandmother, make you bitter?'

'Steady, boy! Don't you go raking over them ashes … get too personal and I'll blow your brains out.'

'You got wax in your ears, sir? For the umpteenth time, I'm telling you … I ain't your "boy". I am your grandson … call me "Jeb" … call me "Prior" … call me "Phelan" … but do not call me "boy".'

The young man's defence of his status … his willingness to stand up and fight, reminded Jeb Montague Prior of himself. He couldn't understand the part of himself that this pleased. He was fighting prejudice. Prejudice didn't fight fair. Prejudice poked you in the eye … twisted your nose … kicked you where it hurt. Sometimes you didn't know you were prejudiced. Sometimes you didn't know who or what you were fighting. You found it hard to differentiate between friend and foe. Was it possible for custom and habit to make an evil … slavery … a fact of nature … like … rain is wet and the sun is hot? He didn't know. He was staring at the sun. 'Truth' was the sun and it was blinding him. His eyes were hurting.

'Ma told me, sir,' continued Jeb, 'she and her step-mother didn't much like each other.'

'True … true,' said Jeb Montague Prior.

He didn't feel well. What he was hearing was confusing him. What he was hearing had picked him up, turned him upside down and was shaking him violently by the legs. His bellum way of life was no more than a pocketful of nickels. His beloved way of life was being shaken out of him the way coins fall out of pockets.

'Ma's step-mother … your second wife, sir … she didn't like Ma being friendly with Byron … my pa. But you see, sir, Ma liked Byron, and Byron liked my ma. They liked being together. When they were children they'd played hopscotch together. When they were babes in arms their difference in colour hadn't count for much. They were children in the Garden of Eden before Adam ate the apple. I ask you, sir … Grandfather … is it a crime for a man and a woman to fall in love? Shoot me! You … my own grandfather and people like you, have made me weary of life. Steam … sail back to Atlanta … feel proud. Puff out your chest. Proclaim: "For my cause I have purchased one hundred Armstrong Guns. For the cause of the "Peculiar Institution" I murdered my grandson in cold blood".'

Jeb's outburst acted upon his grandfather the way resuscitation revives a man on the cusp of passing over to the other side.

'They were in love,' sighed Jeb Montague Prior. 'They were in love. To stop them falling in love would have been like trying to make the Mississippi flow north. They were "star crossed lovers".'

'Love!' exploded Lafayette. 'Your daughter was raped. All of Virginia knows she was raped. If you won't shut this uppity boy up, I will. I ain't your grandfather, boy–' cocking the Colt he was holding and pointing it at this uppity black man who claimed kinship with Jeb Montague Prior.

AS IN ORIGAMI PAPER CAN BE FOLDED TO MAKE AN ARMSTRONG GUN, OUR STORY IS NOW FOLDED TO A CONCLUSION.

What was taking place in the parlour between Jeb Montague Prior, Jeb Prior Phelan and Francois Lafayette was the New World.

In the lobby, outside the closed parlour door, the Old World was biting its nails. It was pondering whether or not to stay put or to burst into the parlour and find out what the hell was going on.

Doris sat in a straight backed chair, sipping a brandy and ginger ale.

'Waft me,' she told Emma, 'in this situation my fan is useless. I need air … waft me.'

Emma obliged by wafting a tea towel in Doris's face the way Apaches use a buffalo skin to make smoke signals.

Edwin Wakefield, as a clock maker, eased his uneasiness at what might be going on inside the parlour, by exploring the innards of a grandmother clock; looking at its cogs, pulleys and wheels took him for a walk in Saltwell Park.

To control her anxiety, Meggie screwed the top on and off a bottle of smelling salts.

Sir William told Richard: 'The old stone bridge, Richard … it has to go.'

'Yes, sir.'

'Progress is a galloping horse, Richard. I do hope those Americans in there are being sensible.'

To pass the 'waiting time', Phillips was testing the patience of the three policemen Richard had commandeered from Pilgrim Street police station. He wanted them to tap him on the heed with their truncheons.

'Gan on … divent be scared. You'll dee nee harm. Me and lignum vitae have the same mother and fatha.'

Rowley and Henry stood, staring at the closed parlour door, either side of a potted fern standing on top of a tripod pedestal.

Every so often, Sir William advised everyone to be patient.

The waiting ended when there was an almighty bang and a bullet splintered its way through the closed parlour door. The bullet's ricochet smashed Doris's glass of brandy. It hit the lobby's wood panelling with an audible … thwack!

'Truncheons!' exclaimed the sergeant in charge of the constables. 'Sir William, sor, is that door locked?'

'It is unlocked.'

'Reet lads … I apologise, Sir William, for giving oot orders in your own house but this is a job for the Peelers. Is that gun loaded, sor?' tapping Rowley on the shoulder with his truncheon.

'No.'

'Thank the lord for that … ready, lads?'

'Police!'

'Police!'

'Police!'

In the room, Jeb Montague Prior lay flopped in a chair. In his lap there lay a Colt Revolver.

On the floor, Jeb was trying to wrestle a Colt revolver off Lafayette.

'Leave this to me,' said Phillips. 'If a bad guy's on the ground yuh divent hesitate to give him a headache.'

The kick Phillips gave Lafayette's head was the sort of kick a goalkeeper gives a ball when he's taking a goal kick.

Only when Lafayette had been disarmed and had ceased to struggle, did Jeb accept Phillips' helping hand.

'Thank you,' said Jeb. 'Thank you …'

'Jeb, you alright?' said Henry, pushing his way to the fore.

Jeb nodded that he was alive and well. A few seconds later, when his breath had more or less returned to normal, he began to talk in a fast, non-stop, excitable way … the way one can imagine Paul of Tarsus explaining his conversion to Christianity.

'My grandfather saved my life. If he hadn't upset his aim–' gesturing at Lafayette– 'I would be dead. Grandfather, look at me. You saved my life …look at me … call me "grandson".'

Jeb Montague's vision was blurred. Why did the black man he was looking at so remind him of his daughter? When he looked at the black man he saw his daughter. He was seeing, as if through a frosted glass … not a black man … not a Union agent … not an enemy of the Secessionist states … but the face of the daughter he loved.

'You recognised the lullaby, sir?' said Jeb. 'Shall I play it again? Where's my banjo?'

Jeb Montague Prior raised an arm, not to indicate to Jeb the whereabouts of his banjo but, to bless his grandson with the sign of the cross.

'I don't like the look of him,' said the police sergeant, 'his blood's gannin to his boots. He's as white as the whitewash inside me gran's pantry. Are you not well, sir? Yuh nar what,' looking at Jeb, 'am thinking he's on the way out … he's a-going. We'll need more than smelling salts to bring him back to wearing a waistcoat. Here, sir, let me undo your collar. You need air, sir. You're a horse, sir, that nars it's heading back to its stable. What's that, sir?' bending down to better hear Jeb Montague Prior's mutterings. 'What you trying to tell me, sir? Pocket … letter. Howay, sir … fight. Divent hear harps and angels, hear the Blaydon Races. He's gannin. He's a sinking ship. His bow's under watta and his stern's up in the air like a duck's when it's pecking seaweed. Oh, dear me … he's pissed himself. Begging your pardon, ladies. I was forgetting

I was in mixed company. When you goes to join the angels you always travels light. A spirit don't need a bladder … likewise a dead man don't need one either. He's a staring but I knows he don't see my helmet. If nee one's any objections I'll dee the honours,' whereupon he closed Jeb Montague Prior's eyes. 'If it's not done afore the rigger sets in it's like trying to get a good price for a teapot in a pawnshop.'

'You killed him, boy,' said Lafayette. 'Your reminiscing killed my compatriot. You killed him as surely as if you'd shot him between the eyes with a Colt 45.'

'Now, now, sir,' said the police sergeant. 'We'll have nee talk like that. You'll be needing stitches in ya heed, I'm thinking.'

Jeb, staring wide eyed at his grandfather… the man who had murdered his father, strummed a discord. He strummed his banjo the way someone smashes plates to take the sting out of their rage.

'He was my grandfather,' he said to anyone who might be listening. 'If he had lived … would we have become friends? To have become friends, how high a hurdle would he have had to jump over? How deep seated were his prejudices? How loath would he have been to give up the bellum way of life? If he didn't have slaves was he frightened he'd have to go out in the fields himself and pick cotton?'

'Now, now, sir,' said the police sergeant, 'your grandfatha has left us to gan walkies with angels. He'll not be hearing discords. He'll be a hearing harmony. He is at peace, sir. As a keel man needs wind and tide, your grandfatha needs a requiem. Sing him a requiem, sir. If you are musical, sir, you might be able to turn that lullaby you and him were so fond of into one. After aal, sir, dying is like ganin to sleep. A requiem is a lullaby what sings us to eternal rest. Aye, sir, your grandfatha needs hymns, not oaths or affidavits. And you, sir, will be wanting the letter he mentioned. The last words he muttered with his last breath … his dying breath. A dying breath is like watching a fire gan out … aye, in my job I see a lot of dying fires. And you, sir,' nodding at Lafayette, who was tottering, 'will be wanting the doctor.'

'I've got him covered,' said Rowley, pointing the unloaded Colt at Lafayette.

'Last words, sir,' continued the police sergeant, 'means a lot to a dying man … or, woman. The last words me mother said to me were …'

'I love you,' suggested Rowley.

'You sure that gun's unloaded, sir?'

'I unloaded it, sergeant,' said Sir William.

'Mr Harrison … Geordie Black … I know who you are … you are not on stage. Sir William's parlour is real life and so was me mother's dying words to me. She telt me to wash the dishes … very house proud me mother was. Now then, which pocket might this letter be in … eeny-meeny-miny-mo …'

'There's only one way to find out,' said Jeb, moving to search his grandfather's pockets.

'If you don't mind, sir, I'll do the honours. We don't want civilians touching evidence, do we? Let's use our heeds. Gentlemen keep important stuff in their inside coat pockets. And here we have it, I'm thinking, as the fisherman said when he landed a fifty-pound cod. Here's the letter, sir. I'll keep the Colt in the deed gentleman's lap. Loaded guns is like wives when yuh tell them yuh divent like their cooking … they ricochet aal ower the place.'

A gurgling noise coming from the corpse made everyone, except the police sergeant, look as if they'd seen a ghost.

'Deed or alive,' said the police sergeant, 'wind is better out than in.'

The letter was addressed to: Captain Byron Prior c/o The Mosque South Shields. Breaking its seal, Jeb read:

'Dear Byron, I have heard from my spies that since I aided and abetted your escape from my planation you have prospered. That you have become the captain of a collier fills me with pride. Pray do not think, I lie. I do not. I have further heard that you have become a Muslim.

You are, I know, well aware that without my help you would have been lynched. I remind you of our bargain. As far as my daughter is concerned you are a dead man.

Your love child is called Jeb Prior Phelan. My spies tell me he is a fine strapping lad. He is, so I have been told, fond of music. My dear daughter named him after me. I am vain enough to like that.

"Phelan" is the name of his step-father. He is a wealthy New Yorker. Your son lacks for nothing money can buy. As far as I am aware, my daughter's marriage is a happy one.

I am here, on Tyneside to buy the Armstrong Gun for the Secessionist states. You will, I know, disapprove. It is my opinion that slavery will wither away of its own accord. It does not need a civil war to help it on its way.

I am not at all sure that this letter will ever each you; if it does and pray god it does, forgive me my sins. So much water has flowed under our respective bridges I know not how to sign off. Are you my slave? Are you my son-in-law? Taking the plunge, I am yours, with all his faults,
Jeb Montague Prior.'

It took many seconds for Jeb to take in the facts that his father was alive and that his grandfather … the old, white haired man slouched dead in a chair in front of him … was not a murderer.

To Jeb the letter was a revelation. He felt awed … humbled … bewildered. He was Peter, seeing Jesus after Jesus had been crucified.

For many seconds he stared at the letter the way a man stares at a mirage. Was what he was seeing real, or was it an optical illusion?

He looked for many seconds at his dead grandfather. The white-haired old man was not as bigoted as he'd thought. His grandfather had been, like most men, a mixture of the good and the bad.

Unbidden, like a wild dog chasing sheep, his mind raced on to other possibilities. Would he be able to meet his father? Should he tell his mother that his black father … her lover, was alive and well?

'Henry,' he said, handing Henry the letter, 'my father lives.'

'Your pa is dead, boy,' said Lafayette. 'Your pa raped a white woman, boy. In Virginia we don't take that on the chin. We got our own way of handling situations like that.'

In lieu of shutting Lafayette up with a knock-out blow to the chin, Phillips folded his pocket handkerchief into the shape of a ball.

'Hold him,' he told the two constables.

'You are …' said Lafayette.

When you have a handkerchief rolled up into the shape of a ball stuffed into your mouth and two big policemen are linking your arms like anchor chains … you have no choice but, in the words of Phillips, 'to gan quiet'.

'Sir,' said the police sergeant to Jeb, 'do you wish to press charges?'

'No, I do not.'

'There will be no charges,' said Henry, 'so long as Sir William agrees not to sell guns to the Secessionist states. Do I make myself clear? In this parlour I am Abraham Lincoln's representative. My father is America's legate to Great Britain. I speak with all the authority of the New World.'

'England, Mr Adams,' said Sir William, 'is a neutral country in your civil war. You know as well as I do that that is our position.'

'It is my experience, Sir William, that private individuals often ignore official positions.'

Spitting out his gag … an act that made Phillips mutter … 'I'm losing me touch … dear me,' … Lafayette said: 'We have paid for those guns, Sir William. Your sales manager in Paris has our money. A Confederate steamer, the Alabama, is off the Tyne waiting to collect them.'

'The Alabama will not be loaded with my guns,' said Sir William. 'It will, sir, be loaded with your good self. If your fellow countryman does not wish to press charges, I have concluded that the sooner you quit England the better. Sergeant, would it be possible for the constabulary to escort Mr Lafayette to North Shields?'

'Where a paddle-wheel tugboat will take him across the bar to the Alabama?'

Sir William nodded.

'It's irregular but practical.'

'I came to Newcastle by express train, First Class, from Liverpool,' said Lafayette. 'I have a return ticket.'

'And I have two constables with me and a pair of handcuffs,' said the police sergeant.

'Handcuffs, Mr Policeman, are for slaves. I am not a slave. I own slaves. I have a bellum mansion. I have a pond full of goldfish. I have … why are you shaking your heads and looking at me as if you think I am a mad man?'

'It's the kick to the heed,' said a constable.

'He's delirious,' said the other constable.

'Divent let him fall doon,' said the police sergeant, 'he's a-tottering like a horse that's ready for the knacker's yard. Nivva mind the bracelets … this is an under the armpit job … and remember, when yuh put him in the wagon that he's a human being and not a bag of coal.'

'They are not treating him kindly,' said Meggie. 'I hope it is not forgotten he has been kicked in the head.'

'They are treating him the way he treats his slaves,' said Doris, 'that's my opinion. They are giving him a dose of his own medicine … serve him right. That's what I think. If I could make an origami slave owner's head, I'd stick pins in it. That's "sympathetic magic". I have read about "sympathetic magic" in Mr Dickens's "All the Year Round".'

The one-horse cart, with POLICE stencilled on its canvas awning, into which the constables had thrown Lafayette as if he had been a bag of coal, moved off at a walking pace. As it did so, Sir William and his guests heard the stirring music of a brass band. They heard the sort of stirring music that on a cold and frosty night makes icicles tingle like tambourines.

The Salvationists marched up Sir William's drive playing the 'Battle Hymn of the Republic'. At the front of this noisy army of twelve, were Major Starkey and her husband, Captain Starkey. They were sharing the holding of a banner, proclaiming: JESUS SAVES.

When the band stopped playing all exclaimed: 'Down with slavery … halleluiah!'

In Rowley's ear, Edwin Wakefield whispered: 'I heeded your advice. I told Annie of your part in helping to abolish slavery. She thinks you are a hero. The Salvationists are here, Rowley, because of you.'

'Phillips,' said Sir William, 'I'm thinking, tea and coffee for the Salvationists.'

'Sor …'

'And biscuits,' said Meggie.

'And brandy,' said Doris.

'No, Doris,' said Meggie, 'you are forgetting, they are Salvationists. They are "Temperance". They are against alcohol.'

It was over a hot mug of tea, sweet with sugar, shared with Annie in Sir William's frozen drive – Annie sipping from one side, Rowley from the other – that Rowley … emboldened by their camaraderie for the abolition of slavery … asked Annie if she and he might one day become an item.

'You mean, Rowley, you want to wed me?'

'Aye, I do.'

'Course I will, Rowley. My lips are cold with playing the trombone.'

'What about if I warmed them with a kiss?'

'Would you?'

'Come here, me bonny lass. This is not a stage kiss.'

'Watch me trombone.'

EPILOGUE

Sir William did not sell guns to the Confederates; not at least on this occasion. What happened to the money the Confederates had paid upfront, disappeared into thin air.

Rowley and Annie did wed. Throughout their married life 'temperance' and a 'medicinal toddy' warred with each other. It was rumoured that Rowley and Captain Starkey met up in the 'Old Grey Horse'.

Jeb tried to meet his father. The imam in charge of the mosque at South Shields told him his father, seeking adventure, had signed on as first mate on a whaler. His father was heading for the southern ocean. It took many years for Jeb to track down his father. When they met … that is another story.

The Coxons did not hang. They were transported to Australia. In Australia Geordie married a widow called Kelly. Her son, Ned, was the apple of his step-father's eye.

Oh, and Billy did learn to read and write.

ACKNOWLEDGEMENTS

In some dialogue I have used Rowland Harrison's original script. For example: 'I'm a draughtsman.' 'What do you draw?' 'He draws the boogie round the yard.' As I am Rowley's great-grandson, I don't think he'd mind. It is not plagiarism. It is keeping it in the family.